Vera Axyonova (ed.)

EUROPEAN ENGAGEMENT UNDER REVIEW

Exporting Values, Rules, and Practices to the Post-Soviet Space

**AN INTERDISCIPLINARY SERIES
OF THE CENTRE FOR INTERCULTURAL AND EUROPEAN STUDIES**

**INTERDISZIPLINÄRE SCHRIFTENREIHE
DES CENTRUMS FÜR INTERKULTURELLE UND EUROPÄISCHE STUDIEN**

CINTEUS • Fulda University of Applied Sciences • Hochschule Fulda

ISSN 1865-2255

11   *Vera Axyonova*
     The European Union's Democratization Policy for Central Asia
     Failed in Success or Succeeded in Failure?
     ISBN 978-3-8382-0614-1

12   *Lisa Moessing*
     Lobbying Uncovered?
     Lobbying Registration in the European Union and the United States
     ISBN 978-3-8382-0616-5

13   *Andreas Herberg-Rothe (ed.)*
     Lessons from World War I for the Rise of Asia
     ISBN 978-3-8382-0791-9

14   *Agnieszka Satola*
     Migration und irreguläre Pflegearbeit in Deutschland
     Eine biographische Studie
     ISBN 978-3-8382-0692-9

15   *Vera Axyonova (ed.)*
     European Engagement under Review
     Exporting Values, Rules, and Practices to the Post-Soviet Space
     ISBN 978-3-8382-0860-2

Series Editors

Gudrun Hentges
Volker Hinnenkamp
Anne Honer †
Hans-Wolfgang Platzer

Fachbereich Sozial- und Kulturwissenschaften
Hochschule Fulda University of Applied Sciences
Marquardstraße 35
D-36039 Fulda
cinteus@sk.hs-fulda.de
www.cinteus.eu

Vera Axyonova (ed.)

EUROPEAN ENGAGEMENT UNDER REVIEW

Exporting Values, Rules, and Practices to the Post-Soviet Space

ibidem-Verlag
Stuttgart

Bibliografische Information der Deutschen Nationalbibliothek
Die Deutsche Nationalbibliothek verzeichnet diese Publikation in der Deutschen Nationalbibliografie; detaillierte bibliografische Daten sind im Internet über http://dnb.d-nb.de abrufbar.

Bibliographic information published by the Deutsche Nationalbibliothek
Die Deutsche Nationalbibliothek lists this publication in the Deutsche Nationalbibliografie; detailed bibliographic data are available in the Internet at http://dnb.d-nb.de.

∞
Gedruckt auf alterungsbeständigem, säurefreien Papier
Printed on acid-free paper

ISSN: 1865-2255
ISBN-13: 978-3-8382-0860-2

© *ibidem*-Verlag
Stuttgart 2016

Alle Rechte vorbehalten

Das Werk einschließlich aller seiner Teile ist urheberrechtlich geschützt. Jede Verwertung außerhalb der engen Grenzen des Urheberrechtsgesetzes ist ohne Zustimmung des Verlages unzulässig und strafbar. Dies gilt insbesondere für Vervielfältigungen, Übersetzungen, Mikroverfilmungen und elektronische Speicherformen sowie die Einspeicherung und Verarbeitung in elektronischen Systemen.

All rights reserved. No part of this publication may be reproduced, stored in or introduced into a retrieval system, or transmitted, in any form, or by any means (electronic, mechanical, photocopying, recording or otherwise) without the prior written permission of the publisher. Any person who does any unauthorized act in relation to this publication may be liable to criminal prosecution and civil claims for damages.

Printed in Germany

Editorial

This series is intended as a publication panel of the Centre of Intercultural and European Studies (CINTEUS) at Fulda University of Applied Sciences. The series aims at making research results, anthologies, conference readers, study books and selected qualification theses accessible to the general public. It comprises of scientific and interdisciplinary works on inter- and transculturality; the European Union from an interior and a global perspective; and problems of social welfare and social law in Europe. Each of these are fields of research and teaching in the Social- and Cultural Studies Faculty at Fulda University of Applied Sciences and its Centre for Intercultural and European Studies. We also invite contributions from outside the faculty that share and enrich our research.

Gudrun Hentges, Volker Hinnenkamp, Anne Honer, Hans-Wolfgang Platzer

Editorial

Die Buchreihe versteht sich als Publikationsforum des Centrums für interkulturelle und europäische Studien (CINTEUS) der Hochschule Fulda. Ziel der CINTEUS-Reihe ist es, Forschungsergebnisse, Anthologien, Kongressreader, Studienbücher und ausgewählte Qualifikationsarbeiten einer interessierten Öffentlichkeit zugänglich zu machen. Die Reihe umfasst fachwissenschaftliche und interdisziplinäre Arbeiten aus den Bereichen Inter- und Transkulturalität, Europäische Union aus Binnen- und globaler Perspektive sowie wohlfahrtsstaatliche und sozialrechtliche Probleme Europas. All dies sind Fachgebiete, die im Fachbereich Sozial- und Kulturwissenschaften der Hochschule Fulda University of Applied Sciences und dem angegliederten Centrum für interkulturelle und Europastudien gelehrt und erforscht werden. Ausdrücklich eingeladen an der Publikationsreihe mitzuwirken sind auch solche Studien, die nicht 'im Hause' entstanden sind, aber CINTEUS-Schwerpunkte berühren und bereichern.

Gudrun Hentges, Volker Hinnenkamp, Anne Honer, Hans-Wolfgang Platzer

Acknowledgements

This volume evolved from the young researchers workshop "An exercise in normative and real power: Promoting European values in the post-Soviet space", held at Fulda University of Applied Sciences, Germany, in October 2013. I would like to thank the German Academic Exchange Service (DAAD) for sponsoring this event, which brought together young scholars from Germany and former Soviet states.

I am also indebted to the Centre for Intercultural and European Studies and the Department of Social and Cultural Studies at Fulda University, who supported the organisation of the workshop and this publication. I am particularly grateful to Prof. Dr. Hans-Wolfgang Platzer for his support and insightful comments that helped to develop the volume to its present shape.

I would further like to express my appreciation to everyone who provided valuable feedback on the concept of the volume and individual chapters, especially to Olga Burlyuk, Eamonn Butler, Eduard Klein, and Alla Leukavets. I am grateful to Bastian Heck for his editorial assistance in putting this book together and to Nate Breznau for his excellent work on proofreading the text that went far beyond language-related aspects. Special thanks go to all workshop participants, also those who are not represented in this volume. Finally, I would like to thank my fellow contributors for their intellectual effort, fruitful cooperation, and extensive patience.

Vera Axyonova
October 2015

Contents

Editorial V

Acknowledgements VII

Vera Axyonova
On the export of European values, rules and practices:
Introducing the debate 1

Elena Kropatcheva
The EU's policy of democracy promotion and Ukraine's bumpy path
to the Association Agreement—amidst a major crisis in Europe 11

Shushanik Minasyan
Provisionally unsuccessful?
European democracy promotion in the South Caucasus 41

Aron Buzogány
Governance and governmentality of EU Neighbourhood Policy.
Two perspectives on the role of civil society
in external democracy promotion 59

Aijan Sharshenova
The European Union's assistance to Kyrgyzstan:
Good intentions, mixed results 85

Tsveta Petrova
Poland's democracy promotion in Belarus—
closer to the US' or the EU's approach? 109

René Lenz
Academic cooperation with Russian higher education institutions:
German organisations as transfer agents? 125

Bettina Bruns and Helga Zichner
That's what friends are for—external migration management
of the European Union in its eastern neighbourhood 151

Olga Burlyuk
Inescapable partners: The European Union
and the Council of Europe as rule of law promoters in Ukraine 177

List of contributors 203

On the export of European values, rules and practices: Introducing the debate

Vera Axyonova

A spread of values, rules and practices across time and space is not a new research field. It has been viewed by scholars with different perspectives, involving a variety of conceptual and methodological approaches. A substantial literature evolved around this phenomenon addressing it as a process of transfer of rules and policies, i.e. *"a process in which the knowledge about policies, administrative arrangements, institutions etc. in one time and/or place is used in the development of policies, administrative arrangements and institutions in another time and/or place"* (Dolowitz & Marsh, 1996, p. 344). Following this definition, the objects being transferred are not limited to rules and policies and may include instruments, institutions and structures, but also more general ideas, values and conceptions of "normal" (Manners, 2002, p. 239).

A range of actors may participate in the process of transfer, both as aggregate entities such as supra-national institutions, state agencies, political parties and civil society organisations, and as individuals, e.g. elected officials, civil servants, members of pressure groups, and policy entrepreneurs (Dolowitz & Marsh, 1996, p. 345). Depending on the role of these actors and the instruments they use, scholars distinguish various types of transfer mechanisms. These range from processes of diffusion (that lack any specific agency) and lesson-drawing (a voluntary adoption of ideas, norms or policies from without) to socialisation or social learning (a process in which a socialiser is attributed with a more active role as a facilitator or instructor), and active promotion of policies wherein promoters may go as far as coercing their targets into the adoption of these policies.[1]

---

[1] This list is by no means exhaustive. Scholars use a variety of terms to conceptualise different types and mechanisms of transfer, often without a strict differentiation between them. For different conceptual approaches see e.g. Bennett, 1991; Majone, 1991; Rose, 1991, 1993; Haas, 1992; Börzel, 1999; Checkel, 2001, 2005; Schimmelfennig & Sedelmeier 2004. For an overview of approaches see Dolowitz & Marsh, 1996.

While the process of transfer in its various forms is central to this volume, we have deliberately chosen to use a somewhat more narrow term of *export* in its title. The reason is the emphasis of this term on the existence of origin and destination in the process of (a cross-border) transfer, which is of particular interest to authors of this volume. In addition, the concept of export implies a presence of actors who (equally) participate in the process, i.e. exporters and importers. It grants these actors greater and more specific roles than the frameworks of diffusion or lesson-drawing could allow. At the same time, while exporters remain in the spotlight, importers are not deprived of agency. Export is thus not limited to promotion, which ascribes an intrusive nature to one part of actors by distinguishing between promoters (subjects) and their targets (objects) in the process of transfer.

Drawing on these concepts, the book seeks to contribute to the scholarly debate on transfer of values, rules and practices to former Soviet countries by mapping the multi-faceted engagement of various European actors—both in active promotion and facilitation—in this broader region. Among the European actors, the European Union (EU) is a frontrunner in terms of the number of publications that address European involvement in transfer processes. Reviewing them all would be an impossible task for this brief introductory chapter, but several major works need to be mentioned. Burlyuk (2013, pp. 29–31) identifies among them those that apply the concept of isomorphism developed within organisational theory to explain policy diffusion within the EU (Radaelli, 2000), approach institutions (including the EU) as promoters and sites of socialisation (Checkel, 2001, 2005), and make a strong case for conditionality policies in explaining rule transfer through the EU external governance (Schimmelfennig & Sedelmeier, 2004).

Starting with the enlargement debate, a vast literature emerged on the modes and mechanisms of EU rule transfer and EU transformative power, both within the process of accession of new member states and beyond. A specialised cluster focuses on the role played by and transfer of values and principles in EU foreign affairs (e.g. Manners, 2002; Lucarelli & Manners, 2006; Cremona, 2011), while a considerable number of studies are devoted specifically to the EU's promotion of democratic and human rights norms (Schimmelfennig, Engert, & Knobel, 2002; Fierro, 2003; Kubicek, 2003; Börzel & Risse, 2004; Vachudova, 2005; Jünemann & Knodt, 2007; Freyburg, Lavenex, Schimmelfennig, Skripta, & Wetzel, 2009, to name just a few). These studies reveal that neither EU documents nor scholarly literature provide a clear differentiation between the concepts of values, norms and principles that are promoted by the EU. In fact, these terms are often used interchangeably (Cremona, 2011, pp. 280–281; Ghazaryan, 2014, p. 17) and commonly include (yet are not limited to) liberty, democracy, respect for human rights, rule of law, and good governance. These values[2] are also central to this volume. Although the transfer of European rules and practices in other spheres, such as higher education and migration management, that are illustrative of the European engagement in post-Soviet countries, are equally included in selected chapters.

Apart from the EU, other European actors advancing their values, rules and practices have attracted less scholarly attention. Systematic analyses of rule transfer beyond European borders initiated specifically by European national (i.e. governments of EU Member States) and societal (i.e. civil society organisations) actors have been rare.[3] The same is true for the analyses of normative engagements by multilateral actors, such as the Council of Europe (CoE) and the Organization for Security and Co-operation in Europe (OSCE). Some recent larger works include a book by Andrea Gawrich (2014) conceptualising democracy promotion by the CoE and the OSCE and an earlier monograph by Solveig Richter (2009) on external democratisation through the OSCE in South Eastern Europe.[4] While studies of EU engagement also dominate this volume, it seeks to exercise a more inclusive approach and incorporates accounts of other European actors: the CoE, the EU Member States' governments, and non-governmental organisations.

Finally, the countries under study, where these European actors are engaged, include the independent states that emerged as the result of the disintegration of the Soviet Union, excluding the Baltics. These countries have rarely been brought together in studies of European value and rule transfer. Instead, scholars tended to examine European engagement in separate

---

[2] In this volume, we follow the definition of *"values"* provided by Sonia Lucarelli (2006, p. 10) as *"notions laden with an absolute (i.e. non-instrumental) positive significance for the overall order and meaning we try to give to our world"*.

[3] For some exceptions see e.g. Mikulova & Simecka, 2013; Petrova, 2014; Pospieszna, 2014.

[4] See also policy-oriented papers by Evers (2010) and Boonstra (2007).

states, especially in the case of Russia (e.g. Fischer, 2007; Gänzle, 2008; Saari, 2009), or sub-regions (the six countries addressed by the Eastern Partnership framework of the EU: Belarus, Moldova, Ukraine, Armenia, Azerbaijan and Georgia (e.g. Kubicek, 2005; Beichelt, 2007; Gordon & Sasse, 2008; Sasse, 2008; Bosse & Korosteleva, 2009), the latter three South Caucasus republics (e.g. Jawad, 2007; Pardo Sierra, 2011; Börzel & Pamuk, 2012), or the five states in Central Asia: Kazakhstan, Kyrgyzstan, Tajikistan, Turkmenistan and Uzbekistan (e.g. Crawford, 2008; Warkotsch, 2009; Hoffmann, 2010; Urdze, 2010; Axyonova, 2014)). The present volume deliberately focuses on the broader post-Soviet region, as we assume that all the countries retain certain similarities, e.g. they remain affected—even if to different extents—by their communist legacies. At the same time, we admit that European actors have varying degrees of influence in these states, considering the latter's commitments to the OSCE and the CoE, their relations with individual European countries, and the lacking EU membership perspective in all post-Soviet states.

The book does not intend to provide a structured comparative perspective, but rather a set of in-depth case studies shedding light on various aspects of transfer processes. It consciously engages in "analytical eclecticism" (Katzenstein & Okawara, 2002), and uses an author-driven approach, meaning that the contributing authors are given the freedom to choose their analytical lens and define concrete objects of their studies within the given thematic framework.

Elena Kropatcheva opens this set of studies with an analysis of EU democracy promotion policy for Ukraine. She focuses specifically on the presidency of Victor Yanukovych, the turbulent period of transition to the presidency of Petro Poroshenko, and the signing of the Association Agreement which was the main instrument the EU used to encourage democracy in Ukraine. Kropatcheva also discusses other political, diplomatic, economic and assistance instruments applied by the EU. In doing so, the author examines three factors that impacted the EU's Ukraine policy, namely the capacities of the EU to act as a normative power, the Russian factor, and the domestic constraints in Ukraine. Kropatcheva emphasises shortcomings in the EU's policies towards both Ukraine and Russia, yet shows a certain evolution of the EU approach from an underestimation of Russia's role in the shared neighbourhood to more decisive measures (sanctions) against the Kremlin.

Despite this evolution, the author questions the EU's ability to stabilise the situation in Ukraine under the conditions of the major crisis in Europe.

Following Kropatcheva, *Shushanik Minasyan* also engages in the debate of successes and failures of the EU's external democratisation policy. She looks at EU democracy promotion in the three South Caucasus republics: Georgia, Armenia and Azerbaijan. Focusing on conditionality instruments applied by the EU, Minasyan reveals a limited impact of EU involvement on political regimes in the region, which she attributes to considerable misconceptions and inconsistencies in the EU's approach. The author makes a strong case for limitations of the use of conditionality policies towards countries that lack EU membership prospects, in particular in the framework of the European Neighbourhood Policy.

Continuing the line of authors who focus on the EU's Eastern Partnership countries, *Aron Buzogány* argues for including civil society into the analysis of EU democracy promotion. In doing so, he employs two approaches towards conceptualising the role of civil society in external democratisation: a functionally-driven external governance perspective, which has been a preferred way of analysing the role of civil society in EU democracy promotion, and a Foucault-inspired governmentality perspective that emphasises the practices embedded in governance networks and devotes particular attention to how power is constituted therein. Using these two lenses, Buzogány investigates the role of civil society organisations in the Neighbourhood Policy framework both at the EU-level and in the Eastern Partnership countries.

Also focusing on the EU's democratisation policy, *Aijan Sharshenova* examines EU efforts beyond its immediate neighbourhood. She scrutinises assistance provided by the EU to Kyrgyzstan, one of the five post-Soviet Central Asian republics. Being the most liberal state in Central Asia, Kyrgyzstan has a potential to provide a fruitful environment for democracy promotion from abroad. Yet, Sharshenova observes that the EU's good intentions are distorted by a variety of negative external and domestic influences. A lack of clear economic and security interests on the part of the EU with regard to the country, the EU's inability to compete with other international aid donors, and the fusion of formal and informal practices in Kyrgyzstan hinder the EU from inducing genuine democratic change in the country.

Remaining in the domain of democratisation policies, *Tsveta Petrova* introduces a new actor into the analysis of external democracy promotion. She looks at the engagement of one of the EU's post-communist member states, namely Poland, whose democratic history is comparably short. Petrova examines Polish democracy promotion in Belarus from 1989 to 2009, and compares it to the democracy promotion efforts of the United States and the European Union. The author finds out that, having transitioned from a recipient to a supplier of democracy support, Poland exercises a democratisation policy that incorporates both a US-like approach of political pressure and a non-intrusive EU-like approach. At the same time, unlike both of these actors, Poland prefers to persuade and pressure through quiet diplomacy and chooses engagement over sanctions, which gives it a comparative advantage in the context of the authoritarian regime in Belarus.

René Lenz breaks the line of authors focussing on democracy promotion and brings the analysis to a new (sub-national) level. He discusses whether and how academic institutions and individual actors diffuse organisational models and practices. More specifically, Lenz concentrates on academic exchange between German organisations and Russian higher education institutions. He observes that, while working in Russia, German organisations and individual academics transfer their ideas and methods of teaching and organising work to the new environment. In doing so, they use the Bologna-Process as a framework that provides the instruments, rhetoric means, and models in the process of transfer. Yet, while some practices are successfully adopted by Russian actors, more far-reaching institutional reforms encounter severe impediments. Thus, the diffusion of institutional models remains largely superficial.

Following the chapter by Lenz, *Bettina Bruns* and *Helga Zichner* return to the EU, yet focus on a completely different sphere of its engagement. They investigate the EU's attempts to involve Ukraine, Moldova and Belarus in its migration management, with a specific focus on asylum policy and refugee matters. The authors present an in-depth study of the EU-funded Regional Protection Programme (RPP), which aims to enhance asylum capacities in the three countries and enable the states to observe high international standards in refugee protection. Opposite to their expectations, Bruns and Zichner find that in reality the harmonisation with EU provisions leads to a lowering of precisely these standards in the three countries.

Finally, in her chapter, *Olga Burlyuk* remains at the supra-national level of analysis and looks at two actors, the EU and the CoE, that find themselves pursuing similar tasks in similar fields: promoting the triptych of European values—democracy, human rights and the rule of law—in post-Soviet states. Bulyuk scrutinises the nature of the relationship between the EU and the CoE by zooming in on their rule of law promotion efforts in Ukraine. Her findings reaffirm that the EU and the CoE are in a complex interactive relationship, with elements of both cooperation and competition, and reveal three important tendencies therein. First, cooperation prevails over competition at substantive, political and operational levels, while competition is concentrated at the institutional level. Second, cooperation at the political and operational levels precedes and even triggers cooperation at the institutional level, bending the reluctant institutional structures of the two organisations. And, third, the growing political, financial and normative leadership of the EU does not cancel out the traditional and special relevance of the CoE in this particular region and policy area.

The chapters thus address different aspects of export (active promotion and facilitation) of values, e.g. democracy, human rights and the rule of law, as well as rules and practices in the fields of education and migration management. The studies examine motives, mechanisms or effects of the European engagement, while the (process of) transfer of values, rules and practices remains central to each contribution. The synthesis of perspectives on various European actors' engagements in the post-Soviet space provides the value-added of this collective exercise.

References

Axyonova, V. (2014). *The European Union's democratization policy for Central Asia: Failed in success or succeeded in failure?* Stuttgart: ibidem.

Beichelt, T. (2007). Externe Demokratisierungsstrategien der Europäischen Union: Die Fälle Belarus, Moldova, Ukraine. In A. Jünemann & M. Knodt (Eds.), *European external democracy promotion* (pp. 207–230). Baden-Baden: Nomos.

Bennett, C. J. (1991). What is policy convergence and what causes it? *The British Journal of Political Science, 21*, 215–233.

Bosse, G. & Korosteleva, E. (2009). Changing Belarus? The limits of EU governance in Eastern Europe. *Cooperation and Conflict, 44*(2), 143–165.

Boonstra, J. (2007). OSCE democracy promotion: Grinding to a halt? *FRIDE Working Paper*, No. 44. Madrid: FRIDE.

Börzel, T. (1999). Towards convergence in Europe? Institutional adaptation to Europeanization in Germany and Spain. *Journal of Common Market Studies*, 37, 573–596.

Börzel, T. & Pamuk, Y. (2012). Pathologies of Europeanisation: Fighting corruption in the Southern Caucasus. *West European Politics*, 35(1), 79–97.

Börzel, T. & Risse, T. (2004). One size fits all! EU policies for the *promotion of human rights, democracy and the rule of law*. Paper presented at the Workshop on Democracy Promotion, October 4–5, 2004, Center for Development, Democracy, and the Rule of Law, Stanford University.

Burlyuk, O. (2013). *European Union rule of law promotion in Ukraine: Exploring the effects of interaction between the institutional contexts*. PhD Dissertation, University of Kent, Canterbury/Brussels.

Checkel, J. T. (2001). Why comply? Social learning and European identity change. *International Organization*, 55(3), 553–588.

Checkel, J. T. (2005). International socialization and socialization in Europe. Introduction and framework. *International Organization*, 59(4), 801–826.

Crawford, G. (2008). EU human rights and democracy promotion in Central Asia: From lofty principles to lowly self-interests. *Perspectives on European Politics and Society*, 9(2), 172–191.

Cremona, M. (2011). Values in EU foreign policy. In M. Evans & P. Koutrakos (Eds.), *Beyond the established orders: Policy interconnections between the EU and the rest of the world* (pp. 275–315). Oxford: Hart Publishing.

Dolowitz, D. P. & Marsh, D. (1996). Who learns what from whom: A review of the policy transfer literature. *Political Studies*, XLIV, 343–357.

Evers, F. (2010). OSCE efforts to promote the rule of law: History, structures, survey. *CORE Working Paper*, No. 20. Hamburg: Centre for OSCE Research, Institute for Peace Research and Security Policy at the University of Hamburg.

Fierro, E. (2003). *The EU's approach to human rights conditionality in practice*. The Hague: Martinus Nijhoff Publishers.

Fischer, S. (2007). The EU and Russia: Democracy promotion in a "Strategic Partnership"? In A. Jünemann & M. Knodt (Eds.), *European external democracy promotion* (pp. 247–267). Baden-Baden: Nomos.

Freyburg, T., Lavenex, S., Schimmelfennig, F., Skripka, T., & Wetzel, A. (2009). EU promotion of democratic governance in the neighbourhood. *Journal of European Public Policy*, 16(6), 916–934.

Gänzle, S. (2008). The EU's policy towards Russia: Extending governance beyond borders? In J. DeBardeleben (Ed.), *The boundaries of EU enlargement: Finding a place for neighbours* (pp. 53–70). Houndsmills: Palgrave.

Gawrich, A. (2014). *Demokratieförderung von Europarat und OSZE: Ein Beitrag zur europäischen Integration*. Wiesbaden: VS Verlag.

Ghazaryan, N. (2014). *The European Neighbourhood Policy and the democratic values of the EU: A legal analysis*. Oxford, Portland: Hart Publishing.

Gordon, C. & Sasse, G. (2008). *The European Neighbourhood Policy: Effective instrument for conflict management and democratic change in the Union's eastern neighbourhood?* MIRICO EU Framework VI Project, Work package 5 special report. Bolzano, Italy: EURAC.

Haas, P. (1992). Epistemic communities and international policy coordination. *International Organisation,* 46, 1–36.

Hoffmann, K. (2010). The EU in Central Asia: Successful good governance promotion? *Third World Quarterly,* 31(1), 87–103.

Jawad, P. (2007). The European Union as an external democracy promoter in the South Caucasus region? In A. Jünemann & M. Knodt (Eds.), *European external democracy promotion* (pp. 269–292). Baden-Baden: Nomos.

Jünemann, A. & Knodt, M. (Eds.) (2007). *European external democracy promotion.* Baden-Baden: Nomos.

Katzenstein, P. J. & Okawara, N. (2002). Japan, Asian-Pacific security, and the case for analytical eclecticism. *International Security,* 26(3), 153–185.

Kubicek, P. (Ed.). (2003). *The European Union and democratization.* London, New York: Routledge.

Kubicek, P. (2005). The European Union and democratization in Ukraine. *Communist and Post-Communist Studies,* 38, 269–292.

Lucarelli, S. (2006). Introduction. In S. Lucarelli & I. Manners (Eds.), *Values and principles in European Union foreign policy* (pp. 1–18). London, New York: Routledge.

Lucarelli, S. & Manners, I. (Eds.) (2006). *Values and principles in European Union foreign policy.* London, New York: Routledge.

Majone, G. (1991). Cross-national sources of regulatory policy-making in Europe and the United States. *Journal of Public Policy,* 11, 79–106.

Manners, I. (2002). Normative power Europe: A contradiction in terms? *Journal of Common Market Studies,* 40(2), 235–258.

Mikulova, K. & Simecka, M. (2013). Norm entrepreneurs and Atlanticist foreign policy in Central and Eastern Europe: The missionary zeal of recent converts. Europe-Asia Studies, 65(6), 1192–1216.

Pardo Sierra, O. B. (2011). Shaping the neighbourhood? The EU's impact on Georgia. Europe-Asia Studies, 63(8), 1377–1398.

Petrova, T. (2014). *From solidarity to geopolitics: Support for democracy among post-communist states.* Cambridge: Cambridge University Press.

Pospieszna, P. (2014). *Democracy assistance from the third wave: Polish engagement in Belarus and Ukraine.* Pittsburgh, Pa.: University of Pittsburgh Press.

Radaelli, C. M. (2000). Policy transfer in the European Union: Institutional isomorphism as a source of legitimacy. *Governance,* 13(1), 25–43.

Richter, S. (2009). *Zur Effektivität externer Demokratisierung: Die OSZE in Südosteuropa als Partner, Mahner, Besserwisser?* Baden-Baden: Nomos.

Rose, R. (1991). What is lesson-drawing? *Journal of Public Policy,* 11(1), 3–30.

Rose, R. (1993). *Lesson-drawing in public policy: A guide to learning across time and space*. Chatham, NJ: Chatham House Publishers.

Saari, S. (2009). European democracy promotion in Russia before and after the "colour" revolutions. *Democratization*, 16(4), 732–755.

Sasse, G. (2008). The European Neighbourhood Policy: Conditionality revisited for the EU's eastern neighbours. *Europe-Asia Studies*, 60(2), 295–316.

Schimmelfennig, F., Engert, S., & Knobel, H. (2002). Costs, commitment, and compliance. The impact of EU democratic conditionality on European non-member states. *EUI Working Paper RSC 2002, 29*.

Schimmelfennig, F. & Sedelmeier, U. (2004). Governance by conditionality: EU rule transfer to the candidate countries of Central and Eastern Europe. *Journal of European Public Policy*, 11(4), 661–679.

Urdze, S. (2010). *Die Externe Demokratieförderung der EU in den zentralasiatischen Staaten*. Baden-Baden: Nomos.

Vachudova, M. A. (2005). *Europe undivided: Democracy, leverage and integration after communism*. Oxford: Oxford University Press.

Warkotsch, A. (2009). The European Union's democracy promotion approach in Central Asia: On the right track? *European Foreign Affairs Review*, 14, 249–269.

The EU's policy of democracy promotion and Ukraine's bumpy path to the Association Agreement— amidst a major crisis in Europe[1]

Elena Kropatcheva

Introduction

On March 21, 2014 Ukraine and the EU signed the Association Agreement (AA), which advanced their political relations to a new level, and then on June 27, 2014 the parties signed the economic part, involving close economic cooperation and the creation of the Deep and Comprehensive Free Trade Area (DCFTA). This happened after a "Euro-Maidan revolution," Russia's annexation of Crimea, and grave destabilisation in the East of Ukraine; thus, amidst a major crisis in Europe.

This chapter analyses the EU's policy of democracy promotion towards Ukraine from February 2010, when Victor Yanukovych was inaugurated as president, until June 27, 2014 when the new Ukrainian president, Petro Poroshenko, signed the economic part of the AA. The study examines the following factors, which have impacted the EU's Ukraine policy: 1) availability of the necessary capacities for the EU to act as a normative power in Ukraine, 2) the Russian factor, and 3) domestic conditions in Ukraine. The importance of both domestic and international factors for the success of democracy promotion is noted in most studies on democracy promotion and conditionality (Carothers, 1999; Kelley, 2004; Schimmelfennig, 2005).

The chapter starts with a short overview of EU-Ukraine relations before President Yanukovych came to power. Then it examines the EU's democracy promotion (meaning, more generally, democratic practices and standards) during the Yanukovych presidency via political and diplomatic as well as financial/economic and assistance instruments. It then considers the role of the Russian factor during this period and domestic conditions in Ukraine. Next the transition period from the "Euro-Maidan" to Poroschenko's signing

---

[1] An earlier version of this manuscript was published in: Kropatcheva 2014. The author would like to thank the anonymous reviewer for the very helpful comments and Elizabeth Hormann for making the language more eloquent.

of the DCFTA is discussed. The last section draws conclusions regarding the EU's policy.

Overview of EU-Ukraine relations before Victor Yanukovych's presidency: On the slow way to the AA

EU-Ukraine relations were established in 1991.[2] However, Ukraine started pursuing a European integration policy only during Leonid Kuchma's presidency (1994–2004) in 1994,[3] when Ukraine and the EU signed a 10 year Partnership and Cooperation Agreement (PCA), which went into force in 1998 (a year after the PCA with Russia went into force). This is why the EU was criticised for its "Russia first" approach (Tocci, 2008, p. 62; Solonenko, 2009, p. 715). The PCA with Ukraine went into force earlier than with some other Commonwealth of Independent States (CIS) countries, who in turn criticised the EU for its "Ukraine first" policy.

In the 1990s, EU policy was overall quite passive towards Ukraine (Moshes, 2003), with the focus on stability and market economy reforms (Solonenko, 2009). Only with enlargement, did the EU become more active in general and in promoting democracy in particular. Ukraine played a special role in the considerations of the EU about a "Wider Europe" policy and, in 2004 the country was included in the European Neighbourhood Policy (ENP). Nonetheless, EU-Ukraine relations mostly remained "binding in rhetoric but shallow in action" (Korosteleva, 2012, p. 84). Kuchma's foreign policy became notorious because of its multi-vector character, which in practice meant that the ruling elites instrumentalised and prioritised either the Russian or the Western vector at different times, without a real commitment to either (Kuzio, 2003; Kropatcheva, 2010a; Wolczuk, 2003). The country was not moving forward on democracy (Wilson, 2005).

The "Orange Revolution" in Ukraine in the winter of 2004–2005 and the coming to power of the pro-Western President Victor Yushchenko raised many futile hopes, both within Ukraine about its quick prospect for membership in the EU, as well as in the EU about a quick democratic transfor-

---

[2] Statement by EPC Ministerial Meeting concerning Ukraine. Declaration. Document 91/427. December 2, 1991, Brussels, The Hague.
[3] The EC's Delegation to Ukraine. Ukraine-EU: Chronology of Bilateral Relations. Accessed July 10, 2014. http//www.delukr.ec.europa.eu/page4824.html.

mation of Ukraine. On January 22, 2007 the Council of the EU adopted the negotiating directives for an "enhanced agreement" between the EU and Ukraine (Council of the EU, 2007). This was a procedural window of opportunity, which coincided with a political one: the PCA had to be replaced with a new agreement in any case. This gave the EU a chance to support Ukraine and enhance the level of their relations without giving Ukraine a clear membership prospect. In September 2008, the EU and Ukraine decided that their new agreement would be an AA with a DCFTA.[4] In 2008, Ukraine was also included in the Eastern Partnership (EaP) Initiative (European Commission (EC), 2008).

Despite this, Yushchenko's presidency was notorious for constant internal strife and political crises (Kropatcheva, 2010b) as well as "stagnated Europeanization" (Korosteleva, 2012, p. 85). Nevertheless, there were some important democratic achievements such as free elections and mass media.

The 2010 presidential election reversed the political situation in Ukraine once again, by transferring power from Yushchenko to his former rival Yanukovych. Overall, neither the EU nor Ukraine showed enough commitment to build a long-term strategy for developing their relationship. The EU failed to understand complex domestic processes in Ukraine, especially after the "Orange Revolution," which led to its overly optimistic expectations and later to mutual disappointment.

The mismatch between EU efforts at democracy promotion and Ukraine's performance during the presidency of Victor Yanukovych

At the start, EU-Ukraine relations seemed to develop positively after Victor Yanukovych's election. During his pre-election campaign, he promised to strengthen the strategic partnership with the EU, while also resetting relations with Russia (Kropatcheva, 2013). Yanukovych chose the EU for his first foreign policy visit as president. Representatives of the new Ukrainian government consistently reaffirmed Ukraine's commitment to proceed on the path towards European integration (Delo.ua, 2012), and the government

---

[4] EU-Ukraine Summit. Joint Declaration on the EU-Ukraine Association Agreement, September 9, 2008, http://www.mfa.gov.ua/mfa/en/news/print/15263.htm.

of Yanukovych did much more within the country to promote EU integration than his predecessor.[5]

To support Ukraine, the European Parliament (EP) passed a resolution that explicitly acknowledged that Ukraine "may apply for membership of the EU like any European state that adheres to the [EU] principles ..." (EP, 2010b). Economic relations were developing well.[6] In 2011, Ukraine became a member of European Energy Community. By the end of 2011, Ukraine completed negotiations on the AA, the first EaP country to do this, as well as on the DCFTA.

Nonetheless, the overall record of achievements by the Yanukovych government in terms of approximating EU democratic values and practices was negative. Though there were specific advances in a few sectors, the Ukrainian government implemented EU rules selectively and was prepared to work only on reforms that would not undermine the power of the ruling elite, just like the past Ukrainian governments (Casier, 2011; Razumkov Centre, 2012; Natorski, 2013).

President Yanukovych had centralised power by undertaking such steps as changing legislative procedures to create a pro-presidential parliamentary majority, expanding the president's formal powers through a return to Ukraine's original constitution, creating a party of power (Party of Regions) and using different coercive approaches against his (potential) opponents (Kudelia, 2014, pp. 19–23). As a result of frequent attacks on the mass media, human rights activists and the opposition, as well as the dependency of the judicial system on executive power and the growing role of the security services (Korrespondent, 2011), the situation in the country was described in terms of "Putinisation" (Zhdanov, 2010) or even "Lukashenization" (Bezsmertny, 2012). According to the Bertelsmann-Transformation-Index (BTI, 2012), Ukraine was the only country of 128 studied by BTI in which all aspects of political participation had worsened by comparison to the situation in 2010. Freedom House downgraded Ukraine's rating from "free" in 2010 to "partly free" in the following years (cf. Freedom House, 2010 and

---

[5] This was admitted by many Ukrainian EU experts in interviews with the author in October 2013, Kyiv.

[6] More information on EU-Ukraine economic relations in: DG Trade, "Ukraine," January 10, 2012.

2013) and the Organization for Security and Co-operation in Europe (OSCE)/Office for Democratic Institutions and Human Rights (ODIHR) (2012) assessed the parliamentary elections in 2012 as "a step backwards." The EU tried to counteract these developments, by "diffusing" its norms and values and "socialising" Ukraine.[7] Thereby, the EU addressed different levels of society—government officials, business representatives, local authorities, educators and civil society activists (Casier, Korosteleva, & Whitman, 2013). The EU used many political and diplomatic channels, such as various joint EU-Ukraine executive bodies and communication formats, and bilateral and regional agreements reflecting and reiterating the EU's acquis (Korosteleva, 2012). Most of the EU-Ukraine documents signed in this period stress the "common values" of the two parties and task Ukraine with strengthening them through reforms with the guidance and assistance of the EU.

The main leverage that the EU had vis-à-vis Ukraine during Yanukovych's presidency was exerting influence based on his pledge to sign the AA and DCFTA during his term. He saw this as a way to achieve more domestic and international legitimacy for his rule and strengthen his chances of being re-elected. The next sections take a closer look at the political/diplomatic and economic/financial instruments the EU applied in promoting democracy in Ukraine.

The EU's use of political and diplomatic instruments in the Tymoshenko case

The most obvious example of the EU's inability to have a serious impact on Ukraine was the imprisonment of Yulia Tymoshenko, former Prime Minister of Ukraine. In 2011, she was found guilty of exceeding her powers while in office by ordering the state energy firm, Naftogaz, to sign a burdensome gas deal with Russia in 2009. This case was used politically by Yanukovych to eliminate his opponent.[8] Before the court ruling on the Tymoshenko case was made, the EU condemned the trial and tried to influence it (Kudelia,

---

[7] On socialisation see, for example: Schimmelfenning, 2005; Schimmelfennig, Engert & Knobel, 2006; on diffusion see: Gilardi, 2012; Börzel & Risse, 2012.

[8] Before this gas case Yanukovych was also searching for other cases to raise criminal charges against her. For more information see: Kudelia 2013, pp. 34-36.

2013). However, overall, the EU was rather passive at that time because European officials did not believe that a guilty verdict was possible.[9] This is why the EU belatedly became more active, after the imprisonment of Tymoshenko. The focus of this section is largely on the actions of the European Parliament, because of its very active role in this case, but also because this helps to demonstrate the different positions and indecisiveness within the EU.

The EU used statements, calls and resolutions, attempting to employ "blaming and shaming," promises and warnings that all amounted to rather futile efforts to impact the Ukrainian government's conduct. On October 27, 2011 the EP adopted a harsh resolution on Ukraine, criticising the imprisonment of Tymoshenko and warning that a failure to review her conviction would "jeopardize" the conclusion of the AA, pushing the country further away from "the realization of its European perspective" (EP, 2011b).

Even though the EU was unified in condemning the case, there was no unity about what to do next. This reflects the lack of a long-term strategy towards Ukraine in general, but also the divergent specific interests of EU member states. For instance, Polish representatives, who aimed to make their presidency in the Council of the EU as well as the Poland-driven EaP look successful, argued that negotiations on the AA "should be completed and the document should be initialled as planned under the Polish Presidency... Subsequently, its signature and ratification could be declined if no changes take place in Ukraine" (EP, 2011a). Poland was also afraid that a strict EU position could push Ukraine towards closer relations with Russia. A Romanian representative, on the contrary, wondered "why we need to continue doing what we have been doing for a good few months. ... Yanukovych was not at all receptive to this message..." (EP, 2011a).

At the Ukraine-EU summit in November 2011 "a common understanding" was reached on the text of the AA, but the document was not initialled. The joint declaration revealed the pressure that the EU exerted on Ukraine: "Ukraine's performance, notably in relation to respect for common values and the rule of law, will be of crucial importance for the speed of its political

---

[9] Author's interviews in the European Commission and Parliament, Brussels, April 2012.

association and economic integration with the EU, including in the context of conclusion of the Association Agreement."[10]

Subsequently, the EU's critique of the deterioration of democracy in Ukraine continued in 2012 and 2013. Nonetheless, instead of granting Tymoshenko amnesty, new charges of fraud and tax evasion were raised against her. In 2012, the former Interior Minister Yury Lutsenko was also sentenced. The EU criticised this verdict as well.[11]

The critical positions of the EU were presented by the Yanukovych government as something positive. For instance, according to Kostyantyn Gryshchenko the then Minister of Foreign Affairs, the critique of the EP reaffirmed that Ukraine was on course towards European integration (RBC Ukraine, 2011). Another example is the official response of Ukraine to a very critical article written by the heads of Ministries of Foreign Affairs of five EU states (Bildt, Hague, Schwarzenberg, Sikorski, & Westerwelle, 2012): the Ukrainian MFA saw in it a "confirmation of Ukraine's belonging to the European family" and the EU's readiness "to contribute to Ukraine's Eurointegration."[12] These messages were addressed to a domestic audience and were intended to show Yanukovych's confidence and progress in negotiations with the EU, but they also indicate that the Ukrainian government was not taking EU criticism seriously enough. It believed that the EU would proceed with the AA in any case.

Indeed on March 30, 2012 the AA and DCFTA were initialled. In December 2012, the Council of the EU (2012) set requirements, which Ukraine needed to fulfil, for the AA to be signed. However, in practice, the main focus was on the Tymoshenko case, while other conditions remained in the background. The EP set up a special mission, which undertook 22 visits to Ukraine, requesting Tymoshenko's pardon (Cox & Kwasniewski, 2013).

---

[10] Ukraine-EU Summit Joint Declaration, November 25, Brussels, http://eeas.europa.eu/delegations/ukraine/press_corner/all_news/news/2011/2011_12_20_01_en.htm.

[11] Statement by High Representative Catherine Ashton and Commissioner Stefan Füle on the verdict of Yuriy Lutsenko in Ukraine, February 27, 2012, Memo 12/140, http://europa.eu/rapid/pressReleasesAction.do?reference=MEMO/12/140&format=HTML&aged=0&language=EN&guiLanguage=en.

[12] Alexander Diskusarov, press secretary in Ukraine's MFA, cited in: "MID Ukrainy ras'tsenil kritiku ES kak gotovnost' pomoch evrointegratsii," *Zerkalo Nedeli*, March 6, 2012, http://zn.ua/POLITICS/mid_ukrainy_rastsenil_kritiku_ec_kak_gotovnost_pomoch_evrointegratsii.html.

Even though officially the EU did not set deadlines for its partner countries to decide on signing the AA, different representatives of EU member states emphasised that the EaP summit in Vilnius was an important deadline for Ukraine in terms of "now or never"—otherwise the prospect of its European integration would be delayed "for years."[13]

Nonetheless, new charges were raised against Tymoshenko in 2012 and 2013. The only achievement was that Lutsenko was released in April 2013. Just before the EaP summit in 2013, the Ukrainian Rada failed to pass a resolution, which would have been a compromise solution allowing Tymoshenko to go abroad for a medical treatment, even though this refusal could have endangered the signing of the AA.

Again, the EU was divided on whether to sign the AA with Ukraine during the Vilnius EaP summit. Some members argued for strict conditionality, that Ukraine had to fulfil the conditions first ("more for more" principle), while others wanted "to avoid giving Putin the time and opportunity" to exploit Ukraine's vulnerability (Emerson, 2012). Gradually the latter argument became predominant, because throughout 2013 Russia increased pressure on Ukraine. Another argument was that the EU could not punish the whole country and especially pro-EU forces in Ukraine because of Yanukovych. As a consequence, by autumn 2013 the EU became ready to sign the AA with Ukraine, even though the government had not fulfilled its requirements.

In summary, the EU was using its traditional method of diplomatic and political pressure to bind the Yanukovych government to democracy values and norms and a European integration course. Thereby, however, the EU's normative agenda became mixed with geopolitics. The latter intervened in the conditionality politics of the EU. The EU competed with Russia in their common neighbourhood, and, as a consequence, conditionality became less important. There was no urgency to push Ukraine to sign the AA at the Vilnius Summit. The issue could have been postponed until Ukraine fulfilled the EU requirements.

At the same time, the EU applied influence belatedly, selectively, too softly and without a longer-term strategy in mind. The Yanukovych government felt the EU's indecisiveness and internal divisions and even tried to exploit

---

[13] See, for example: Interview with Pieter Jan Wolthers, Ambassador of the Netherlands to Ukraine, in: Razumkov Centre 2013a, p. 68.

them. For instance, the EU could have threatened to boycott the 2012 European Football Championship, but it did not do so. The EU did not threaten the Yanukovych government with sanctions. Instead, it initialled the AA with Ukraine, which was considered by the Yanukovych government a sign of EU weakness and a signal that it could go on with its status quo policies.

The EU's insufficient use of financial/economic and assistance instruments

Besides political/diplomatic influence, the EU also had some financial means and economic aid and assistance tools to try to impact Ukraine. The usage of these instruments had increased greatly over the years. The EU began to operate in Ukraine in early 1992 within the scope of the Technical Assistance to the Commonwealth of Independent States (TACIS) programme.[14] Until 2007, it paid for the ENP programmes out of TACIS funds. In 2007, the European Commission established a special budget to implement the ENP and later EaP, the ENP Instrument (ENPI).

Most EU Ukraine-related programmes ran under the ENPI, but there were also special democracy-related interregional programmes within the European Instrument for Democracy and Human Rights (EIDHR) and, since 2013, within the European Endowment for Democracy (EED). In 2011–2013, €470.1 million were allocated for programmes in the areas of good governance and rule of law, facilitation of entry into force of the AA and DCFTA, and sustainable development.[15] Overall, there were more than 400 programmes and smaller projects running in Ukraine in 2011–2013.[16] They dealt with different aspects of EU-Ukraine relations, from democracy promotion, support for human rights and civil society *per se*, to different projects in the areas of economy, security, environment and education, which also promoted EU values and standards.

Most of these programmes, however, were rather brief (running for just 2–3 years), involved only small groups of think tanks or experts and were, thus,

---

[14] See tables summarising the allocation of TACIS resources, 1991-1999, available at: http://www.eu.int.
[15] European Neighbourhood and Partnership Instrument. Ukraine. National Indicative Programme 2011-2013, http://ec.europa.eu/world/enp/pdf/country/2011_enpi_nip_ukraine_en.pdf, pp. 9, 34 and 35.
[16] Ibid.

largely invisible in the country. Their focus was narrowly technical, processes were overly bureaucratic, and the projects left "no space for long-term planning and strategic thinking and provid[ed] little hope for sustainability" (Jarabik & Kobzova, 2011). Some programmes were criticised for their "technocratic and inflexible approach, and for setting low political expectations" (Rotter, 2012). Many of these projects were planned in advance and were not updated to account for the negative political developments on the ground in Ukraine at the time of their implementations.

Nonetheless, the EU made some attempts to provide or suspend other economic and financial assistance instruments in attempts to impact the situation in Ukraine. In 2011, for example, the EU suspended some €100 million worth of support programmes because of Ukraine's adoption of a new law on public procurement, growing corruption and lack of transparency. The EU simply did not know how supporting monies were spent (Thomson Reuters Foundation, 2011).

The EU also discussed the possibility of aiding the drastic economic situation in Ukraine (World Bank, 2013) with €500 million in macro-financial assistance (EP, 2010a). However, this did not happen because the EU tied its macro-financial assistance to the International Monetary Fund's (IMF) assistance (EC, 2011), and Ukraine's cooperation with the IMF was problematic. In August 2010, the IMF approved a €15.1 billion standby loan for Ukraine to support the country's implementation of reforms (Roudet, 2010). Ukraine received two tranches (worth a total of over €3.4 billion). However, further aid was suspended in December 2010 because the Ukrainian authorities were not fulfilling the necessary requirements for this loan, such as the introduction of higher tariffs for gas for domestic consumption, reform of the housing and communal services sector, pension reform and measures to fight corruption and increase transparency. All other negotiations with the IMF were fruitless, and the last IMF report prior to the Vilnius EaP summit repeated that Ukraine would not get the loan. Thereby the EU's tied macro-financial assistance was also blocked.

Ukraine, for its part, expected much more financial support from the EU, especially since the signing of the AA and DCFTA would not have only long-run positive consequences for the Ukrainian economy, but also short-term losses for industries with connections to Russian enterprises. Nonetheless, the EU did not plan any support beyond the regular programmes.[17]

In sum, the EU's use of its financial, economic and assistance instruments in relation to Ukraine was inadequate, often invisible and too weak. The "sticks" were not hard enough, while the "carrots" were not provided by the EU. The EU ignored the financial and economic concerns that Ukraine had. It lacked the political will to mobilise resources to help Ukraine, though, as a much stronger economic actor than Russia, it had the capability of doing so. Many measures required by the EU and IMF could have weakened and endangered the position of Yanukovych and elites in power and thus, it was naïve to expect that the government would implement them.

The destructive influence of the Russian factor on the EU's policy

Russia's policy and influence in the EaP region was considered disruptive for the EU's policies of democratisation (Delcour, 2011, pp. 51–70; Dimitrova & Dragneva, 2009).[18] During the presidency of Yanukovych, the impact of the Russian factor increased, pushing him to turn his back on the AA.

From the start of his presidency, many analysts expected Yanukovych to become a pro-Russian president (Kuzio, 2010). Some of his first presidential decisions seemed to prove this: the notorious Kharkiv accords (the so-called "gas for fleet" agreement, according to which Russia's stationing of the Black Sea Fleet (BSF) in Sevastopol was prolonged and Ukraine received discounts on the price of Russian gas deliveries), and changing Ukrainian legislation and adopting a non-bloc status (that is introducing a pause in Ukraine's NATO membership aspirations). He also tried to mitigate some other contentious issues in relations with Russia, concerning history and language. As Arkady Moshes (2013) observed, the concessions that Ukraine made were not reciprocated by Russia. Most importantly, Russia did not decrease the gas price for Ukraine. As Moshes (2013, p. 66) explained, "neither the proximity of views on domestic norms of governance nor Yanukovych's readiness to be 'pragmatic'" in Ukraine's foreign policy

---

[17] Author's interviews with EU experts in Kyiv, October 2013.
[18] EU-Russia relations play an important role, but it is possible to consider them here only in the background.

brought harmony in relations between the two states. The main reason for this was Ukraine's focus on its sovereignty and freedom to make foreign policy choices.

Yanukovych did not become a pro-Russian president after all. Ukraine did not make all the concessions Russia was pushing for. It resisted Russia's attempts to get control over its energy transportation system and Naftogaz. Ukraine rejected participation in the Russian-led Eurasian Customs/Economic Union. This became a point of friction not only in Russian-Ukrainian, but also in Russian-EU relations (Shumylo-Tapiola, 2012; Dragneva & Wolczuk, 2012; Emerson, 2014). The EU insisted on the incompatibility of the Russian project and DCFTA (Füle, 2013a). Russia also raised many issues, such as the potential negative DCFTA impact on its economy, the overflow of EU goods under Ukrainian labels in the Russian market under cheaper customs regime and, thereby, the inability of Ukraine to participate in the CIS free trade area (Aleksashenko, 2014a; Emerson, 2014). However, this is a case of strong politicisation of the issue by both the EU and Russia, and the incompatibility arguments may be more rhetorical than realistic (Aleksashenko, 2014a).

For Russia, Ukraine's EU integration means different kinds of losses. Russia perceives Ukraine's turn to the EU as a strategic geopolitical loss vis-à-vis the West. Russia is afraid that Ukraine's closer relations with the EU will be a preparatory step for its accession to NATO (Izvestia, 2013). For instance, during Yushchenko's presidency, Ukraine applied for a Membership Action Plan (MAP) in NATO. Russia is also afraid that the Black Sea could become a "NATO sea" (Richter, 2014, p. 5). Access to the Black Sea is important because it gives Russia access to the Mediterranean Sea and contributes to its ability to influence developments in the Middle East and North Africa (ibid.). The question of withdrawal of Russian BSF, dislocated in Crimea, was often raised by pro-Western politicians.

Besides strategic considerations, Ukraine's symbolic importance as the "cradle of Russian statehood" and Russia's perception of Ukraine as not being a real nation, but rather subordinate and "brotherly" to the Russian nation-state, also played a role (Molchanov, 2002). Russia was afraid that traditional cultural and linguistic ties between the two nations would be disrupted. The EU's as well as other Western policies toward Ukraine were perceived as challenging and destructive for traditional Russian-Ukrainian relations, especially because Russian-Western relations were characterised by mistrust and increasing aggravation.

Finally, taking into account the changes in Russian domestic policy towards more nationalism and authoritarianism (Zevelev, 2014), the EU's democracy promotion policy towards Ukraine challenged not only Russia's status as a "great power" actor and its integration projects in the post-Soviet space, but also its domestic situation. Russian policy making elites were afraid of possible "colour revolutions" in Russia and Ukraine which could set a "bad" example for Russian liberal opposition who took to the streets after falsified elections in 2011–2012. A successful, stable and democratic Ukraine would mean a real alternative to authoritarian models in the post-Soviet space. All this explains why Ukraine's closer steps to integration with the EU were counter to Russia's objectives.

Thus, Russia increased pressure on Ukraine in 2013, using both sticks and carrots, trying to compel Yanukovych not to sign the AA and DCFTA with the EU. It used warnings of such dire consequences for Ukraine's economy as disruption of "traditional manufacturing and industrial relations" between the two countries (Interfax, 2013). Russia had leverage over Ukraine because of the latter's dependence on Russian gas, its accumulating debt and its worsening economic situation. Naftogaz's debt to Gazprom reached $806 million by November 2013 (Interfax-Ukraine, 2013). In summer 2013, Russia used a stricter customs regulation, which led to a stop of exports of Ukrainian products to Russia for several days. The export of some Ukrainian products, e.g. confectionery, was banned entirely. According to Fyodor Lukyanov (2013), all these "sticks" had one goal: "to shake up the Ukrainian elite ... and to make them aware that the forthcoming ceremony [of signing the AA] is not a formal act ... but a real decision with consequences." As a result, Mykola Azarov, the then Ukrainian Prime Minister, claimed that a decrease in exports to Russia by more than one quarter hit the Ukrainian economy hard explaining why "the normalization of relations with Russia is question No. 1 in our national policy" (Coalson, 2013).

Russia also used "carrots," by indicating that it could significantly decrease the price of gas deliveries for Ukraine, give it considerable credits, discounts and orders to the Ukrainian military-industrial enterprises to the sum of around $15 billion and without demanding difficult reforms (Echo Moskvy, 2013). In the words of First Deputy Prime Minister Igor Shuvalov, Russia was ready to help Ukraine, but not "without commitments on their part" (Reznik & Meyer, 2013).

Thereby, the Russian factor explains to a great extent why, several days before the EaP Summit, Ukraine officially announced its decision to "postpone" signing the AA/DCFTA (Gotev, 2013). In response, the EP adopted a critical resolution on Russia and Stefan Füle (2013b), Commissioner for Enlargement and ENP, criticised Russia's "enormous pressure". Russian representatives, in turn, accused the EU of putting pressure on Ukraine (Izvestia, 2013). Thus, Russia was playing geopolitics vis-à-vis the EU, using economic pressure and posturing. However, this was also a case of normative geopolitics for Russia: it was defending the status quo normative regime, which was closer to Russia's authoritarian course.

Russia's pressure turned out to be more effective than the EU's democracy promotion, which lacked strong economic support for Ukraine. While the EU insisted on the freedom of the EU and Ukraine to decide on their bilateral future and rejected Russia's proposal to discuss this in a trilateral format, it underestimated the Russian factor and had no adequate response to it. However, while Russia was able to win against the EU in the short run, it does not have long-term attractiveness as a sustainable model for development. According to Sergei Aleksashenko (2014b), the Kremlin wants to make all its neighbours "homeless" and "beggars," who constantly need Russia's discounts on energy, help and credits, which will not be returned, without offering any other alternatives.

Domestic impediments for EU policy in Ukraine

Conditionality works when "benefits of EU rewards exceed the domestic adaptation costs" (Schimmelfennig & Sedelmeier, 2005). Ukrainian domestic factors were a strong impediment to the EU's policy and enabled Russian pressure to work. These can explain Yanukovych's decisions, in particular his refusal to free Tymoshenko and to implement necessary, but difficult, political and economic reforms, and his decision to "postpone" signing of the AA/DCFTA.

First of all, the pre-election conditions in the country need to be taken into account. The presidential election was scheduled for 2015. Yanukovych was afraid of Tymoshenko as the strongest political opponent, who could challenge his power. This is why—despite the EU's demands—he did not free her, even though this endangered signing the AA. Thereby, he also wanted to show all other opponents that he was a strong president (Kudelia, 2013). Yanukovych wanted to maintain his regime, because, in addition to the rewards of being president, the maintenance of political power is often equal to personal security and the security of one's own belongings in corrupt political systems. A change of power could have led to accusations and procedures against him similar to those he had initiated against Tymoshenko.

The pre-election conditions also explain why the potential long-term economic prospects and benefits of a DCFTA with the EU were insufficient for Yanukovych, who urgently needed short-term financial inflows, to mitigate the economic situation in the country and thereby strengthen his pre-election ratings. Yanukovych's approval rating constantly declined: if in February 2010 about 28 per cent did not support his actions, by March 2013 their numbers had reached 53 per cent (Razumkov Centre, 2013b). Thus, he simply could not afford to implement the difficult economic reforms the EU demanded as a condition for providing more loans and assistance to Ukraine, without risking further damage to his chances of being re-elected.

Secondly, EU conditionality did not work under the Ukrainian oligarchic political system (Puglisi, 2008; Stuart, 2011). Members of the political elite, who backed Yanukovych, were striving to maintain the power and financial benefits rooted in corruption and criminal actions (Aslund, 2013). This is why implementation of many of the EU conditions, directed at a fight against corruption and an increase in transparency, was blocked by the oligarchic political elite. According to Marc Franco, the EU required an export of the model that meant the "hara-kiri" of the economic and political elite of Ukraine, a fundamental geopolitical change and a disruption of old alliances and economic links (EurActiv.com, 2014).

Furthermore, during the presidency of Yanukovych, the balance among various oligarchic groups in Ukraine was upset, because a new group of oligarchs, linked to the family and close associates of Yanukovych, appeared and alienated other oligarchs (Kobzova, 2013; Kudelia, 2014). According to some Ukrainian experts, the government's decision to postpone signing the AA reflected the struggle between two groups of oligarchs: the "old group" formed during the Kuchma presidency, which wanted to legalise their capital by going to the European market, and the younger generation of oligarchs, which emerged during Yanukovych's presidency and was more interested in re-distributing and acquiring property and in no hurry to get into European markets (Ivzhenko, 2013).

Thus, these domestic factors hindered the effectiveness of the conditionality of the EU and increased the influence of the Russian factor. "Domestic adaptation costs" were too high for the ruling Ukrainian elite. The EU's demands were not realistic. The EU acted as if these important domestic impediments were not factors in Ukrainian decision making.

From Victor Yanukovych to Petro Poroshenko through "revolution", loss of territory and war

Because of the pro-EU integration campaign during Yanukovych's presidency and also due to Russian pressure, 45 per cent of Ukrainians supported the AA by October 2013 and only 14 per cent preferred the Russia-led Customs Union (Coalson, 2013). After Ukrainians were convinced of the benefits of the AA they became confused and even angry when the government suddenly pulled back from signing the AA. As a result, the first pro-EU "Maidan" protests started in Kyiv in November. Both the Ukrainian political elite in power and the Russian government underestimated the civil society factor and the political awareness of Ukrainians, as well as the attractiveness of the EU for them.

The "Euro-Maidan" protests took place not only in the pro-Western regions of Ukraine, but also to some extent in traditional pro-Russian parts, where the population wanted a change from the corrupt Yanukovych regime. Nonetheless, the factor of the geographic division of Ukraine, which was reflected in all post-Soviet elections, remained relevant: "Euro-Maidan" gained more support in the West and the centre and "Anti-Maidan" in the East and the South of the country.[19] This regional division, the active role of

---

[19] See opinion polls for November-December 2013 in: Ukraine-Analysen, No. 126, January 28, 2014, pp. 13-15.

civil society in the Western regions of Ukraine and the existence of strong opposition parties were among the factors explaining why the protests took place and why Yanukovych was unable to create a strong authoritarian regime (Kudelia, 2014).

From the start of the protests, EU representatives expressed their support of the Ukrainian people[20] and called on all sides to remain peaceful.[21] Nonetheless, the EU had not anticipated the level the Ukrainian crisis would reach and continued to engage in negotiations with Yanukovych[22] and to issue calls for some of its programmes in a "business as usual" manner. At the same time, the EU criticised the anti-democratic actions of the Ukrainian government and its use of violence on many occasions and appealed to it to use mediation and negotiation formats.[23]

On February 21, Yanukovych and representatives of the opposition (Vitali Klitschko, Arseniy Yatseniuk and Oleh Tiahnybok), with the mediation of the foreign ministers of France, Germany and Poland, signed an agreement on de-escalation (also in the presence of a special representative of the Russian president). However, this agreement was not accepted by Maidan activists. On February 22, Yanukovych fled the country and one day later the Rada elected the new cabinet of ministers (more on these events in: Fesenko, 2014; Simon, 2014).

Russia assessed the developments in Ukraine as a Western-sponsored coup d'état, directed not only at undermining its strategic interests in this country and in the region, but also Putin's regime. During February 24–27, Russian forces appeared in Crimea to, according to the official explanation, strengthen the Russian BSF, dislocated there; to prevent violence against

---

[20] Statement of Jan Tombinski, the EU Ambassador to Ukraine, November 25, 2013, http://eeas.europa.eu/delegations/ukraine/press_corner/all_news/news/2013/2013_11_25_1_en.htm.

[21] The EU Delegation to Ukraine takes note of the pro-European aspirations, November 29, 2013, http://eeas.europa.eu/delegations/ukraine/press_corner/all_news/news/2013/2013_11_29_1_en.htm.

[22] Yanukovych and Barroso hold a telephone conversation, December 3, 2013, http://eeas.europa.eu/delegations/ukraine/press_corner/all_news/news/2013/2013_12_03_2_en.htm.

[23] See, for example: Statement by Commissioner Füle on the decisions adopted by the Verkhovna Rada, 17 January 2014, http://eeas.europa.eu/delegations/ukraine/press_corner/all_news/news/2014/2014_01_17_2_en.htm.

the (pro-)Russian population by the pro-Western "fascists" and "Bandera followers" who came to power in Kyiv; as well as to prevent the appearance of NATO forces in Ukraine (Putin, 2014). On March 16, a so-called referendum took place in Crimea, and on the basis of its results Crimea became a part of the Russian Federation on March 18. The legitimacy of this referendum has not been recognised internationally. At the moment of writing, destabilisation (with a great deal of Russia's presence and responsibility) continues in Ukraine, mostly in the East, with the clashes between pro-Russian/Russian separatists and the Ukrainian military, leading to many casualties and injuries and a crisis of internally displaced people and refugees.

The EU has strongly criticised Russia's annexation of Crimea and continuously expressed its support for the unity of Ukraine (Council of the EU, 2014b). In response to the situation, since March 2014 the EU has introduced a series of diplomatic and economic sanctions against close Yanukovych's associates as well as against Russia.[24] However, as of October 2015, there has been no unity within the EU on how to deal further with Russia, with some member states demanding stricter economic sanctions, while others willing to continue trade as normal. The EU's response to Russia is limited by its dependence on Russian energy and the Russian market, but also by the fear of destabilising many weak CIS countries who are dependent on trade with Russia (Aris, 2014).

Besides these punitive measures for Russia, the European Commission presented a package of supportive measures for Ukraine, including expediting the visa liberalisation process and a seven-year financial assistance package of at least €11 billion in loans and grants (EC, 2014). The IMF macroeconomic assistance was de-frozen, with a stand-by loan facilitating the amount of $14–18 billion to be granted for macroeconomic stabilisation of Ukraine.[25] The new Ukrainian government passed a new version of the law concerning government procurement on April 10, 2014 adjusting the

---

[24] See, for example: Council of the EU 2014a. EU's Russia policy during this crisis goes beyond the scope of this study. For more information on EU sanctions see: Aris 2014; Raik, Helwig, & Jokela 2014.

[25] IMF announces staff level agreement with Ukraine on 14-18 billion USD Stand-by Agreement, *Press Release* No. 14/131, March 27, 2014, http://www.imf.org/external/np/sec/pr/2014/pr14131.htm.

relevant regulation to EU legislation (Sidenko, 2014). The EU also unilaterally set to zero about 98 per cent of trade customs for Ukrainian goods until November 1, 2014. According to EU estimates, this agreement may save Ukraine about €500 million.[26] Thus, the EU started using economic assistance tools to help Ukraine in an unprecedented manner.

Besides economic/financial help, the EU also showed strong political support to the new Ukrainian government. It separated the political and economic parts of the AA, so that the easier political part could be signed on March 21. The AA is the most advanced agreement the EU has ever offered to its partners outside of accession. It is intended to expedite Ukraine's process of adopting the EU's acquis. Ukraine itself needs the reforms demanded by the EU to reduce corruption, to become more efficient and, thereby, to save funds. The AA reiterates democratic values. Furthermore, the EU shows flexibility in how certain parts of the AA will be applied through "provisional application", that is before the ratification process is over, as it may take a long time. Finally, on June 27, 2014 Ukraine and the EU signed the economic part of the AA.

Another important political step was the EU's support for conducting the early presidential election in Ukraine on May 25, 2014 as a vital step to stabilising the country through legitimate elections (OSCE/ODIHR, 2014). Petro Poroshenko became the new Ukrainian president. There is some paradox in this, as an oligarch was brought into power by an anti-oligarchic protest movement. His election programme was pro-European and all his statements speak of "European choice", "European values", "to be real Europeans", and "Ukrainian is European" (Grabovskii, 2014). In his inauguration speech, Poroshenko (2014) declared that the AA was the first step to Ukraine's membership in the EU. According to the Ukrainian Ambassador to the EU, Kostyantin Yelisieiev, the EU needs to start "revitalizing discussions" on a clear membership perspective for Ukraine, which would be "the light at the end of the tunnel," especially since Ukraine has "paid in blood" for it (EurActiv.com, 2014). There is also more pressure on the EU and the new Ukrainian government from the Ukrainian civil society and educational

---

[26] S 15 maya Evrosoyuz otkryl dlya Ukrainy svoi rynok, *Zerkalo nedeli*, May 15, 2014, http://zn.ua/ECONOMICS/evrosoyuz-otkryl-svoy-rynok-dlya-ukrainskih-tovarov-145059_.html.

elite. Alyona Getmanchuk (2014) writes that "...it is now crucial that the EU should finally determine where it wants to see Ukraine in the long term: Within the European Union, or outside it," pointing out that its other initiatives are not adequate substitutes for EU membership.

According to polls by the Razumkov Centre, as of June 2014, about 53 per cent of the population would like to see their country be a member of the EU. The number of opponents of Ukraine's participation in the Russian-led Customs/Eurasian Union has grown to 61 per cent. The regional division of Ukraine still comes through, though to a lesser extent: Support for EU membership is strongest in the West (88 per cent) and in the centre of Ukraine (64 per cent). In the South and in the East support for the AA and for the Customs Union is approximately the same, excluding Donbass (where 68 per cent support integration in the Customs Union).[27]

The EU is still divided and ambivalent on the issue of Ukraine's long term membership prospects. Many EU member-states are not ready to give Ukraine a clear promise.[28] According to Jan Tombinski, EU Ambassador to Ukraine, reaching an agreement on signing the AA with Ukraine was a difficult task (EurActive.com, 2014). For now, the EU is continuing its policy of "The door is neither closed nor open" (Youngs, 2009, p. 367), which has led to much disappointment in Ukraine in the past.

Finally, with respect to the security situation in Ukraine, the EU is also trying to be a liberal peace power, acting as a mediator between Russia and Ukraine. The EU uses the available bilateral ties (especially Germany and France with Russia and Ukraine), multilateral frameworks (especially the OSCE) and multilateral negotiation formats. It has rejected military involvement in the crisis from the start, but in July it established the EU Advisory Mission for Civilian Security Sector Reform in Ukraine (EUAM Ukraine), a civilian, unarmed, non-executive mission under the EU's Common Security and Defence Policy (Council of the EU, 2014c).

---

[27] *Zerkalo Nedeli*, June 26, 2014, http://zn.ua/article/print/POLITICS/podderzhka-vstupleniya-v-es-v-ukraine-vyrosla-do-50-v-tamozhennyy-soyuz-upala-do-20-147891_.html.

[28] MID Franzii: Evrosoyuz ne gotov prinyat' Ukrainu v svoy sostav, *Zerkalo nedeli*, June 8, 2014, http://zn.ua/POLITICS/mid-francii-evrosoyuz-ne-gotov-prinyat-ukrainu-v-svoy-sostav-146722_.html.

Summing up, the EU's policy towards Ukraine has developed during this crisis from initially being blind to its scale and implications and trying to conduct a "business as usual" approach to taking unprecedented more recent measures to support Ukraine and punish Russia, and thus to change its status quo policy. However, most of the measures taken by the EU are of short-term character, and the EU lacks a strategic plan of how to provide Ukraine all of the political and especially financial/economic help it will need to avoid state bankruptcy and to mitigate the difficult internal situation. Furthermore, the current sanctions against Russia may turn out to be insufficient to stop Moscow from further destabilising Ukraine. It is questionable whether the EU will be bold enough to take more effective sanctions, which could hurt European interests to a larger extent (for example, concerning energy deliveries from Russia).

Conclusion

During the Presidency of Victor Yanukovych the EU's policy of democracy promotion in Ukraine focused on signing the AA and DCFTA. This objective was achieved in the end after a major political crisis and change of power in Ukraine and amidst the most dramatic crisis in European and Russian-Western relations since the end of the Cold War.

The EU used a variety of diplomatic, political and financial/economic assistance tools to act as a normative power and influence the conduct of the then Yanukovych government. However, the success of their application was undermined by disagreements within the EU, its unclear position on the long-term membership prospects of Ukraine and, especially, the lack of political will to commit itself to it. Furthermore, the EU's policy was undermined by a number of misperceptions.

Russia was able to block the EU's policy towards Ukraine, and the EU was taken by surprise both by Russia's strong pressure on Ukraine before the Vilnius Summit as well as its aggressive actions afterwards. The EU thought that it could ignore the triangle of relations—Ukraine, EU and Russia—and just focus on its bilateral EU-Ukraine component. In the EU's logic, it did not perceive itself as a threat to Russia and thus it did not take into account how Russia viewed the EU—as a challenger and a threat to its strategic interests and values as well as to its policies in the neighbourhood and domestically. The EU also overestimated the importance of the European foreign policy vector for Russia as a constraining factor. Nevertheless, Russia's pressure could have been expected. This shows that the EU did not and does not have a clear Russia strategy nor does it understand Russian domestic developments and the motives behind its foreign policy. It also underestimated the importance of the Russian factor in its relations with Ukraine.

The EU *volens nolens* got into a geopolitical fight with Russia. Thereby, Russia wanted to win Ukraine regardless of the material costs and so did the EU, regardless of whether Ukraine fulfilled its conditions and followed its principles. Ukraine tried to balance between the two actors since the collapse of the USSR. Yet, the EU and Russian policies *de facto* pushed Ukraine to make a choice of one over the other; thus bringing its internal politics out of balance. No one, neither the then Ukrainian government nor the EU, nor Russia, was prepared for the internal crisis that followed in the country.

The EU policy was also undermined by domestic factors in Ukraine and by its own misperception and lack of understanding of these. The EU ignored the challenges the country was facing. The drastic economic situation in Ukraine which pushed Yanukovych closer to Russia and further from the EU had been there since 2008, but the EU did not do much to support Ukraine financially.

While the EU has strong normative attractiveness for a majority of the Ukrainian people, this was insufficient during the Yanukovych presidency given the conditions of different internal power games in the context of the approaching elections and oligarchism. The EU's Ukraine policy was unrealistic: It expected to be able to influence the Yanukovych government to adopt more EU acquis in its domestic policies, despite the high costs and risks for the ruling regime. The EU has been present in Ukraine on the ground. Still, it acted without taking the Ukrainian context into account. As a result, the EU set unrealistic conditions for Ukraine, which the then government was simply unable to fulfil. In addition, while the main debate in EU-Ukraine relations during the Yanukovych presidency focused on Ukraine's signing the AA during the EaP Summit in Vilnius and the release of Tymoshenko as the main precondition for this, there were no discussions on what would come next, after the AA had been signed.

However, the period under study shows a certain evolution of the EU's policy in response to the dramatic developments in/around Ukraine. The EU still acts as a normative power, insisting on international norms and democratic values, but it has also shown that it can take some hard measures and be a stronger actor. The EU was able to agree on sanctions on Russia, which go counter to the interests of some of its member states. While the EU lacked the political will and seemed to lack the necessary resources to help Ukraine before the Vilnius Summit, simply making distant promises, it was able to use the acute crisis to find the political will and mobilise some resources to support Ukraine in the short run. Thereby, it proved that it can be flexible and decisive.

It is still unclear, however, how the Ukraine conflict will be resolved. The EU needs to find ways to act as an effective mediator and security provider in the region, to contribute to restoring peace in Ukraine's territory and to stop Russia from further aggressive actions. Already this task is one of the biggest political and security challenges the EU has ever faced. Furthermore, the signing of the AA is not the end but rather the beginning of a difficult process of domestic changes in Ukraine. The EU needs to support the country in implementing constitutional reform and de-centralisation, stabilising the economy, fighting corruption and oligarchism, and supporting different difficult reforms—and all this under even more challenging domestic political, economic and wider geopolitical conditions than before. It is unclear whether the EU realises the scope of these tasks and how many financial/economic and political resources it will need to commit to Ukraine in the long run to help it. The question of the EU's long-term strategy towards both Ukraine and Russia is unresolved and the EU is divided on many related issues.

References

Aleksashenko, S. (2014a). *For Ukraine, Moldova, and Georgia free trade with Europe and Russia is possible*. Carnegie Moscow Center, July 3. Retrieved from http://carnegie.ru/eurasiaoutlook/?fa=56074.

Aleksashenko, S. (2014b). *O prave natsii na samoopredelenie*. Echo Moskvy Blog. Retrieved from http://www.echo.msk.ru/blog/aleksashenko/1345330-echo/.

Aris, B. (2014). Impact of sanctions on Russia: An assessment. *European Leadership Network Policy Brief*, June.

Aslund, A. (2013). Payback time for the "Yanukovych family". Peterson Institute for International Economics, December 11. Retrieved from http://blogs.piie.com/realti me/?p=4162.

Bezsmertny, R. (2012). 'Lukashenizatsiiia' Ukrainy. *Zerkalo nedeli*, March 2. Retrieved from http://zn.ua/POLITICS/lukashenizatsiya_ukrainy-98189.html.

Bildt, C., Hague, W., Schwarzenberg, K., Sikorski, R., & Westerwelle, G. (2012). Ukraine's slide. *New York Times*, March 5. Retrieved from http://www.nytimes.com/2012/03/05/opinion/05iht-edbildt05.html.

BTI. (2012). *Politische Trends*. Retrieved from http://www.bertelsmann-stiftung.de/bst/de/media/xcms_bst_dms_35765_ 35766_2.pdf.

Börzel, T. A. & Risse, T. (2012). From Europeanisation to diffusion: Introduction. *West European Politics*, 35(1), 1–19.

Carothers, T. (1999). *Aiding democracy abroad. The learning curve*. Washington, D.C: Carnegie Endowment for International Peace.

Casier, T. (2011). To adopt or not to adopt: Explaining selective rule transfer under the European Neighbourhood Policy. *Journal of European Integration*, 33(1), 37–53.

Casier, T., Korosteleva, E., & Whitman, R. G. (2013). Building a stronger Eastern Partnership: Toward an EaP 2.0. *Global Europe Center Policy Paper*, No.1.

Coalson, R. (2013). Ukraine's choice: East or West? *RFE/RL*, November 15. Retrieved from http://www.rferl.org/articleprintview/25169110.html.

Council of the EU. (2007). *Council Conclusions concerning the negotiation of a new Enhanced Agreement between the EU and Ukraine*. 2776th External Relations Council Meeting. Brussels, January 22.

Council of the EU. (2012). *Council Conclusions on Ukraine*, 3209th Foreign Affairs Council meeting, Brussels, December 10.

Council of the EU. (2014a). *Decision 2014/119/CFSP*. Retrieved from http://eur-lex.europa.eu/LexUriServ/LexUriServ.do?uri=OJ:L:2014:066:0026:0030:EN:PDF.

Council of the EU. (2014b). EU condemns Russia's actions in Ukraine, calls for dialogue and remains ready for further measures. *EU @ UN—Partnership in Action*, March 4. Retrieved from http://eu-un.europa.eu/articles/en/article_14680_en.htm.

Council of the EU. (2014c). EU establishes mission to advise on civilian security sector reform in Ukraine. *Press Release*, ST 11974/14, Brussels, July 22.

Cox, P. & Kwasniewski, A. (2013). *European Parliament Monitoring Mission to Ukraine, Mission Update on April 18*, Strasbourg.

Delcour, L. (2011). *Shaping the post-Soviet space? EU policies and approaches to region-building*. Surrey: Ashgate.

Delo.ua. (2012). *Klyuyev: Evrointegratsiya ostaetsya prioritetom dlia Ukrainy*, February 29. Retrieved from http://delo.ua/ukraine/kljuev-evrointegracija-ostaetsja-prioriteto m-dlja-ukrainy-174172/.

Dimitrova, A. & Dragneva, R. (2009). Constraining external governance: Interdependence with Russia and the CIS as limits to the EU's rule transfer in the Ukraine. *Journal of European Public Policy,* 16(6), 853–872.

Dragneva, R. & Wolczuk, K. (2012). Russia, the Eurasian Customs Union and the EU: Cooperation, stagnation or rivalry? *Chatham House Briefing Paper*, August. Retrieved from http://www.chathamhouse.org/sites/files/chathamhouse/public/Research/Russia%20and%20Eurasia/0812bp_dragnevawolczuk.pdf.

EC. (2008). *Communication from the Commission to the European Parliament and the Council. Eastern Partnership.* Brussels, December 3, Doc. COM(2008) 823 final. Retrieved from http://eeas.europa.eu/eastern/docs/index_en.htm.

EC. (2011). *Proposal for a regulation of the European Parliament and of the Council laying down general provisions for macro-financial assistance to third countries.* Brussels, July 4, COM (2011) 396 final, 2011/0176 (COD). Retrieved from http://eur-lex.europa.eu/LexUriServ/LexUriServ.do?uri=COM:2011:0396:FIN:EN:PDF.

EC. (2014). *European Commission's support to Ukraine. IP/14/219.* Retrieved from http://europa.eu/rapid/press-release_IP-14-219_en.htm.

Echo Moskvy. (2013). *Interview by V. Varfolomeeva with A. Venediktov "O situatsii na Ukraine"*, December 7. Retrieved from http://www.echo.msk.ru/programs/beseda/1213257-echo/.

Emerson, M. (2012). The Ukraine Question. *European Neighbourhood Watch,* No. 80.

Emerson, M. (2014). Trade policy issues in the wider Europe—that led to war and not yet to peace. *CEPS Working Document,* No. 398.

EP. (2010a). *MEPs approve €500 million EU loan to Ukraine. Press release,* May 17. Retrieved from http://www.europarl.europa.eu/sides/getDoc.do?language=en&type=IM-PRESS&reference=20100517IPR74656.

EP. (2010b). *Resolution of February 25, 2010 on the situation in Ukraine.* Doc. P7_TA-PROV(2010)0035.

EP. (2011a). *Debates. Current developments in Ukraine*, October 12, 2011, Brussels. Retrieved from http://www.europarl.europa.eu/sides/getDoc.do?pubRef=-%2f%2fEP%2f%2fTEXT%2bCRE%2b20111012%2bITEM-017%2bDOC%2bXML%2bV0%2f%2fEN.

EP. (2011b). *Resolution of October 27, 2011 on the current developments in Ukraine.* Retrieved from http://www.europarl.europa.eu/sides/getDoc.do?pubRef=-//EP//TEXT+TA+P7-TA-2011-0472+0+DOC+XML+V0//EN.

EurActiv.com. (2014). *Diplomats polemicise over Ukraine's EU membership perspective*, 3 June. Retrieved from http://www.euractiv.com/sections/europes-east/diplomats-polemicise-over-ukraines-eu-membership-perspective-302549.

Fesenko, V. (2014). Krizis v Ukraine v vospriyatii ukraintsev. *Pro et Contra,* 18(3–4), 26–35.

Freedom House. (2010). *Freedom in the world. Ukraine.* Retrieved from https://freedomhouse.org/report/freedom-world/2010/ukraine#.VIs-GLG5WUk.

Freedom House. (2013). *Freedom in the world.* Retrieved from http://www.freedom house.org/report/freedom-world/2013/ukraine#.U8jlGkBkxQA.

Füle, S. (2013a). *ENP—priorities and directions for change*, Speech/13/661, July 25, Warsaw: Annual Conference of Polish Ambassadors. Retrieved from http://euro pa.eu/rapid/press-release_SPEECH-13-661_en.htm.

Füle, S. (2013b). *Statement on the pressure exercised by Russia on countries of the Eastern Partnership.* EP Parliament Plenary, Strasbourg, 11 September, Speech/13/687.

Getmanchuk, A. (2014). Tracing the origins of the Ukraine crisis: Should the EU share the blame? *Europe's World*, June 15. Retrieved from http://europesworld.or g/2014/06/15/tracing-the-origins-of-the-ukraine-crisis-should-the-eu-share-the-bla me/#.U9D9KqPX_ct.

Gilardi, F. (2012). Transnational diffusion: Norms, ideas, and policies. In W. Carlsnaes, T. Risse, & B. Simmons (Eds), *Handbook of International Relations* (pp. 453–477). Thousand Oaks: SAGE Publications.

Gotev, G. (2013). Ukraine stuns EU by putting association deal on ice. *EurActiv.com*, November 21. Retrieved from http://www.euractiv.com/global-europe/ukraine-stu ns-eu-putting-associa-news-531873.

Grabovskii, S. (2014). Deistvovat' po-evropeiski. *Den'*, June 27. Retrieved from http:// www.day.kiev.ua/ru/print/425430.

Interfax. (2013). Russian deputy PM paints black picture of Ukraine's future in EU. *David Johnson's Russia List*, No. 204, November.

Interfax-Ukraine. (2013). *Naftogaz reduces debt to Gazprom to $806 million*, 6 November 6. Retrieved from http://en.interfax.com.ua/news/economic/173688.html.

Ivzhenko, T. (2013). Ukrainian expert warns oligarchs may back pro-EU demonstrations. *Nezavisimaya Gazeta*, November 27.

Izvestia. (2013). Konstantin Volkov's interview with the head of the State Duma international affairs committee Alexey Pushkov "The EU does not explain where to take funds to modernize Ukraine". *David Johnson's Russia List*, No. 2016, November.

Jarabik, B. & Kobzova, J. (2011). European Neighbourhood Policy: Addressing myths, narrowing focus, improving implementation. *CES Paper*, June. Retrieved from http://martenscentre.eu/sites/default/files/publication-files/european_neighbourho od_policy.pdf.

Kelley, J. (2004). International actors on the domestic scene: Membership conditionality and socialization by international institutions. *International Organization*, 58(3), 425–457.

Kobzova, J. (2013). The EU's relationship with Ukraine: Fling or partnership? *ECFR*, March 14. Retrieved from http://www.ecfr.eu/article/commentary_the_eus_relat ionship_with_ukraine_fling_or_partnership.

Korosteleva, E. (2012). *The European Union and its eastern neighbours: Towards a more ambitious partnership?* London: Routledge.

Korrespondent. (2011). *Vsia vlast' – Ya! Pochemu Yanukovych nachinaet otdaliat ot sebia silnye politicheskie figury i kontsentrirovat' vlast' v svoikh rukakh*, November 15. Retrieved from http://korrespondent.net/ukraine/politics/1282877/print.

Kropatcheva, E. (2010a). *Russia's Ukraine policy against the background of Russian-Western competition*. Baden-Baden: Nomos.

Kropatcheva, E. (2010b). Stable instability in Ukraine. *OSCE Yearbook 2009*, 137–152. Baden-Baden: Nomos.

Kropatcheva, E. (2013). Ukraine's foreign policy choices after the 2010 presidential election. In V. Feklyunina & S. White (Eds.), *The international economic crisis and the post-Soviet states* (pp. 186–206). New York: Routledge.

Kropatcheva, E. (2014). Ukraine's EU integration during the presidency of Victor Yanukovych. *CEURUS EU-Russia Working Paper*, February 16.

Kudelia, S. (2013). When external leverage fails. The case of Yulia Tymoshenko's trial. *Problems of Post-Communism,* 60(1), 29–42.

Kudelia, S. (2014). The house that Yanukovych built. *Journal of Democracy,* 25(3), 19–34.

Kuzio, T. (2003). EU and Ukraine: A turning point in 2004? *Institute for Security Studies Occasional Paper*, 47, November 1.

Kuzio, T. (2010). First 100 days of Viktor Yanukovych explodes six myths. *Eurasia Daily Monitor,* 7(109).

Lukyanov, F. (2013). Strana somneniy. *Rossiya v globalnoy politike*, November 7. Retrieved from http://globalaffairs.ru/redcol/Strana-somnenii-16192.

Molchanov, M. A. (2002). *Political culture and national identity in Russian-Ukrainian relations*. College Station: Texas A&M University Press.

Moshes, A. (2003). Dvoinoe rasshirenie i rossiisko-ukrainskie otnosheniia. In A. Moshes & K. Koktysh (Eds.), *Mezhdu vostokom i zapadom. Ukraina i Belorussiia na evropeiskom prostranstve* (pp. 7–28). Moscow: Gendalf, Carnegie Endowment for International Peace.

Moshes, A. (2013). A marriage of unequals: Russian-Ukrainian relations under President Yanukovych. In S. Meister (Ed.), *Economization versus power ambitions. Rethinking Russia's policy towards post-Soviet states* (pp. 59–72). Baden-Baden: Nomos.

Natorski, M. (2013). Reforms in the judiciary of Ukraine: Domestic practices and the EU's policy instruments. *East European Politics,* 29(3), 358–375.

OSCE/ODIHR. (2012). *Ukraine parliamentary elections 28 October 2012. OSCE/ODIHR election observation mission final report*. Retrieved from http://www.osce.org/odihr/98578.

OSCE/ODIHR. (2014). *Ukraine. Early presidential election May 25, 2014: Final report*. Retrieved from http://www.osce.org/odihr/elections/ukraine/120549.

Poroshenko, P. (2014.) *Inaguratsionnaya rech Poroshenko: polnyi tekst i video*, June 7, Retrieved from http://korrespondent.net/ukraine/politics/3375056-ynauhuratsyonnaia-rech-poroshenko-polnyi-tekst-y-vydeo.

Puglisi, R. (2008). A window to the world? Oligarchs and foreign policy in Ukraine. In S. Fischer (Ed.), *Ukraine: Quo vadis?* (pp. 55–86). Paris: EU Institute for Security Studies.

Putin, V. (2014). *Soveshanie poslov i postoiannykh predstavitelei Rossii*. Retrieved from http://news.kremlin.ru/news/46131/print.

Raik, K., Helwig, N., & Jokela, J. (2014). EU sanctions against Russia. Europe brings a hard edge to its economic power. *FIIA Briefing Paper*, No. 162.

Razumkov Centre. (2012). EU-Ukraine-Russia relations: Problems and prospects. *National Security and Defence*, 4(5), 2–3.

Razumkov Centre. (2013a). Ukraine's European integration: Internal factors and external influences. *National Security and Defense*, 4(5), 141–142.

Razumkov Centre. (2013b). *Sociological poll "Do you support the activity of the President of Ukraine?"* (recurrent, 2000–2013). Retrieved from http://www.razumkov.org.ua/eng/poll.php?poll_id=67.

RBC Ukraine. (2011). *Grishchenko: Resolutsiia Evroparlamenta podderzhivaet integratsionnyi kurs Ukrainy*, October 27. Retrieved from http://www.rbc.ua/rus/top/show/grishchenko-rezolyutsiya-evroparlamenta-podderzhivaet-evrointegratsionnyy-27102011195700.

Reznik, I. & Meyer, H. (2013). Russia offers Ukraine cheaper gas to join Moscow-led group. *Bloomberg*, December 2. Retrieved from http://www.bloomberg.com/news/2013-12-01/russia-lures-ukraine-with-cheaper-gas-to-join-moscow-led-pact.html.

Richter, W. (2014). Die Ukraine-Krise. Die Dimension der paneuropäischen Sicherheitskooperation. *SWP-Aktuell*, No. 23.

Rotter, M. E. (2012). *Good governance. Sensible but insufficient*. Retrieved from http://www.dandc.eu/articles/220194/index.en.shtml.

Roudet, S. (2010). *IMF approves $15.1 billion loan for Ukraine*. Retrieved from http://www.imf.org/external/pubs/ft/survey/so/2010/car081110a.htm.

Schimmelfennig, F. (2005). Strategic calculation and international socialization: Membership incentives, party constellations, and sustained compliance in Central and Eastern Europe. *International Organization*, 59 (Fall), 827–860.

Schimmelfennig, F., Engert, S., & Knobel, H. (2006). *International socialization in Europe: European organizations, political conditionality and democratic change*. Basingstoke: Palgrave Macmillan.

Schimmelfennig, F. & Sedelmeier, U. (2005). Introduction. Conceptualizing the Europeanization of Central and Eastern Europe. In F. Schimmelfennig & U. Sedelmeier (Eds.), *The Europeanization of Central and Eastern Europe* (pp. 1–28). Ithaca, N.Y.: Cornell University Press.

Shumylo-Tapiola, O. (2012). Ukraine at the crossroads: Between the EU DCFTA and Customs Union. *Russie.Nei.Reports*, No. 11, Russia/NIS Center IFRI.

Sidenko, V. (2014). Economic and social challenges of Ukraine after the change of power. *China Policy Review*, May, 114–118. Retrieved from http://uceps.org/eng/article.php?news_id=1120.

Simon, G. (2014). Zusammenbruch und Neubeginn. Die ukrainische Revolution und ihre Feinde. *Osteuropa*, 5/6, 9–40.

Solonenko, I. (2009). External democracy promotion in Ukraine: The role of the European Union. *Democratization*, 16(4), 709–731.

Stuart, S. (2011). Regionen und Oligarchen: Einflüsse auf die ukrainische Außenpolitik. *SWP-Studien*, 2011/S23, September.

Thomson Reuters Foundation. (2011). *EU suspends aid to Ukraine over procurement law*, February 23. Retrieved from http://www.trust.org/item/?map=eu-suspends-aid-to-ukraine-over-procurement-law.

Tocci, N. (Ed.). (2008) *Who is a normative foreign policy actor? The European Union and its global partners*. Brussels: Centre for European Policy Studies.

Wilson, A. (2005). *Virtual politics. Faking democracy in the post-Soviet world.* New Haven/London: Yale University Press.

Wolczuk, R. (2003). *Ukraine's foreign and security policy 1991–2000*. London/New York: RoutledgeCurzon.

World Bank. (2013). *World Bank Group – Ukraine Partnership: Country program snapshot*, October. Retrieved from http://www.worldbank.org/content/dam/Worldbank/document/Ukraine-Snapshot.pdf.

Youngs, R. (2009). "A door neither closed nor open": EU policy towards Ukraine during and since the Orange Revolution. *International Politics*, 46, 358–375.

Zevelev, I. (2014). Granitsy russkogo mira. *Rossiia v globalnoi politike*. Retrieved from http://globalaffairs.ru/number/Granitcy-russkogo-mira--16582.

Zhdanov, I. (2010). Novaia vlast' na Ukraine. Vyzovy i tendentsii. *Zerkalo nedeli*, 16(796). Retrieved from http://gazeta.zn.ua/POLITICS/novaya_vlast_v_ukraine_vyzovy_i_tendentsii.html.

Provisionally unsuccessful?
European democracy promotion in the South Caucasus

Shushanik Minasyan

Introduction

The aspiration of the European Union to observe the principles of democracy, rule of law and respect for human rights (European Council, 1987) led to codification of a common set of European values to guide both the internal and external governance of the EU. In addition, following the European Council's intention to establish a ring of politically stable and reliable partner states around the EU's external borders, set out in the European Security Strategy (European Council, 2003), the EU has sought to act as a normatively directed external actor in its immediate neighbourhood. Implementing this value-guided system has proven quite a different matter, however, as there is a considerable gulf between EU rhetoric and actions.

This chapter considers the extensive range of instruments available to the EU for promoting democracy and tackles the question of the extent to which the EU has been successful as a force for transmitting its basic values to the South Caucasus region. Since European democracy promotion cannot take place without a mixture of pressure and incentives, and given that the degree of cooperation in this area is dependent on the conduct of the recipient state, I also consider the question as to how consistently political conditionality has been implemented as an approach within EU democratisation policy. In order to offer a convincing answer to the question posed in the title, this contribution will highlight factors that explain why the EU has aimed at securing enduring system change in some cases but not in others. Finally, the conclusion will look at the effects of the different yardsticks and priorities adopted by the EU on its credibility and capability as a normative political actor.

European Union external democracy promotion

Although an external democratisation policy of the EU only began to acquire a formalised profile in the period after the transformations of 1989–90

(Bredies, 2009), the earlier EU engagement in democracy promotion should not be underestimated. Despite its somewhat tentative and apolitical nature,[1] EU development aid had a considerable impact in stabilising new democracies in Southern Europe.[2] Although democracy promotion initially took the form of issuing general declarations without necessarily sanctioning systematic human rights breaches in third countries (Smith, 1998), the end of the Cold War initiated a fundamental change in the EU approach.

Since the Single European Act of 1987, the EU acquired a new impetus in which diffusion of moral and political values was not only oriented 'inwards' but also "outwards". Given the challenges posed by the political and social transformations in Eastern Europe, adherence to human rights and democratic principles was anchored in the EU's foreign policy activities in the 1991 Luxembourg Declaration (European Council, 1991). This served as the basis for the first European initiative ("instrument") in the field of democracy and human rights (EIDHR), through which this area of activity then expanded over the course of the 1990s. Democracy and the rule of law, building a pluralist civil society and confidence building measures to re-establish peace have now become standard clauses in the EU's relationships with third states.

In accordance with the conditionality principle, the claim of universal validity for European values was promoted with a set of political and economic incentives intended to facilitate the gradual convergence of partner countries with the EU's *acquis*. It was only after the demise of the Eastern bloc that it became possible to test this form of political conditionality in the context of post-Communist states,[3] where EU technical and financial activities were linked to the desired system transformations and progresses in the field of good governance. In addition to market liberalisation, EU support was main-

---

[1] During the period of the Cold War political provisions were deliberately excluded from EC development aid in order to forestall any impression of (neo-)colonialism (Grilli, 1993, p. 102).

[2] Portugal, Spain and Greece after 1974-75.

[3] Two types of conditionality can be distinguished: the first had an economic character and, prior to the collapse of the Soviet bloc, was usually imposed by international financial institutions such as the World Bank and International Monetary Fund, which made financial support dependent on economic reforms. This served as a model for the second type, political conditionality, which was first established with the emergence of new independent states in the EU's eastern periphery (Fierro, 2003).

ly conditional on reforms aimed at establishing the rule of law and respect for human rights. Discussion around the prospect of the eastern enlargement of the EU legitimised the use of political conditionality for promoting democracy (Smith, 2008). The Copenhagen Summit in 1993 represented the creation of a precedent for the EC/EU to use political conditionality on a large scale, initiating a number of far-reaching changes in how Europe would seek to export democracy. In order to raise the effectiveness of external democracy promotion, recipient countries would be offered the prospect of future EU membership as an incentive.[4]

This fundamental shift in thinking placed cooperation between the EU and third states on a new footing where shaping the international environment in accordance with the European canon of values would now be a central task for all areas of EU foreign relations. Jünemann and Knodt (2006, p. 287) have termed this fragmentation of the export of democracy into diverse policy areas as "democracy mainstreaming", which amongst other things is manifested in so-called "democracy clauses" that the European Union included in all its agreements with third states since 1995.

Drawing on such fundamental milestones in the EU's stance on democratisation, this analysis will consider how instruments have been applied in the South Caucasus region. This is followed by an assessment of their impacts on democratisation processes in Armenia, Azerbaijan, and Georgia in the period since the intensification of political and economic dialogue with the EU.

The EU's instruments for democracy promotion in the South Caucasus

The first European attempts at rapprochement with the states in the South Caucasus region took place in December 1989 when the European Community and the prospectively independent Soviet Republics laid the basis for economic cooperation (Council of the European Economic Community,

---

[4] I have consciously excluded the issue of whether this new approach to enlargement achieved a satisfactory outcome. Detailed consideration of this approach, and the subsequent academic controversies, would go beyond the limits of this contribution. Not to mention "satisfactory" is subjectively linked to whose interests are under consideration.

1990). However, the EU's democratisation approach in the post-Soviet space only became explicit with the Technical Assistance to the Commonwealth of Independent States (TACIS) programme. While this programme included projects for propagating democratic principles in the eastern recipient countries,[5] in light of the chaotic political and economic situation in Armenia, Azerbaijan and Georgia the priority was seen as providing support for economic transformation (Mayer, 2007). The threats and potential conflicts in this region were not seen as urgent by the EU (Lynch, 2003). Rather, the EU's fundamental interest in South Caucasus in the period from 1991 to 1999 was confined to helping these states become full members of the international community and facilitating their integration into the global economy.

The prospect of the EU's eastern enlargement changed the perspective of European policy towards the South Caucasus region in the late-1990s. In 1997, for example, the European Parliament reaffirmed European interest in taking greater account of these countries in European foreign policy in response to a Communication from the European Commission on future cooperation with the southern Caucasus states. Noting the strategic significance of the region, the Parliament called on the Commission and the Council to adopt a more targeted approach to pursue an active European presence in South Caucasus, ensure a common European position, and implement the Common Foreign and Security Policy (CFSP) in the region (European Parliament, 1997). The outcome of this process was the conclusion of Partnership and Cooperation Agreements with Armenia, Azerbaijan, and Georgia.

Although this legal instrument was viewed by some experts as a critical step towards future cooperation between the EU and the states of the South Caucasus with EU policy becoming more consistent and targeted (Mayer, 2007), this view is not fully shared by the present author. In fact, the Partnership and Cooperation Agreements (PCA) were insufficient to bridge the distance between the EU and the three South Caucasus republics. Implementing the programme's objectives also foundered with the lack of a convincing EU presence in the region. And although these treaties reflected the EU's wish to extend the European value system into its periph-

---

[5] That is Ukraine, Belarus, and Moldova.

ery, the enterprise as a whole was dominated by economic considerations (Lynch, 2003). Despite the new format for political dialogue that the treaties offered, transferring democratic values was "more rhetorical in nature" (Jawad, 2006, p. 16) and took a back seat to the economic interests that were highlighted in the emphasis on new trade opportunities.

Eastern enlargement meant that the European Union could no longer maintain a hands-off approach towards political developments in the South Caucasus republics (Dannreuther, 2006). The new geopolitical realities after September 11, 2001 also necessitated developing a fresh approach to the region. These considerations culminated in the European Security Strategy, in which the European Council (2003) acknowledged the significance of the South Caucasus republics for security in Europe as a whole. The upshot of this process was the March 2003 European Commission Strategy Paper on European Neighbourhood Policy (ENP), the aim of which was to overhaul EU policy towards its immediate neighbours, including the South Caucasus region.

Compared with previous instruments, the ENP offered more incentives for incremental convergence towards and opened up new prospects for integration with the EU for the designated partner states. In this context, the states targeted by the ENP were regarded by the EU as preferred partners that would pursue the objective of jointly building a zone of political and economic stability (Koopmann, 2006, p. 23).

Strengthening existing cooperation with the neighbourhood states and their full integration within a single organisational framework was intended to facilitate the key priority of transferring European fundamental principles, values and norms to neighbouring regions (Prodi, 2002). The ENP's core consists of the association agreements, in which the EU and the respective partner state individually negotiate the framework for cooperation. The customary areas are strengthening the rule of law and democracy, convergence towards the *acquis communautaire*, and the development of a competitive market economy (European Commission, 2004).

Despite this fresh direction, the approach also exhibited serious deficiencies and faced critical scrutiny by many experts. The first stumbling block in the ENP was the EU's tactic of "copying and pasting" the requirements originally envisaged for the EU's enlargement. The initial drafts of the ENP country action programmes had marked similarities with previous association agreements that were intended to lay the legal foundation for future EU membership (Kelley, 2006). The nearly identical character of the two approaches was also reflected in the strong conditionality articulated by Commission President Romano Prodi in his vision for a future ENP. In his speech on future cooperation with neighbouring regions, he raised the prospect of a type of "Copenhagen Neighbour Criterion" (Prodi, 2002, p. 6). For example, the Commission's Strategy Paper makes the extent of cooperation dependent on the behaviour of the partner state—that is, implicitly subject to conditions. However, despite insisting on conditionality, the ENP is not oriented towards offering EU accession. In order to create an appropriate legal foundation for political dialogue and regional integration, partner countries are offered access to the EU's internal market, a deepening of economic relations, and the step-by-step removal of trade barriers. Although the ENP is intended as a kind of middle course between partnership and membership, the logic of imposing conditionality without simultaneously offering the powerful incentive of EU membership would appear to be a questionable tactic.

This discrepant incentive structure noted above raised considerable criticism over the lack of clarity and "double standards" (Knodt & Jünemann, 2007, p. 27) implicit in the EU's approach to democracy promotion. By applying conditionality selectively, the EU's implicit message is that the policy's central concern, compliance with the principles of democracy, human rights and the rule of law, is not in fact the most pressing task for its democratisation policy. While democratisation is accorded a high priority in the case of those states that are heavily dependent on the EU, the application of the democratisation instruments is subjectively flexible for partner states with extensive raw material resources (Bendiek, 2008). This multi-lane strategy diminishes the attractiveness of Europe as a community of values and generates justifiable doubts as to the sustainability of democracy achieved through the (lack of) imposition of political conditionality.

The final difficulty lies in the character of the ENP, and in particular the fact that competences for foreign policy are divided and Community policy can collide with the foreign policy of Member States. As a result of the considerable divergences between the interests of Member States, it is difficult to establish effective policy towards neighbourhood states (Bendiek & Kramer,

2009). Even the institutional changes in the CFSP as a result of the Lisbon Treaty did not ensure clear guidance for elaborating a consistent EU external policy towards the South Caucasus region. This simply led to the creation of a typical hybrid construct that neither made EU foreign policy more consistent nor strengthened the capacity of the Union to operate as an effective normative actor (Lippert & Schwarzer, 2011).

In 2008, the Eastern Partnership (EaP) was established following a Polish-Swedish initiative. Its aim was to add a new dimension to the ENP and maintain some balance between the EU's southern and eastern peripheries following France's development of the Mediterranean Union (Kempe, 2010). The treaty basis was laid in May 2009 in Prague at a meeting of high-level representatives of the EU and the eastern ENP states. By committing itself to this initiative, the EU signalled its willingness to offer greater support to the reform efforts of the partner countries and engage in intensive civil society dialogue (Minasyan, 2013).

Although this most recent set of proposals have been celebrated as a profound innovation in relationships with eastern neighbourhood states (European Commission, 2008a), the Eastern Partnership built on the existing structures of the ENP and, aside from the establishment of interparliamentary committees,[6] did not create any fresh scope for cooperation with the states of the South Caucasus. For example, there were no additional resources made available to finance the programme, all of which was covered out of the ENP budget (Kempe, 2010). Moreover, the plan was beset from the onset by the weaknesses that had typified the ENP. Lack of engagement on the part of EU Member States[7] also diminished the effectiveness of the plan. Even the Swedish government itself, which had cooperated in initiating the EaP, refused further support during its Presidency of the Council in 2009 (Meister & May, 2009), further detracting from the initia-

---

[6] On the initiative of the European Parliament, the interparliamentary committee EuroNest was established within the framework of the Eastern Partnership. The intention was to intensify cooperation and exchange between national parliaments (European Commission, 2008b).

[7] The fact that the heads of government of some Member States, such as France, Spain, Italy and the UK, cancelled their participation in the founding summit suggests that these countries accorded little significance to the new approach (Böttger, 2009).

tive. Given the political and economic turmoil in the EU triggered by the global economic crisis and continuing uncertainty about whether the Lisbon Treaty would come into force, the main focus of the Swedish Presidency was on EU internal matters. Furthermore, in the run-up to the Copenhagen Climate Conference in December 2009, a second overarching aim of the Presidency was to bolster the EU's efforts on climate policy (Swedish Presidency of the European Council, 2010). Thus, cooperation with the EU's eastern neighbours was largely neglected.

The EU's legitimacy was severely damaged by these events, alongside the lack of credibility and selective application of its strategy. Within the South Caucasus region, there was a conscious stress on Georgia (Kempe, 2010), with Armenia and Azerbaijan clearly given a much lower priority. As a consequence, the EU lost both these EaP states. This lack of support from Europe left Armenia unable to resist Russian pressure (Smith, 2013) and Azerbaijan announced that it was no longer interested in European cooperation frameworks (Euractiv, 2010).

A provisional assessment of democratisation in the South Caucasus

Based on the aims and direction of the European democratisation instruments noted above, the following section aims to offer a provisional assessment of the development of democracy in Georgia, Armenia and Azerbaijan.

Following the transfer of political power in 2003, the new administration in *Georgia* was able to register substantial progress in a number of areas and for some time was seen by the EU as the model for a peaceful and democratic change of government. However, hopes of a shift to a democratic system were dashed by the overbearing and autocratic ruling style of the new, young and reformist power elite (Halbach, 2008). Reforms intended to combat corruption and criminality led to major legal restrictions and an unbalanced separation of powers that favoured the office of the president (De Waal, 2011). This process culminated in the consolidation of a semi-authoritarian presidential regime with a weak parliament and a justice system that was subject to strong external control (Bendiek, 2008).

According to the democracy indices compiled by Freedom House, the scores for Georgia have stagnated since its intensification of relationships with the EU. In 2013, Georgia achieved a score of 4.75 (where 1 is highest and 10 lowest) for its democratic governance compared with 4.86 in 2006 (Freedom House, 2013c). Following the parliamentary elections in 2007, criticism soon emerged against the authoritarian governing style of President Micheil Saakashvili, throwing a negative light on the peaceful "Rose Revolution" and subsequent efforts to reform and renew the political system in Georgia (Halbach, 2007). The everyday experience of widespread nepotism, mounting corruption, and the lack of press freedom, together with the declining legitimacy of the presidency combined to dampen the popular enthusiasm of the post-revolution period.

The change of government following the 2012 parliamentary elections enabled Georgia to recover its international reputation and pass a significant test of its capacity for democratic governance (Atilgan, 2012). However, these changes turned out to be nothing more than paper promises. At the time of writing, there is a nervous sense of expectation as to whether the current government and newly-elected president Georgi Margvelashvili will carry out the promised constitutional reform to prevent future authoritarian government and facilitate fundamental changes towards a parliamentary democracy.

Although the future of relationships with the EU remained uncertain in view of the clear external shift in Georgia's foreign policy and the ending of confrontation with Russia following the installation of the new head of government, the initialisation of the association and free trade agreement at the Eastern Partnership summit in November 2013 in Vilnius brought some clarity. In light of attempts by Russia to exert pressure on EaP partner countries (Rukomeda, 2013), the EU feared a similar scenario in the case of Georgia, a development that would have signalled the failure of the EU's engagement in the entire South Caucasus region. However, Russia lacked any effective means of putting pressure on Georgia—which was able to diversify its energy supplies (Civil Georgia, 2008) and redirect its trade to western markets to allow it to decouple itself entirely from Russia's sphere of influence—meaning that the Tbilisi government could not be prevented from signing the agreement. By unilaterally recognising the seceded territories of Abkhazia and South Ossetia (Radio Free Europe, 2008), the Kremlin also sacrificed any remaining dominance over its southern neighbour.

Given the pressure previously exerted by Russia on Eastern Partnership countries and following the successful initialing of the agreement, there was concern about whether the Georgian government would go ahead and sign the association agreement, as scheduled, on June 27, 2014. According to the German Foreign Minister Frank-Walter Steinmeier, this agreement would represent a "significant milestone in relationships between Georgia and the EU" (*Süddeutsche Zeitung*, 2014). Georgia's immunity to Russian pressure meant that Tbilisi was able to decide its own foreign policy preferences and its signature of the association agreement in June 2014 indicated its intention to deepen economic and political cooperation with the EU (European Council, 2014).

Although the government of *Armenia* is occasionally the recipient of praise from the EU (European Commission, 2011), the country is generally characterised by an absence of the rule of law. In contrast to the political changes that were promised in order to meet cooperation conditions of the EU (European Communities, 1999), reforms have led to an ossification of political decision-making by an elite. In 2009, the independent Armenian analyst Richard Giragosian (2009) expressed his concern that the prospects for democratisation in Armenia were gradually being extinguished. Parliament, whose legitimacy remains highly contested at the time of writing, consists mainly of the representatives of the oligarchy and big business owners who exercise considerable dominance over the political and economic life of the country and who are highly averse to any democratic developments. Political life is marked by unconstitutional interference in governing institutions by the president and other influential politicians.

The country's "democracy score", according to Freedom House, has barely changed in recent years, with the rating actually declining between 2006 (5.14) and 2013 (5.36) (Freedom House, 2013a). The position of the media continues to be a cause for anxiety. Despite some ostensibly positive developments in the area of press freedom, members of the media report few real changes (Reporters without Borders, 2013). Although the regime avoids resorting to open force against any mass media that is critical of the government, it imposes a wide range of restrictions. For example, in 2009 a new media law was adopted that limited the rights and independence of representatives of the press. This allows the suspension of journalists whose reports are deemed not to correspond with reality and which impugn "the interests, honour and dignity" of members of parliament (Freedom House, 2010).

It was predictable that Russia would not be amenable to the foreign policy likely pursued by Armenia as a result of the intensification of political dialogue with the EU within the framework of the Eastern Partnership. Armenia plays a particularly significant role for Russian policy in the South Caucasus. Armenia is the only state in the region that is both politically and economically completely dependent on Russia. Although the Kremlin does not directly extract a profit from this dependence in financial terms, it views Armenia as a key partner in maintaining its sphere of influence on its southern periphery. As a consequence, the penetration of new confident actors, such as the EU, is seen as a potential for a dangerous shift in the balance of power to the detriment of Russia. Accordingly, and shortly before the initialisation of the association agreement in Vilnius in September 2013, the Kremlin deployed the full spectrum of its political arsenal to put pressure on the Armenian government. This included deepening military and economic cooperation between Russia and Azerbaijan and raising the price of Russian natural gas exports to Armenia from \$180 to \$250 per 1000m^3. The lack of its own energy resources and inadequate EU support meant that the government in Yerevan was unable to resist Russian pressure and, despite considerable public criticism and mass protests, in September 2013 indicated it would join the Russian-led Eurasian Customs Union (Smith, 2013). Irrespective of the motives behind this decision, the Armenian government not only undermined several years of intensive cooperation with the EU but also succeeded in isolating itself from non-Russian political and economic exchange.

The government's interest in cooperation with the EU is limited under current circumstances. The most recent developments threaten to freeze relations with the EU, despite many years of negotiation within the framework of the Eastern Partnership (Atilgan, 2013). Although Brussels has expressed the desire and determination to continue its cooperation with the Armenian government (European Commission, 2013), any such future framework for cooperation remains, as yet, unspecified.

The failure of the EU's engagement cannot simply be attributed to a pro-Russian stance on the part of the Armenian government or the increased pressure brought to bear by the Kremlin in the very recent past (Emerson & Kostanyan, 2013). The prime factor is Brussels' lack of willingness to negotiate. For example, the EU rejected the proposal made by the Armenian government that, in order to avoid exacerbating conflict with Russia, only the economic part of the association agreement should be signed. This removed Armenia's option of being able to proceed on two fronts. Brussels' line towards the Armenian government had the effect of an ultimatum. Fully aware that a requirement for an "either/or" decision could trigger a dangerous train of events for Armenia, given its asymmetric interdependence on Russia, Brussels simply refused to engage with the Armenian request for a compromise.

The EU's stance towards Armenia has been overwhelmingly confined to words rather than deeds (Gordon & Sasse, 2008). The concerns expressed by Armenian civil society about the alarming political situation and the concealment of obligations that the government had already entered into were consistently ignored by the EU, which repeatedly led to doubts about the credibility of the EU as a reliable and capable actor. Furthermore, the EU was unable to offer a coherent plan for Armenia's national security especially concerning Turkey and Azerbaijan thus limiting the persuasiveness of the incentives offered by the EU (Emerson & Kostanyan, 2013).

The effectiveness of EU democracy instruments in *Azerbaijan* tends to be judged more critically than in Georgia or Armenia (Bendiek, 2008). In view of the dynastic transfer of power within the Aliyev family, Azerbaijan is characterised by a monopoly of power held by the ruling clan and a lack of political pluralism. The country is ruled by a de facto presidential regime and decision-making machinery is largely in the hands of the president's family. The government uses political power to maximise its own gains and demands obedience and submission from the population as the price for a guarantee of years of stability. Belief in this rhetoric on the part of large sections of the population is so ingrained that those who choose to think otherwise or criticise the government are viewed as destructive and treacherous public enemies (Badalow, 2004). The analyses by Freedom House make for sobering reading. Since the intensification of dialogue between Brussels and Baku, there has been scarcely any movement in the democracy index suggesting that the governments guarantee is merely a myth. Compared with the score for 2006 (5.93), the index has clearly deteriorated (6.64)

(Freedom House, 2013b). In view of the results of the presidential election held in autumn 2013, no fundamental change is expected.

Azerbaijan's absolute independence in the fields of security and trade mean that it is especially unreceptive to the EU's value system. Its leading position in the Caspian energy economy also allows Baku to withstand European pressure for democratic reforms, and to tolerate the implementation of reform objectives with its own restrictions (Freedom House, 2009). The fact that resource-rich countries are customarily less open to reforms also means that EU conditionality lacks leverage. However, this stance is not due to the dominance of another external power, as is evident with Russia in the cases of Georgia and Armenia. Rather, the country's autarchy in the energy field and the interest of western investors in oil extraction from the Caspian basin gave the country sufficient scope for manoeuvre to control its own economy and political life. Given the prospect of political and economic autonomy, Baku considers its position to be bolstered by Washington and its Turkish ally. As a consequence, Russia has scant scope to influence Armenian politics since it also lacks leverage. According to Stewart (2010, p. 5), Baku "has a qualitatively different status in Russian foreign policy" and will not allow "any deterioration of relations" with Russia. The Russian Federation views Azerbaijan as a serious competitor, whose increasingly independent energy policy has made it a key negotiating partner for international firms in the Caspian Sea region.

The capacity of the EU has also been compromised by its own conduct. The declared aim of EU engagement—to diffuse its political and moral values in the region—has clearly been given a lower priority in the case of Azerbaijan compared to economic interests in energy policy. Concerns about the growing legitimacy problems of the Azerbaijan government are often only voiced in vague terms by senior European politicians, given the central role of the country in EU plans for diversifying its energy acquisition from the Caspian region. In view of the crisis of confidence that has beset Russian suppliers in recent years, the EU aims to forge cooperation on energy policy with other countries adjoining the Caspian Sea. Not only access to Azerbaijan's natural gas reserves, but the implementation of the EU's plans for a network of pipelines would also serve to curtail Russia's monopoly in the Caspian region and grant access to the European energy market for resource-rich Central Asia gas producers. This explains the EU's lack of conviction in asserting its values in Azerbaijan.

Conclusion

The reform processes implemented in the South Caucasus region stemming from the EU's external democracy promotion policies are not entirely satisfactory given that the three states involved continue to be characterised by great instability and a low level of democratic governance. Azerbaijan is still ruled by an autocratic leader with parliament having only limited legislative powers. The political system is dominated by the Aliyev dynasty, which based its power on indigenous energy resources. Both in Armenia and Georgia, problems inherent in the transformation process have favoured semi-authoritarian presidential regimes with weak parliaments and justice systems subject to strict political control. Despite the many positive changes that have taken place in these countries, their intrinsic democratic deficits and the lack of the rule of law mean that sustainable political and socio-economic development remains a remote prospect.

I do not claim that EU democracy promotion in South Caucasus failed entirely as its engagement led to the strengthening of civil society structures. However, selective conditionality, limited capacity for inclusion, and inconsistencies in European planning greatly diminished the effect of EU democracy promotion in the South Caucasus region. This lack of success derives partly from domestic problems of transformation in these three states. But the absence of a clear-cut strategy in the EU's democratisation policy certainly contributed to the countries' poor democratic records. The absence of effective incentives for closer integration with the EU and conflicting criteria have generated counterproductive side-effects that have made it more difficult to achieve democratisation in the South Caucasus. It is hoped that the EU will succeed in setting appropriate incentives that will enable it to place its engagement for democracy and the rule of law on a more consistent footing in the future. This is not only to enable other states to chart a better course but also to ensure that a concept that European heads of government and heads of state repeatedly invoke does not entirely lose its credibility: that is, the European Union as community of values.

References

Atilgan, C. (2012). *Kann Iwanashwili den 'Traum' erfüllen? Wahlen in Georgien*. Tbilisi: Konrad-Adenauer-Stiftung.

Atilgan, C. (2013). *Strategische Kehrtwende. Armeniens geplanter Beitritt zur Zollunion*. Tbilisi: Konrad-Adenauer-Stiftung.

Badalow, R. (2004). Die Demokratie in Aserbaidschan zu Beginn des 21. Jahrhunderts. In W. Kaufmann (Ed.), *Diaspora, Öl und Rosen* (pp. 179–204). Berlin: Heinrich Böll Stiftung.

Bendiek, A. (2008). Wie effektiv ist die Europäische Nachbarschaftspolitik? Sechzehn Länder im Vergleich. *SWP-Studien*, 2008/S24, September.

Bendiek, A. & Kramer, H. (2009). Die EU als globaler Akteur. *SWP-Studien*, 2009/S12, April.

Böttger, K. (2009). Im Osten nichts Neues? Ziele, Inhalte und erste Ergebnisse der Östlichen Partnerschaft. *Integration*, 32(4), 372–387.

Bredies, I. (2009). Leistungen und Grenzen europäischer Demokratieförderung in Osteuropa. *soFid Osteuropaforschung*, 2, 9–21.

Civil Georgia. (2008). Socar takes over gas distribution networks in Georgia. *Civil Georgia*, December 27. Retrieved from http://www.civil.ge/eng/article.php?id=20209.

Council of the European Economic Community. (1990). Council Decision of February 26, 1990 on the conclusion by the European Economic Community of an Agreement between the European Economic Community and the European Atomic Energy Community and the Union of Soviet Socialist Republics on trade and commercial and economic cooperation. *Official Journal of the European Communities*, No. L 68/1, March 15.

Dannreuther, R. (2006). Developing the alternative to enlargement: The European Neighbourhood Policy. *European Foreign Affairs Review*, 11, 183–201.

De Waal, T. (2011). Talking to grown-ups in the Caucasus. *The National Interest*, December 15. Retrieved from http://nationalinterest.org/commentary/talking-grown-ups-the-caucasus-6245.

Emerson, M. & Kostanyan, H. (2013). Putin's grand design to destroy the EU's Eastern Partnership and replace it with a disastrous neighbourhood policy of his own. *CEPS Commentary*, September 17. Retrieved from http://eap-csf.eu/assets/files/Articles/ME%20&%20HK%20EU%20and%20the%20Eastern%20Partnership.pdf.

EurActiv. (2010). EU's eastern initiative, not adequate for Azerbaijan. *EurActiv.com*, November 3. Retrieved from http://neuronick.stage.euractiv.com/east-mediterranean/eus-eastern-initiative-adequate-news-499387.

European Commission. (2004). *European Neighbourhood Policy Strategy Paper*, COM (2004) 373 Final. Brussels: Commission of the European Communities.

European Commission. (2008a). The Eastern Partnership—an ambitious new chapter in the EU's relations with its Eastern neighbours. *Press Release*, IP/08/1858, Brussels, December 3.

European Commission. (2008b). *Communication from the Commission to the European Parliament and the Council: Eastern Partnership,* COM (2008) 823 Final. Brussels: Commission of the European Communities.

European Commission. (2011). *Country Report Armenia. Implementation of the European Neighbourhood Policy in 2010. Joint Staff Working Paper,* SEC (2011) 639. Brussels: Commission of the European Communities.

European Commission. (2013). EU-Armenia: New context but same resolve to take partnership forward. *Press Release,* Memo/13/1117, Brussels, December 9.

European Council. (1987). Single European Act. *Official Journal of the European Communities,* 87/L 169/1, June 29.

European Council. (1991). *Presidency Conclusions,* June 28–29, Luxembourg. Retrieved from http://www.europarl.europa.eu/summits/luxembourg/lu1_en.pdf.

European Council. (2003). *A secure Europe in a better world. European security strategy.* Brussels.

European Council. (2014). Statement at the signing ceremony of the Association Agreements with Georgia, Republic of Moldova and Ukraine. *Press Release,* 375, EUCO 137/14. Herman Van Rompuy. President of the European Council, Brussels, June 27.

European Parliament. (1997). Resolution on the Communication from the Commission 'Towards a European Union strategy for relations with the Transcaucasian Republics', COM (95) 0205 — C4-0242/96. *Official Journal of the European Union,* No. C 33/133, January 17.

Fierro, E. (2003). *The EU's approach to human rights conditionality in practice.* The Hague/New York: M. Nijhoff.

Freedom House. (2009). *Freedom in the world 2009. Azerbaijan.* Retrieved from https://www.freedomhouse.org.

Freedom House. (2010). *Freedom of the press 2010. Armenia.* Retrieved from https://www.freedomhouse.org.

Freedom House. (2013a). *Nations in transit 2013. Country Report Armenia.* Retrieved from https://www.freedomhouse.org.

Freedom House. (2013b). *Nations in transit 2013. Country Report Azerbaijan.* Retrieved from https://www.freedomhouse.org.

Freedom House. (2013c). *Nations in transit 2013. Country Report Georgia.* Retrieved from https://www.freedomhouse.org.

Giragosian, R. (2009). Armenia's crisis for the non-democrats. In M. Emerson & R. Youngs (Eds.), *Democracy's plight in the European neighbourhood* (pp. 84–91). Brussels: CEPS.

Grilli, E. R. (1993). *The European Community and the developing countries.* Cambridge/New York: Cambridge University Press.

Gordon, C. & Sasse, G. (2008). The European Neighbourhood Policy: Effective instrument for conflict management and democratic change in the Union's Eastern neighbourhood? *MIRICO EU framework VI report, Work package 5 special report.* Bolzano, Italy: EURAC. Retrieved from http://www.eurac.edu/en/research/institutes/imr/Documents/Web_del29ENP.pdf.

Halbach, U. (2007). Die Krise in Georgien. Das Ende der "Rosenrevolution"? *SWP-Aktuell,* No. 61.

Halbach, U. (2008). Politik im Südkaukasus. Krisen und "doppelte Standards". *SWP-Aktuell,* No. 31.

Jawad, P. (2006). Europas neue Nachbarschaft an der Schwelle zum Krieg. Zur Rolle der EU in Georgien. *HSFK-Report,* 7/2006. Frankfurt/Main: Hessische Stiftung Frieden- und Konfliktforschung.

Jünemann, A. & Knodt, M. (Eds.) (2006). Externe Demokratieförderung der Europäischen Union – die Instrumentenwahl der EU aus vergleichender Perspektive. *Integration,* 4(29), 287–296.

Kelley, J. (2006). New wine in old wineskins: Promoting political reforms through the new European Neighbourhood Policy. *Journal of Common Market Studies,* 44(1), 29–55.

Kempe, I. (2010). Die EU und ihre Nachbarn: Auf der Suche nach neuen Formen der Partnerschaft. In *Import/Export Demokratie. Schriften zur Demokratie,* Band 14 (pp. 93–108). Berlin: Heinrich Böll Stiftung.

Knodt, M. & Jünemann, A. (2007). Theorizing EU external democracy promotion. In A. Jünemann & M. Knodt (Eds.), *Externe Demokratieförderung durch die Europäische Union* (pp. 9–29). Baden-Baden: Nomos.

Koopmann, M. (2006). Die Nachbarschaftspolitik der Europäischen Union. Herausforderungen und Probleme eines anspruchsvollen Politikkonzepts. In M. Koopmann & C. Lequesne (Eds.), *Partner oder Beitrittskandidaten. Die Nachbarschaftspolitik der Europäischen Union auf dem Prüfstand* (pp. 17–30). Baden-Baden: Nomos.

Lippert, B. & Schwarzer, D. (2011). Die EU zwischen Zerfall und Selbstbehauptung: Entwicklungen und Handlungsmöglichkeiten. Entwicklungsperspektiven der EU. *SWP-Studien,* 2011/S18.

Lynch, D. (2003). The EU: Towards a strategy. *Chaillot Papers,* 65(12/2003), 171–191.

Mayer, S. (2007). *Der Südkaukasus als Nachbar der erweiterten Union.* Bremen: Friedrich Ebert Stiftung.

Meister, S. & May, M. (2009). Die Östliche Partnerschaft der EU – ein Kooperationsangebot mit Missverständnissen. *DGAP-Standpunkt,* 7.

Minasyan, S. (2013). Energiepolitische Interessen der EU im Rahmen der Östlichen Partnerschaft. In A. Masát, E. Bos, M. Eckardt, G. Kastner, & D. R. Wenger (Eds.), *Der Donauraum in Europa* (pp. 277–282). Baden-Baden: Nomos.

Prodi, R. (2002). *A wider Europe—a proximity policy as the key to stability.* Speech 02/619, Brussels, December 2002. Retrieved from http://europa.eu/rapid/press-release_SPEECH-02-619_en.html.

Radio Free Europe. (2008). Russia recognizes Abkhazia, South Ossetia. *Radio Free Europe*, August 26. Retrieved from http://www.rferl.org/content/Russia_Recognizes_Abkhazia_South_Ossetia/1193932.html.

Reporters without Borders. (2013). *World report Armenia*. Retrieved from http://en.rsf.org/report-armenia,88.html.

Rukomeda, R. (2013). Russia's response to Ukraine's European choice: What is next? *EurActiv.com*, September 23. Retrieved from http://www.euractiv.com/europes-east/russia-response-ukraine-european-analysis-530644.

Smith, K. E. (1998). The use of political conditionality in the EU's relations with third countries: How effective? *European Foreign Affairs Review*, 3(2), 253–274.

Smith, K. E. (2008). *European Union foreign policy in a changing world*. Cambridge: Polity Press.

Smith, M. (2013). Europe losing battle of influence with Russia. *Foreign Policy Journal*, September 23. Retrieved from http://www.foreignpolicyjournal.com/2013/09/23/europe-losing-battle-of-influence-with-russia.

Stewart, S. (2010). Russische Außenpolitik im postsowjetischen Raum. *SWP-Studien*, 2010/S5.

Süddeutsche Zeitung. (2014). Steinmeier und Fabius wollen Georgien an den Westen binden. *Süddeutsche Zeitung,* April 24. Retrieved from http://www.sueddeutsche.de/politik/besuch-in-tiflis-steinmeier-und-fabius-wollen-georgien-an-den-westen-binden-1.1943037.

Swedish Presidency of the European Council. (2010). *Report on the Swedish Presidency of the Council of the European Union July 1–December 31, 2009*. Retrieved from http://www.government.se/sb/d/12363/a/145451.

Governance and governmentality of EU Neighbourhood Policy. Two perspectives on the role of civil society in external democracy promotion

Aron Buzogány

Introduction

The European Union is often credited as a successful democracy promoter but most if not all positive assessments focus on the EU's enlargement strategy (Vachudová, 2005). Without offering the perspective of membership, the EU's democracy promotion agenda has proved to be much less successful (Schimmelfennig & Scholtz, 2008). Democracy indicators, such as the Freedom House Index, show a rapid increase of democracy during the early nineties all over the post-socialist region. But important differentiation processes took place within this region in the following years. Countries that were granted EU membership prospects, such as the Central and Eastern European states, have achieved democracy levels that basically set them on par with Western European ones. Meanwhile, conflict-ridden South-Eastern European states stagnated at a lower level and the newly independent former member states of the Soviet Union see the least promising democratic developments (Merkel, 2004). In the 2000s, the post-Soviet space differentiated further: While some states, including Moldova, Ukraine, and Georgia developed more or less regular habits of sticking to democratic rules, developments in the other formerly Soviet states made the scholarly community rethink the legitimacy of talking about democratisation. Instead, authoritarian stabilisation has become the typical feature for most of these states (Levitsky & Way, 2010).

From the EU's perspective, the question of how to induce normative change leading to democratisation remains an important strategic goal even if it complements other, potentially more important, targets such as security considerations and market expansion (Rosamond, 2014). An extensive literature on external governance highlights that without the possibility of EU membership, there are several alternative mechanisms like market opening, assistance and monitoring, and horizontal diffusion through networks that might trigger processes of institutional change in the countries around the EU (Langbein & Börzel, 2013; Lavenex & Schimmelfennig, 2013). Such complementary mechanisms of Europeanisation beyond conditionality may involve actors who are empowered to facilitate, legitimise and stabilise the EU's impact on domestic policies, politics and polities. Ultimately, the hope is that (economic, political or cultural) interactions between actors in the Eastern neighbourhood countries (Ukraine, Moldova, Belarus and the three South Caucasian states Armenia, Azerbaijan and Georgia) and the EU will induce democracy. From an "external governance" perspective, the main expectation is that democracy develops from functional cooperation, more or less as a side-product of technical integration in distinct policy fields. From this perspective, EU public policies that become at least partially harmonised in the neighbourhood countries include normative content that increases the transparency, accountability and participation; and allows democratisation "between the lines" (Freyburg, Lavenex, Schimmelfennig, Skripka, & Wetzel, 2011). Two central micro-level mechanisms might be at play here. First, elites in the neighbourhood states might be supportive of alignment with the EU out of rational calculations as this strengthens their domestic positions and/or their economic wealth (Melnykovska & Schweickert, 2008). Second, socialisation into common networks is also expected to become influential in changing normative perceptions of elites (Freyburg, 2015).

The strong focus on elites is not coincidental. Most of the literature on external governance underlines the role of domestic elites and bargaining among different sets of these elites in the success of externally induced reform processes. Others question the willingness of elites to democratise, suggesting that their goals are mainly stability-oriented—an inclination that often sets them on par with the EU, which often prioritises stability to democracy in its foreign policy (Börzel, 2010). While prominent in the external democratisation literature, the role of potential counter-elites, such as factions within the ruling elite, business groups or civil society actors has received less attention in the context of external governance. This is unexpected as the concept of external governance is explicitly open to a variety of state and non-state actors inside and outside the EU's formal boundaries. Nevertheless, most research to date on the European Neighbourhood Policy (ENP) is still focused on intergovernmental activities (for notable exceptions, see Beichelt, Hahn, Schimmelfennig, & Worschech, 2014; Rommens, 2014).

To address this gap in the literature, this chapter proposes two conceptual innovations. First, I will make the case for bringing civil society into analyses of EU democracy promotion in the neighbourhood countries. Second, the chapter also calls for extension of the analytical perspective used to analyse the role of civil society in democratisation processes. Rather than restricting the analytical perspective on the functionally-driven governance agenda (Mayntz, 2004), I propose to combine this with an approach that promises to shed light on some of the more hidden aspects of (external) governance. One of the most prominent criticisms regarding governance research is its neglect of power. Employing a Foucauldian governmentality perspective emphasising the practices embedded in governance networks and attention to how power is constituted therein frames civil society both as a subject and an active object of governance in the EU's Neighbourhood Policy (Sending & Neumann, 2006). Using this dual perspective— governance and governmentality—the chapter argues that a comprehensive analysis of civil society's role in democratisation processes should capture divergent developments with distinct analytical instruments.

The chapter is organised as follows: The next section gives an overview of the literature on external democratisation and civil society, and the ENP in this context. I will show that the literature on the ENP and civil society can be divided using the two analytical perspectives, governance and governmentality. Using both perspectives and focusing on the EU-level, Section 3 describes how and why civil society became a part of the Neighbourhood Policy framework. In Section 4, I turn to the ENP countries and provide examples for both perspectives "on the ground". The final section summarises.

Civil society in the EU's Neighbourhood Policy:
Functional and critical perspectives

Civil society, usually defined as an associational sphere located between the private and the political, is often seen as a "cradle of democracy" which has positive effects on the development and long-term maintenance of pluralism. Among political theorists, Toqueville's work stands out as referencing the benefits of civil society in creating the fabric of political life based on interpersonal trust and confidence. Two centuries later, neo-Toquevellians such as Robert Putnam pointed to the role of social capital and institutions that can lead to the development of trust (Putnam, Leonardi, & Nanetti, 1994). Following Tocqueville's work, much of the research on social capital highlighted cultural and structural effects of civil society and pointed to the role of networks and membership in voluntary organisations as main sources of democratic norms. The success and short rise to prominence and (sometimes) to political power of Eastern European dissidents such as Vaclav Havel, fostered a liberal interpretation of the 1989 revolutions as civil society-led uprisings against the authoritarian state.[1] This reading of regime change fit with the liberal agenda favouring a smaller state and more autonomy and responsibility for individuals. Moreover, this conceptual role of civil society became an important policy goal for external actors, including development agencies and international financial institutions, such as the World Bank.

However, civil society proved to be a problematic concept normatively, empirically, and analytically (Hann & Dunn, 1996; Kopecky & Mudde, 2005). The definitional essence of the term remained contested: Is civil society inherently "good"? What about "uncivil societies" (Glasius, 2010) or civil societies in authoritarian states that are often co-opted by the regime (Lewis, 2013)? Can the concept, which presupposes, *inter alia,* a clear delimitation between state and society, be applied universally? Or, for that matter, should civil society be externally supported (Mercer, 2002)? Looking at the effects of transnational influence on civil society organisations, the literature has contradictory answers to whether external influence in the post-communist world "hijacks" civil society agendas (Fagan, 2006) or ultimately strengthens such groups domestically (Císař, 2010).

Few of these debates are reflected in the current ENP literature. Scholarship dealing with the neighbourhood countries focuses mostly on state actors. Analyses addressing the making of the ENP usually regard the policy process as a tug-of-war between member states with diverging geopolitical

---

[1] Recent assessments of the allegedly civil society-led revolutions of 1989 found that the involvement of civil society was rhetorically overstated. In an influential book, Stephen Kotkin (2009) argues that it was rather the "uncivil" society, i.e. mostly second-rank party cadres that were behind the political changes.

agendas. Countries deeply involved with the Barcelona process, such as Spain and France, supported the inclusion of Mediterranean states into the neighbourhood framework. Germany and the Nordic countries were more interested in enhancing ties with the post-Soviet region. Germany and the Nordic countries received additional support after the accession of the Central and Eastern European states, of which especially Poland was eager to make relations with the "new" Eastern Europe a priority on the EU's external agenda, eventually leading to the establishment of the Eastern Partnership (Vandecasteele, Bossuyt, & Orbie, 2013). At the same time, the European Commission maintained an important role in designing the policies towards the neighbourhood countries. Particularly within-Commission path-dependencies have played a role as institutional models were often directly copied from the enlargement portfolio (Kelley, 2006; Tulmets, 2010). After the Lisbon Treaty, consecutive reforms in the EU's foreign policy set-up resulted in bureaucratic infightings over turf also regarding the Neighbourhood Policy (Kostanyan & Orbie, 2013).

Another part of the literature on the ENP focuses on its domestic impacts. Most of these studies emphasise the EU's willingness, but not so much its ability, to be a "force for good" (Barbé & Johannson-Nogués, 2008). Extant research on the EU's external governance argues that the EU was reluctant or unable to solve "hard" security issues (Popescu, 2010), and instead it sought to be active in democracy promotion or to encourage "good" or "democratic" governance in the neighbouring countries (Freyburg et al., 2011; Börzel & Pamuk, 2012). A growing number of studies of external governance show that the EU's influence results from policy spill-over. This functional spill-over ranges from migration and internal security (Delcour, 2013), through environment and energy (Buzogány, 2013; Schulze & Tosun, 2013), to technical standardisation (Langbein, 2014) or judicial reforms (Natorski, 2013). While only few authors (Freyburg et al., 2011) do explicitly expect that functional policy transfer will lead to democratisation, some kind of "better governance" as a result of EU harmonisation is implicitly assumed by most observers using an external governance perspective.

Another take on the ENP's impact is the argument that EU policies "abroad" do not have much in common with democracy promotion: instead of democracy, the EU values geopolitical stability or increased market access (Reynaert, 2011). Particularly migration policy researchers are sceptical as they regard the securitisation of borders as an aspect that essentially contradicts democracy promotion (Ratzmann, 2012). Only few studies in this tradition take a closer look at what happens on the ground, i.e. inside the neighbourhood countries, but those who do find that the EU's influence is "reshaping civil society" (Dimitrovova, 2009) or promotes neoliberal "economic logics and exercises" (İşleyen, 2014).

The mentioned literatures belong to two ontologically different viewpoints on what the European Union is and what it does. The governance perspective is clearly the dominant one: During the last decade or so, EU studies essentially underwent a "governance turn" (Kohler-Koch & Rittberger, 2006) and this has also diffused to research dealing with external action of the EU. In contrast, the research agenda on governmentality is a relatively new addition to political science (for early work in this direction, see Burchell, Gordon, & Foucault, 1991; Brass, 2000) and is received in EU studies mostly via the Paris School of Critical Security Studies (cf. e.g. Merlingen, 2011). For this chapter, my main interest is how these two perspectives deal with civil society in the EU's external action and how they can be combined to provide a more comprehensive analysis.

The governance perspective promotes an essentially liberal and constructivist understanding of civil society and its actors as intermediaries and subjects that can be helpful in achieving certain policy goals. As argued already in the literature on transnational advocacy networks (Keck & Sikkink, 1998), multi-level polities offer the chance for domestically constrained non-state actors to use the so-called "boomerang-effect", i.e. to appeal to states or citizens of other states to put pressure on their government. Such networks are particularly promising to become catalysts of transnational social learning processes, e.g. by identifying and amplifying issues, connecting different stakeholders or monitoring policies (Brown & Timmer, 2006). In the EU context, civil society networks can contribute to planning, implementing and assessing EU policies. They are essentially transmission belts between national civil societies in the Eastern Partnership (EaP) countries and the EU decision-making arena. In the context of the EaP they aggregate information from local or national-level NGOs and inform decision-makers at the EU-level. They connect NGOs focusing on the EaP countries and inform them about their possibilities and rights. While NGOs are able to provide their policy expertise and can increase the legitimacy of the process by bringing in domestic civil society, the European Commission can strengthen their capacities through targeted funding for their activities. The empowerment of civil society on the ground can happen both indirectly and directly (Börzel & Buzogány, 2010). Indirectly, the EU might be influential in altering the domestic structures governing civil society organisations. Directly, it can provide attention, training or financial support to these organisations. Particularly when lacking capacities on the ground, strengthening the influence of NGOs on third-country governments through capacity-building can become an important tool for the European Commission to reach its policy goals (Dimitrova & Buzogány, 2014).

The reason why civil society actors' activities might result in better governance and why this might lead to democratisation is articulated in the literature about the quality of democracy. Following Mitchell Orenstein (2002), improvements in the quality of democracy include not only the establishment of formal democratic institutions, but also employment of a broader definition of democracy that takes into account procedural aspects of democratic policy making processes, including public consultation, participation, review of administrative decisions, and access to information. If civil society actors seek the EU's involvement, the formal EU rules can result in better governance in two ways. Firstly, the active invocation of formal rules as rules-in-use strengthens the rule of law. Secondly, domestic actors maintain and use their links to the EU institutions as a way to guarantee checks and balances in the policy making process. In this way, the existence of coalitions between domestic and supranational actors can empower reformers and prevent or limit democratic backsliding (cf. Dimitrova & Buzogány, 2014).

In sum, liberal and constructivist analyses focus on NGOs' roles in mediating conflict, putting checks on power and promoting social learning (Brown & Timmer, 2006). Meanwhile, scholars using the governmentality research agenda are characterised by a focus on power and micro-practices and ask what EU empowerment does to civil society actors and what broader consequences this brings. From this perspective, the role of civil society actors in "shaping and carrying out [global] governance-functions is not an instance of transfer of power from the state to non-state actors but rather an expression of a changing logic or rationality of government" (Sending & Neumann, 2006, p. 651). While governance approaches underline the goal-oriented, conflictive or consensual ways of solving problems, governmentality oriented explanations stress the role of power in governance processes, which overshadows deliberation and joint learning (Merlingen, 2011).

More recently, the governmentality research agenda has been fruitfully applied to EU external action, taking the EU-level as its analytical "micro-site" (Merlingen, 2011). Using a discourse analysis of the European Commission's strategy paper on setting up the European Instrument for Democracy and Human Rights (EIDHR), a core instrument for democracy-promotion, Milja Kurki (2011a) shows how a liberal and technocratic understanding of democracy and the role of civil society therein became the dominant narrative in EU democracy promotion. While consultations with and participation of civil society actors is rhetorically highly valued, what is in fact meant by civil society are often NGO elites that are "based in Europe and in possession of adequate financial and knowledge-making facilities" (Kurki, 2011a, p. 229). In another contribution, Kurki deconstructs the EIDHR's agenda behind local ownership, arguing that this encourages, on the one hand responsibility-taking, but on the other it comes at the price of "fierce form of self-regulation with regard to what constitutes the right kind of rational and responsible action" (Kurki, 2011b, p. 356). Furthermore, the EIDHR perceives civil society as autonomous from the state, and seems to believe that it is holding the potential and willingness to encounter the state in defence of freedom. At the same time, it also presupposes that NGOs are subscribing to the development and democratisation goals of the EU, and hold the capacity to act as entrepreneurial project managers (Kurki, 2011b, p. 357). Both independence and entrepreneurialism are underlying assumptions that are rather difficult to meet in the EaP countries.

While being mostly focused on developments and official discourses at the EU level, more recently researchers using the governmentality framework have started to look also at the effects of EU policies on the ground. Analysing the usage of EU twining instruments in Egypt and Tunisia, İşleyen (2014) shows how EU projects infuse economic rationalities and techniques that change local conditions to make them serviceable to neoliberal governing patterns. Similarly, another piece of research unmasks EU practices supporting "local ownership" of reform initiatives in the Maghreb and challenges the powerlessness assumption of governance relations (Malmvig, 2014). In addition, the author also draws on Foucault's concept of counter-conduct, which shows how domestic actors reinterpret externally induced agendas, including the concept of ownership.

Summarising the above we can highlight that governance and governmentality provide different perspectives on the role of civil society in external democratisation processes. While the governance perspective focuses on functional problem-solving and presupposes equality among governance actors including civil society, the governmentality perspective digs deeper by unearthing power relations in governance structures in a Foucauldian "archaeology of power" tradition. Thus, according to the governance perspective, civil society activity increases the EU's potential to put pressure on reluctant governments to adopt crucial reforms; complementing its top-down approach with a bottom-up push. The governmentality perspective emphasises that the embeddedness of civil society actors in power relations is a form of dependency, which can undermine the original normative policy goals. However, as suggested by the concept of counter-conduct, civil society can equally challenge the EU by rigorously demanding that it acts according to its own principles. Thus, the role of non-state actors in shaping and carrying out different governance-functions empowers and constrains state actors at the same time (Sending & Neumann, 2006). In the next section, I use both the governance and the governmentality perspective to analyse how the notion of civil society became important in the ENP's policy design.

The (re-)making of the Neighbourhood Policy: Bringing civil society in

In May 2004, only a few days following eastern enlargement, the European Commission presented a comprehensive outline of its proximity-policy. Two guiding principles were put forward: *differentiation* and *joint ownership* (Korosteleva, 2012). Differentiation highlights the significant differences between the countries in the ENP and promises to give tailor-made plans of cooperation to each country reflecting the needs and capacities of both the EU and the neighbour country. This was also envisioned as a reform of the Partnership and Cooperation Agreements (PCAs), which provided the legal basis for EU relations with post-Soviet states and were regarded as rather inefficient. The new terms of cooperation were expected to vary according to each partner's particular circumstances, including geographic location, the political and economic situation, current relations with the European Union and other states, and the reform programmes already underway. The principle of "joint ownership" broke with the EU's traditional way of unilateral priority setting as the EU did not seek to impose conditions on its partners, but wanted them to be defined by "common consent".

Joint ownership and common consent were initially understood as a matter to be decided upon intergovernmentally; no meaningful role for other actors than government was envisioned. However, during the following decade gradual change towards inclusion of civil society took place—something we can call a "governance turn". In 2011, after a review of the ENP and following calls from EU-level civil society umbrellas, the Neighbourhood Civil Society Facility was set up. As mentioned above, the EIDHR also embraced a civil society-oriented empowerment agenda—which was, *inter alia*, also available for civil society from the neighbourhood countries. Rhetorically, the Commission went even further: A "partnership with societies" (and not with governments) came to underpin the ENP (Bousac, Delcour, Riháčková, Solonenko, & Ter-Gabrielyan, 2012). As summarised by Jünnemann and Simon (2013, pp. 80–92), the Commission's discourse included detailed conceptions about 1) the *role* of civil society, *inter alia*, "in checking government excesses" and "holding governments to account"; 2) the *necessities* of civil society ("To operate, CSOs [Civil Society Organisations] need a functioning democratic legal and judicial system—giving them the de jure and de facto right to associate and secure funding, coupled with freedom of expression, access to information and participation in public life"); and 3) the *EU's strategies of empowering CSOs* ("Create a favourable environment for civil society/Discuss everything and avoid any taboos in our interaction/Help NGOs to strengthen their capacities").

How can the significant rise in importance of civil society in the EU's Neighbourhood Policy be explained? I will argue that this resulted from several factors. First, civil society organisations working at the EU-level benefited from the "participatory turn" in the EU that followed calls to address the EU's "democratic deficit" in the early 2000s (Saurugger, 2010). Funding lines established especially for civil society organisations and including extensive references to "participation" or "joint ownership" were commonplace following the EU's White Paper on Governance, which was set up to tackle the EU's democratic legitimacy deficit. The "participatory principle", even if rather unclearly defined, started to play a role in ENP related documents already during the 2004–2006 planning period, with civil society being mentioned repeatedly, albeit in a "supplementary and ancillary" manner (Kaca & Kazmierkiewicz, 2010, p. 7).

Second, contingent events, such as the coloured revolutions and, later, the Arab Spring, provided rhetorical support to calls for—in the words of a policy document by CONCORD—"strengthened EU support for civil society to engage in policy reforms and hold governments accountable".[2] Several information networks provided evidence on the beneficial role of civil society, which was strongly echoed by mostly Scandinavian and Eastern European think thanks, Sweden and Poland being the most vocal supporters of these ideas as they were also lobbying for the establishment of the EaP as the successor of the regionally more diverse ENP. Assessing the problems, these analyses pointed both to institutional weaknesses of the civil society sector in the EaP region, and to the closed nature of EU funding structures for CSOs, with only 1.4 per cent of funding allocated to civil society in the region (Hale & Ursu, 2011). As a result, EU financial support often did not meet the social needs of the target countries (Kaca & Kazmierkiewicz, 2010).

Third, the promotion of the above mentioned "participatory norm" by the EU gave leverage to EU civil society networks to call on the EU to "practice, what it preaches" also in its external affairs (Interview, WWF, Brussels, November 2007). Such platforms bringing together non-state actors already existed previously in EU external relations at the regional-level, such as the EUROMED Civil Platform, which brought together NGOs from the Mediterranean countries, but suffered from political interferences (Jünemann, 2002). During the enlargement period, in Central and Eastern Europe (CEE), the EU provided NGOs with linkages to like-minded organisations in the old member states as well as interest groups and transnational networks active at the EU-level. Brussels level NGOs have played important roles in acquainting their CEE counterparts with the rules of EU policy-

---

[2] The CONCORD Working Group on Enlargement, Pre-Accession and Neighbourhood (2011): EPAN position paper: Eastern European Neighbourhood Policy (with regards to the communication on ENP review, 25.05.2011 and the proposal of establishing an ENPI Civil Society Initiative). Retrieved from http://www.trialog.or.at/images/doku/enp_east_response_epan_30may2011.pdf.

making. At the same time, they also gathered practical experience in Eastern Europe and often established regional offices in the accession countries and the neighbourhood states. Many of these regional organisations could build up EU relevant knowledge and use EU funding for consolidating their organisations. However, when the CEE states became EU members in 2004 and 2007, special EU funding supporting NGOs started drying out. Transferring the gathered EU relevant knowledge further east became one of the possible strategies to secure organisational funding (Interview, Polish Ministry of Foreign Affairs, Warsaw, December 2010). The Review of the ENP process by the Commission provided civil society actors with a welcome opportunity to call for a structure which would help to institutionalise their role in the process. Vested interests in the European Commission to follow the well-beaten track of EU enlargement policy were institutionally pre-determined. Policy-borrowing from enlargement schemes and the incremental institutional adaptation process from the former Directorate General Enlargement is often described as one of the main influences on designing the ENP's institutional set-up (Tulmets, 2010). This process also included the transfer of staff previously working on new member state-relevant tasks to related tasks in Directorate General External Relations (Relex) and a growing influx of new officers holding relevant third country knowledge from the Central and Eastern European states (Interviews, European Commission and EU NGOs, Brussels, March 2011). A considerable part of the latter group held active civil society experience from the time of the accession process, while officers with EU enlargement experience often worked closely together with civil society organisations both in the accession states and in EU-level civil society networks. This created a positive attitude within the Commission towards civil society inclusion.

After the European Neighbourhood and Partnership Instrument (ENPI) was launched, a "beauty-contest" began between the different DGs of the European Commission for filling the gaps left open by the policy's documents. Building on their unique expertise gathered during the enlargement period, technical DGs projected their preferences onto the ENP wish-list. On the coat-tails of different bureaucratic units within the Commission, sectorial civil society networks entered the new policy field of Neighbourhood Policy. Also DG Development started co-shaping the new policy field. Reacting to the introduction of the ENPI, Quintet, a platform of development aid platforms lobbied for the inclusion of principles of the European Consensus on Development, of the Millennium Declaration into ENPI's funding lines and has also argued for the establishment of a Civil Society Facility. At the same time, these networks could already point to their policy related work in some of the fields that the Commission planned to emphasise. Such hands-on help to the Commission was provided e.g., by the World Wildlife Foundation for Nature (WWF) and the Heinrich Böll Foundation which issued *Handbook to assess the implementation of the ENP Action Plans in the field of Environment* and ran several pilot projects and established a network of partners in the region early on (Buzogány & Costa, 2009).

The above factors help explain the changes in the architecture of the ENP towards a stronger inclusion of civil society and the timing of these (gradual) reforms, but what does this process say about the power relations built in this policy? Obviously, neither EU member states, nor the Commission could steer the policy process alone, as standard accounts of EU integration would expect. The rise of the civil society agenda was nevertheless partly a spill-over from EU internal debates about the nature of democracy. The discourse was partly used by Brussels NGOs to make sure that their normative and existential goals are placed into the policy content. By calling for ownership and civil society inclusion, the goals of EU-level civil society coincided with those of the Commission: While the Commission wished to secure its independence from the member states, CSOs wanted to secure on-going funding for their various activities. Not coincidentally, the role of local civil society actors in the ENP states, i.e. those who were to be empowered by the "governance turn", remained rather underdeveloped. In the next section, I turn to the domestic level to examine how the change in the governance structure of the ENP has been translated in the neighbourhood countries.

Empowering civil society on the ground?

It is commonplace to describe civil society in Eastern Europe as weak (Howard, 2003). This applies even more to the six countries forming the Eastern Partnership. Many of the civil organisations are donor-driven; they are disconnected from their societies and are regularly met with public distrust. Accordingly, internal cleavages often hinder effective work. Conflicts trace back either to competition for scarce funds or to political affiliations of NGOs, many of which are in fact launched by government elites. At the same time, there are large differences among the EaP countries in the strength of civil society as highlighted in Table 1. Except the case of Ukraine, no positive change occurred during the last decade.

Table 1: Civil society ratings in Eastern Europe and the South Caucasus

	Armenia	Azerbaijan	Belarus	Georgia	Moldova	Ukraine
2003	3.5	4.25	6.5	4	3.75	3.5
2008	3.5	5.25	6.5	3.5	3.75	2.75
2012	3.75	6	6	3.75	3.25	2.75
2014	3.75	6.50	6.5	3.75	3.25	2.50

Source: Freedom House, Nations in Transit annual reports (2003–2013), www.freedomhouse.org
(1 indicates the highest level of democratic progress, 7 the lowest).

What are the deeper consequences of EU influence on civil society? In this section, I describe organisational developments that are related to the local ownership and participation agenda of the EU in line with what a "governance perspective" would suggest. I complement this by pointing to more "hidden" developments by highlighting governmentality-related questions.

Civil society networks were encouraged through capacity building by the EU and transnational civil society organisations, such as the Open Society Foundation and Transparency International, whose funding helps to organise local coalitions and institutionalise civil society participation in monitoring their government's progress in harmonising domestic policies with the EU ones. This process already had a tradition in some EaP countries before the re-launch of the EU's Neighbourhood Policy in 2011. The main outputs were detailed policy implementation reports compiled by NGOs, which provided an alternative "shadow list" to the diplomatic slang used by the EU in its country reports. Preparation of the reports included the development of a common methodology for assessing the policy process for certain sectorial aims of the ENP, based on which the current policy will be monitored, analysed and evaluated, and further recommendations will be developed. Several consortia were established, with partially overlapping scopes (Bousac et al., 2012). For example, the World Wildlife Foundation for Nature (WWF) has been active with local partner organisations to strengthen the environmental dimension of the ENP. In Ukraine, the WWF project developed capacities and formulated a position paper regarding the inclusion of civil society. The local partner of the WWF project, the environmental NGO "Environment – People – Law", worked on issues related to civil society participation and environmental integration in Ukraine (Buzogány, 2013). In Georgia, the Open Society Foundation, and the Heinrich Böll and Eurasia Foundations were involved in financing several rounds of monitoring reports, and providing know-how and contact to their offices in Brussels.

After the re-launch of ENP, civil society organisations working on EU issues received increased attention given to their role in Brussels. Of particular importance was the establishment of an overarching structure to coordinate different monitoring projects, which previously existed in parallel. The founding of the Civil Society Forum (CSF) of the EaP brought a new coordination body into being. While the initial conception did not place an emphasis on the National Platforms of the CSF, these were rapidly established in each EaP state often based on previously existing networks of pro-EU civil society groups. National Platforms replicate the structure of the CSF; there are also sectorial Working Groups that cooperate with the EU-level ones. This also includes several regional components, focusing for example on media independence, monitoring EaP progress or on policy dialogues. Otherwise the National Platforms are autonomous from each other.

As the National Platforms bring together significant on-the-ground expertise, they hold the potential to become the main structures for lobbying and advocacy. However, their access to domestic structures varies. According to the "Vilnius Roadmap" project carried out by Regional Environmental Centre in Moldova and Pasos, a think tank umbrella, only EaP "frontrunner" countries Georgia and Moldova regularly invite civil society organisations to government meetings and provide them access to documents. This is clearly not the case in Ukraine and Armenia, and even less so in Azerbaijan and Belarus (Lovitt, 2013). While the access to domestic structures and to the bilateral leg of the EaP process is problematic in some countries, the National Platforms work is highly valued by the European Commission, which is their "natural partner" (Fuhr-Hahn & May, 2012). Particularly when preparing the yearly progress reports, the Commission is eager to consult with members of civil society and includes their assessments into its reports—

often word-by-word (Interviews, EaP CSOs, Yerevan and Tbilisi, December 2009 and December 2011).

The new structures, such as the CSF, and the inclusion of new monitored outcomes allowed for benchmarking of activities in a policy field specific manner. More importantly, this provided the opportunity to compare across countries. As highlighted already during the accession process (Grabbe, 2002), artificial races induced by benchmarking of governmental behaviour can have some change-inducing power. This is also the main idea behind the European Integration Index for Eastern Partnership Countries (EaP Index), which was promoted as a "speedometer" of European integration for EaP states. This tool—built through considerable experience from practitioners and academics—"is designed to keep countries on the right track and to provide warnings when countries depart from the expected trajectory or progress is at an unacceptable pace".[3] The EaP Index captures legal and institutional developments towards EU membership (approximation and management) as well as more broadly defined political and socio-economic linkages between a neighbourhood state and the EU.[4]

Other developments did not follow the liberal logic of the governance role attributed to civil society. There are several observations which question the assumptions of a governance-centred perspective and lend support to the governmentality view instead. First, given the authoritarian setting in some of the ENP countries, civil society cannot be thought of as independent from the state or its ability to criticise the government is severely restricted. Conflicts related to the legitimacy of representation of domestic civil society's goals among NGOs within national platforms or in different CSF working groups have emerged regularly, as governments have interfered with the process by delegating their own GONGO's (government owned NGOs) into these bodies (Ter-Gabrielyan, 2012).[5]

---

[3] Quote from EaP Civil Society Index (2011). Retrieved from http://www.eap-index.eu/about.

[4] See also the similar Visa Liberalization Index maintained by the Polish Stefan Batory Foundation. Retrieved from http://monitoring.visa-free-europe.eu/.

[5] EaP Civil Society Forum (2014), Statement of the Steering Committee on the incident at the sixth EaP CSF annual assembly side exhibition. Retrieved from http://eap-csf.eu/en/news-events/news/statement-of-the-steering-committee-on-incident-at-sixth-eap-csf-annual-assembly-side-exhibition1/.

Second, the empowerment of NGOs was restricted to elite organisations with professional, i.e. entrepreneurial capacities. Even though awareness-raising projects and other activities of civil society tried to include a wider range of groups, the ENP remained a largely elite project. Research carried out by the Eurasia Foundation shows that in Georgia the role of civil society in monitoring the EU Neighbourhood Policy Action Plan was minimal and limited to only about 10 organisations. In effect, EU empowerment of NGOs reinforced differentiation within the domestic NGO scene through what has been described as the "Matthew-Effect" in the context of Central and Eastern European states (Buzogány, 2011), meaning that already powerful actors get even more resources.

Third, professionalisation of civil society activism went hand-in-hand with its "projectification" (Kovách & Kučerova, 2009). Projectification highlights the everyday practices of civil society that is increasingly integrated into a (seemingly) professionalised managerial system. The funding possibilities available for CSOs are tied to the acceptance of a seemingly rationalised special thinking mode that is largely alien both to traditional public administration and civil society: the planning and control of activities through project management (Sampson, 1996). Induced by participation in EU related programmes, one segment of civil society is increasingly developing into consultancy-like companies with rather symbiotic relationship with donor agencies. At the same time, projectification is far from being only a technical process, but remains an essentially political one as it reconfigures domestic power structures by creating a new "project class" that becomes a broker between the EU, national administration and civil society.

Fourth, using a governmentality perspective highlights not only the power relations between state and civil society actors, but also civil society actors at different levels of the hierarchy. Obviously, civil society empowerment has been mainly an activity where EU-based NGOs have successfully lobbied European institutions. On the one hand, they did that by "representing" the "weak" neighbourhood civil society—whose "weakness" became also a goal in itself as a good argument for funding. On the other hand, neighbourhood CSOs were needed as "local partners" in carrying out the projects that were won by EU civil society organisations. Fund allocations under the ENPI to different grantees are presented in Table 2. The table shows that the largest amounts of the available funds were received by institutional and commercial actors. At the same time, there are important differences in funding received by EU-based CSOs and their partners in the EaP countries: While EU-based NGOs have a share of 14 per cent, civil society from the EaP states receives merely 3 per cent of the funds from the ENPI.

Table 2: ENPI 2012 grants according to type of recipient

Type of grantee	Grant amount 2012 (in €)	Per cent
EU consultancies and communication agencies	1,285,139	19.3
EU-based CSOs	941,172	14.1
EU public bodies	1,216,618	18.3
EaP CSOs	**203,741**	**3.0**
EaP consultancies and private companies (translation services)	89,607	1.3
EaP local authorities	165,853	2.4
International organisations	2,742,806	41.2
Total	6,644,936	100

Source: Rihackova, 2014, p. 13

Finally, as highlighted by the Foucauldian concept of contre-conduite, civil society actors hold the potential to reinterpret and adjust agendas in which they participate. Thus, CSO empowerment by the EU has also other, potentially unexpected effects. Not only are domestic governments targeted by domestic civil society, but also the EU itself. The awareness-raising and capacity-building trainings have brought a great amount of frustration with EU programming to the fore such as complaints about the bureaucratic nature of the application process, lack of transparency and clarity of ENPI funding lines and the short and overlapping timing frames. In stark contrast to the norms promoted by the EU, local civil society actors point out that often it is exactly the EU institutions that proved to have difficulties with issues such as providing access to information or giving access to civil society participation (Interviews, Georgian NGO, December 2011). Instead of regarding the EU only as a "force for good", civil society learned to critically assess EU policies in particular fields. Triggered partly by the critical views of their Western partners on EU activities, EaP NGOs such as the Green Alternative in Georgia have vehemently criticised the unbalanced "neoliberal", pro-business orientation of the ENP and structural investments in environmentally unsustainable projects. In this way, the new structures allow at least for some CSOs to become project partners, but also to use their leverage "against" the donor institution—allowing what Foucault would have called a new art of neoliberal governmentality (cf. Malmvig, 2014).

Conclusion

This chapter investigated the role of civil society organisations in democratisation processes. While the current literature on the EU's Neighbourhood Policy takes a governance perspective that assumes—explicitly or implicitly—that ownership and participation of civil society enhances democracy, this contribution tried to paint a more nuanced picture pointing also toward a governmentality perspective. The question that emerged from this dualism was not only what NGOs do on behalf of the EU when promoting democracy, but also what this process does to them.

Empirically, by discussing EU-level and domestic level developments, the chapter showed that the strategy of EU-level civil society actors was to demand the inclusion of domestic civil society actors also beyond a few human rights projects, this being the case in the 1990s. Under the ENP and the EaP, civil society's calls for more funds and concrete goals, which civil society organisations can monitor, can be considered to be successful. The new, more civil society focused approach of the EU aimed to bring together several, partially conflicting aims. On the one hand, it helped establish cooperation among domestic elites and the NGO sector in partner states. On the other, civil society empowerment led to the establishment of platforms bringing together NGOs from the region, in order for the European Commission to have partners it can address. Adding to this, these new platforms bring together Western and Eastern NGOs where they can exchange views and foster coalitions. Building on the sectorial and regionally secluded monitoring activities funded under different constellations by civil society networks such as the Open Society Foundation or Transparency International, the establishment and consolidation of the Civil Society Forum and the introduction of the "more for more" principle in EU neighbourhood relations have led to more coordinated activities among civil society in the EaP countries. Domestic governments are the main addressees of control exerted by the National Platforms. This is reminiscent of the model of the mutually beneficial coalitions between international NGOs and their domestic networks created using the "boomerang effect" (Keck & Sikkink, 1998), which allow non-state actors to increase their leverage by circumventing central policy actors. At the same time, the chapter also listed a number of developments, which question the straight-forward nature of democratisation by civil society in the EU's neighbourhood. While the reform of the EU's Neighbourhood Policy has indeed uplifted the role of civil society, the underlying assumptions for civil society inclusion are not apolitical or left to the wills of domestic actors. Thus, the governmentality-related perspective applied here highlights how power relations transcend the policy of including civil society and can lead to frictions between state and society, between the EU and civil society, but also among different kinds of civil society actors.

Conceptually, the chapter calls for combining the governance and the governmentality perspective. Both have their merits. The governance perspective shows how functional problem-solving and different sets of interests have shaped the emergence of the ENP's civil society agenda. Despite the criticism voiced, the analysis outlined here shows that the governance perspective is fairly attentive to power relations. Realist or liberal accounts highlight differences between actors and show how self-interested actors have different possibilities to become influential. The added value of the governmentality perspective becomes clear, however, when looking at the "afterlife" of political decisions, i.e. developments that happen *after* institutions are designed and when (domestic varieties of) reality "takes over". In this chapter, some of these emerging "practices" were highlighted. As the domestic implementation of the still new EaP civil society agenda develops further on the ground in the following years, more in-depth analyses would be necessary to complement governance-oriented accounts of this process.

References

Barbé, E. & Johannson-Nogués, E. (2008). The EU as a modest 'force for good': The European Neighbourhood Policy. *International Affairs*, 84(1), 81–96.

Beichelt, T., Hahn, I., Schimmelfennig, F., & Worschech, S. (2014). *Civil society and democracy promotion*. Basingstoke: Palgrave Macmillan.

Börzel, T. A. (2010). The transformative power of Europe reloaded: The limits of external Europeanization. *KFG Working Paper Series,* No. 11. Berlin: Free University Berlin.

Börzel, T. A. & Buzogány, A. (2010). Governing EU accession in transition countries: The role of non-state actors. *Acta Politica*, 45(2), 158–182.

Börzel, T. A. & Pamuk, Y. (2012). Pathologies of Europeanisation: Fighting corruption in the Southern Caucasus. *West European Politics*, 35(1), 79–97.

Bousac, J., Delcour, L., Riháčková, V., Solonenko, I., & Ter-Gabrielyan, G. (2012). *Improving the EU support for the civil society in its neighbourhood: Rethinking procedures, ensuring that practices evolve.* Contract EXPO/B/AFET/2012/32. Bruxelles: European Parliament.

Brass, P. R. (2000). Foucault steals polittical science. *Annual Review of Political Science*, 3(1), 305–330.

Brown, L. D. & Timmer, V. (2006). Civil society actors as catalysts for transnational social learning. *Voluntas: International Journal of Voluntary and Nonprofit Organizations*, 17(1), 1–16.

Burchell, G., Gordon, C., & Foucault, M. (1991). *The Foucault effect: Studies in governmentality.* Chicago: University of Chicago Press.

Buzogány, A. (2011). Stairway to heaven or highway to hell? Ambivalent Europeanization and civil society in Central and Eastern Europe. In H. Kouki & E. Romanos (Eds.), *Protest beyond borders* (pp. 69–85). New York: Berghahn Publishers.

Buzogány, A. (2013). Selective adoption of EU environmental norms in Ukraine: Convergence á la carte. *Europe-Asia Studies*, 65(4), 609–630.

Buzogány, A. & Costa, O. (2009). Greening the neighbourhood? The environmental dimension of the European Neighbourhood Policy in Morocco and Ukraine. *European Foreign Affairs Review*, 14(4), 525–545.

Císař, O. (2010). Externally sponsored contention: The channelling of environmental movement organisations in the Czech Republic after the fall of Communism. *Environmental Politics*, 19(5), 736–755.

Delcour, L. (2013). Meandering Europeanisation: EU policy instruments and policy convergence in Georgia under the Eastern Partnership. *East European Politics*, 29(3), 344–357.

Dimitrova, A. & Buzogány, A. (2014). Post-accession policy-making in Bulgaria and Romania: Can non-state actors use EU rules to promote better governance? *Journal of Common Market Studies*, 52(1), 139–156.

Dimitrovova, B. (2009). Reshaping civil society in Morocco. *CEPS Working Document*, No. 323, December. Brussels: CEPS.

Fagan, A. (2006). Transnational aid for civil society development in post-socialist Europe: Democratic consolidation or a new imperialism? *Journal of Communist Studies and Transition Politics*, 22(1), 115–134.

Freyburg, T. (2015). Transgovernmental networks as an apprenticeship in democracy? Socialization into democratic governance through cross-national activities. *International Studies Quarterly*, 59(1), 59–72.

Freyburg, T., Lavenex, S., Schimmelfennig, F., Skripka, T., & Wetzel, A. (2011). Democracy promotion through functional cooperation? The case of the European Neighbourhood Policy. *Democratization*, 18(4), 1026–1054.

Fuhr-Hahn, I. & May, M.-L. (2012). The Eastern Partnership Civil Society Forum: An important tool with ambivalent interim results. *DGAP Standpunkt*, December 12(4).

Glasius, M. (2010). Uncivil society. In H. Anheier & S. Toepler (Eds.), *International encyclopedia of civil society* (pp. 1583–1588). New York: Springer.

Grabbe, H. (2002). The governance of the EU: Facing the challenge of enlargement. *New Economy*, 9(2), 113–117.

Hale, J. & Ursu, V. (2011). From funder to partner? Prospect for the ENP's Civil Society Facility. *Open Society Institute-Brussels Policy Brief*, October. Retrieved from http://www.soros.org/initiatives/brussels/articles_publications/publications/enp-csf.

Hann, C. & Dunn, E. (1996). *Civil society: Challenging western models*. Abingdon: Routledge.

Howard, M. M. (2003). *The weakness of civil society in post-communist Europe*. Cambridge: Cambridge University Press.

İşleyen, B. (2014). The European Union and neoliberal governmentality: Twinning in Tunisia and Egypt. *European Journal of International Relations*, Early Access.

Jünemann, A. (2002). From the bottom to the top: Civil society and transnational non-governmental organizations in the Euro-Mediterranean Partnership. *Democratization*, 9(1), 87–105.

Jünemann, A. & Simon, J. (2013). Europa und die Arabellions: Zur Wiederentdeckung der Zivilgesellschaft in der EU-Mittelmeerpolitik. In E. D. Stratenschulte (Ed.), *Grenzen der Integration. Europas strategische Ansätze für die Nachbarregionen* (pp. 79–120). Baden-Baden: Nomos.

Kaca, E. & Kazmierkiewicz, P. (2010). *Eastern promises: Supporting civil society in the Eastern Partnership countries*. Warszawa: Institut Spraw Publicznyh.

Keck, M. E. & Sikkink, K. (1998). *Activists beyond borders : Advocacy networks in international politics*. Ithaca, N.Y.: Cornell University Press.

Kelley, J. G. (2006). New wine in old wine skins: Policy adaptation in the European Neighbourhood Policy. *Journal of Common Market Studies*, 44(1), 29–55.

Kohler-Koch, B. & Rittberger, B. (2006). Review article: The 'governance turn' in EU studies. *Journal of Common Market Studies*, 44(1), 27–49.

Kopecky, P. & Mudde, C. (2005). *Uncivil society?: Contentious politics in post-communist Europe*. Abingdon: Routledge.

Korosteleva, E. (2012). *The European Union and its eastern neighbours: Towards a more ambitions partnership?* London: Routledge.

Kostanyan, H. & Orbie, J. (2013). The EEAS' discretionary power within the Eastern Partnership: In search of the highest possible denominator. *Southeast European and Black Sea Studies*, 13(1), 47–65.

Kotkin, S. (2009). *Uncivil society: 1989 and the implosion of the communist establishment.* New York: Random House.

Kovách, I. & Kučerova, E. (2009). The social context of project proliferation—the rise of a project class. *Journal of Environmental Policy and Planning,* 11(3), 203–221.

Kurki, M. (2011a). Democracy through technocracy? Reflections on technocratic assumptions in EU democracy promotion discourse. *Journal of Intervention and Statebuilding,* 5(2), 211–237.

Kurki, M. (2011b). Governmentality and EU democracy promotion: The European instrument for democracy and human rights and the construction of democratic civil societies. *International Political Sociology,* 5(4), 349–366.

Langbein, J. (2014). European Union governance towards the eastern neigbourhood: Transcending or redrawing Europe's East-West divide? *Journal of Common Market Studies,* 52(1), 157–174.

Langbein, J. & Börzel, T. A. (2013). Introduction: Explaining policy change in the European Union's eastern neighbourhood. *Europe-Asia Studies,* 65(4), 571–580.

Lavenex, S. & Schimmelfennig, F. (Eds.). (2013). *Projecting EU rules beyond membership.* Basingstoke: Routledge.

Levitsky, S. & Way, L. A. (2010). *Competitive authoritarianism: Hybrid regimes after the cold war.* Cambridge: Cambridge University Press.

Lewis, D. (2013). Civil society and the authoritarian state: Cooperation, contestation and discourse. *Journal of Civil Society,* 9(3), 325–340.

Lovitt, J. (2013). *The Eastern Partnership roadmap to the Vilnius Summit: An assessment of the roadmap implementation by the Eastern Partnership Civil Society Forum, May 2012–October 2013.* Prague: PASOS.

Malmvig, H.(2014). Free us from power: Governmentality, counter-conduct, and simulation in European democracy and reform promotion in the Arab world. *International Political Sociology,* 8(3), 293–310.

Mayntz, R. (2004). *Governance Theory als fortentwickelte Steuerungstheorie?* Köln: Max Planck Institut für Gesellschaftsforschung, Working Paper.

Melnykovska, I. & Schweickert, R. (2008). Who you gonna call? Oligarchic clans as a bottom-up force of neighborhood Europeanization in Ukraine. *Arbeitspapiere des Osteuropa-Instituts der Freien Universität Berlin, Arbeitsschwerpunkt Politik,* Nr. 67.

Mercer, C. (2002). NGOs, civil society and democratization: A critical review of the literature. *Progress in Development Studies,* 2(1), 5–22.

Merkel, W. (2004). Embedded and defective democracies. *Democratization,* 11(5), 33–58.

Merlingen, M. (2011). From governance to governmentality in CSDP: Towards a Foucauldian research agenda. *Journal of Common Market Studies,* 49(1), 149–169.

Natorski, M. (2013). Reforms in the judiciary of Ukraine: Domestic practices and the EU's policy instruments. *East European Politics,* 29(3), 358–375.

Orenstein, M. A. (2002). *Quality of democratic policy processes in Central and Eastern Europe and the former Soviet Union*. Paper presented at the American Political Science Association Annual Meeting, Boston, MA.

Popescu, N. (2010). *EU foreign policy and post-Soviet conflicts: Stealth intervention*. Basingstoke: Routledge.

Putnam, R. D., Leonardi, R., & Nanetti, R. (1994). *Making democracy work: Civic traditions in modern Italy*. Princeton: Princeton University Press.

Ratzmann, N. (2012). Securitizing or developing the European neighbourhood? Migration management in Moldova. *Southeast European and Black Sea Studies*, 12(2), 261–280.

Reynaert, V. (2011). Preoccupied with the market: The EU as a promoter of 'shallow' democracy in the Mediterranean. *European Foreign Affairs Review*, 16(5), 623–637.

Rihackova, V. (2014). *Taking stock of EU civil society funding in EAP countries*. Bruxelles: EaP Civil Society Forum/Europeum.

Rommens, T. (2014). The Eastern Partnership: Civil society in between the European and domestic level: The case of Georgia. *East European Politics*, 30(1), 54–70.

Rosamond, B. (2014). Three ways of speaking Europe to the world: Markets, peace, cosmopolitan duty and the EU's normative power. *The British Journal of Politics and International Relations*, 16(1), 133–148.

Sampson, S. (1996). The social life of projects: Importing civil society to Albania. In C. Hann & E. Dunn (Eds.), *Civil society: Challenging western models* (pp. 121–142). Basingstoke: Routledge.

Saurugger, S. (2010). The social construction of the participatory turn: The emergence of a norm in the European Union. *European Journal of Political Research*, 4, 471–495.

Schimmelfennig, F. & Scholtz, H. (2008). EU democracy promotion in the European neighbourhood political conditionality, economic development and transnational exchange. *European Union Politics*, 9(2), 187–215.

Schulze, K. & Tosun, J. (2013). External dimensions of European environmental policy: An analysis of environmental treaty ratification by third states. *European Journal of Political Research*, 52(5), 581–607.

Sending, O. J. & Neumann, I. B. (2006). Governance to governmentality: Analyzing NGOs, states, and power. *International Studies Quarterly*, 50(3), 651–672.

Ter-Gabrielyan, G. (2012). Eastern Partnership Civil Society Forum: The view of a participant from Armenia. *Caucasus Analytical Digest*, No. 35–36, 9–12.

Tulmets, E. (2010). Experimentalist governance in EU external relations: Enlargement and European Neighbourhood Policy. In C. F. Sabel & J. Zeitlin (Eds.), *Experimentalist governance in the European Union: Towards a new architecture* (pp. 297–324). Oxford: Oxford University Press.

Vachudová, M. A. (2005). *Europe undivided: Democracy, leverage, and integration since 1989*. Oxford: Oxford University Press.

Vandecasteele, B., Bossuyt, F., & Orbie, J. (2013). Unpacking the influence of the Council Presidency on European Union external policies: The Polish Council Presidency and the Eastern Partnership. *European Integration online Papers,* 17(5), pp. 1–28.

The European Union's assistance to Kyrgyzstan: Good intentions, mixed results

Aijan Sharshenova

> Democracy is a device that insures
> we shall be governed no better than we deserve.
> (Bernard Shaw)

Introduction

As an integral part of the Soviet Union, the Kyrgyz Republic had very limited, if any, contact with the world on the other side of the Iron Curtain. With the collapse of the USSR in 1991, Kyrgyzstan established itself as a sovereign state, embarked upon transition to democracy and a market economy, and engaged in bilateral and multilateral relations with various international actors. The post-Soviet transition in Kyrgyzstan brought significant socio-political, economic and cultural changes. Many of these changes were proposed, encouraged, funded and implemented by Western external actors, who sought to promote liberal democratic values and free market principles in the former Soviet space. However, some externally promoted values and principles were not fully adopted, and others became distorted or re-routed by local realities in the complex post-Soviet environment. As a result, Kyrgyzstan transformed into a complex and somewhat bizarre political and social system, where Soviet traits are intertwined with newly acquired democratic features and pre-Soviet socio-cultural traditions. This awkward combination of "new ways", "old ways" and "ancestors' ways" is not exactly a success or total failure of transitioning to a democratic order. This uneven record of external democracy promotion and socio-economic transformation in Kyrgyzstan proves one more time that a transfer of values and principles is an unpredictable process that is susceptible to the influence of numerous impeding or facilitating factors.

This chapter examines the European Union's efforts to promote democratic principles in Kyrgyzstan. The EU has been a major donor to and democracy promotion agent in Kyrgyzstan since the early 1990s. The Union now pursues a more coordinated and unified support to democratisation processes[1] in third states and in the presence of development cooperation and a gradual consolidation of EU common policies, Kyrgyzstan became the most democratic country in the region and the Kyrgyz political elites declare formal commitment to expanding democratic principles. Given these developments, one would expect that EU democracy promotion was highly successful here, but the reality does not match this claim. EU democracy assistance to Kyrgyzstan is affected by certain challenges that impede the dissemination of liberal democratic norms and values, and distort the ostensible outcomes of this process. These challenges stem from certain inconsistencies on the European side, a resistant local context in Kyrgyzstan, and the nature of a largely authoritarian regional environment. Understanding why seemingly favourable local conditions do not lead to the success in external democratisation efforts might provide some insights to improve democracy promotion policies and implementations in the post-Soviet space.

The chapter is structured as follows. First, a brief overview of EU democratisation policies and some conceptual clarifications provide a framework for understanding EU motivations, legal and normative foundations and delivery mechanisms of democracy promotion. These theoretical and conceptual considerations are followed by an analysis of EU's activities in Kyrgyzstan. Next, the factors impeding and distorting the outcomes of EU normative engagement are examined. The analysis draws on insights from numerous expert interviews conducted in Bishkek, Kyrgyzstan, in August-September, 2012. Finally, the conclusion summarises the findings and the main argument of the study.

At the outset some important limitations should be stated. Firstly, the period discussed in this chapter extends from 2007 to 2013 as it was a full EU

---

[1] In its most basic sense democratisation refers to the transition to a democratic political system. However, this is a broad, complex multi-faceted process, which includes institution building and consolidation, legislative reform, socio-economic transformation and other components. Democracy promotion is a more specific process, which implies deliberate efforts to promote democratic principles, practices and values; this process might be driven, shaped and implemented by domestic or external forces, or by both. Democracy assistance is understood here as various kinds of support provided to countries, processes, and institutions to ensure introduction, adoption and consolidation of democratic principles, practices and values.

budget cycle and the timeframe for the cornerstone EU Strategy towards Central Asia issued in 2007 under the German Presidency at the Council of the EU. Secondly, due to complexity of the issue and the plethora of external and domestic democracy promotion agents, it is virtually impossible to calculate the precise EU contribution to the success or failure of Kyrgyz democratisation. For this reason, I rather raise issues than provide thorough answers.

Theorising EU democracy promotion

A comprehensive understanding of EU democracy promotion policy abroad requires familiarity with such key aspects as the contents of democracy promotion, motivations behind it, and tools and mechanisms employed to implement it. In other words, one needs to understand the reasons why democracy is promoted, what exact contents are promoted, and how promotion policy is implemented by the EU.

The essence of democracy is an overwhelmingly large and complex subject, which finds itself in the spotlight of hot debate. For this study, I draw on the European Parliament's notion of democracy as applied in foreign policy and referenced on official EU websites. The European Parliament might not be the most significant actor in EU external affairs, but it is the strongest advocate of normative foreign policy within the EU institutional structure.

In 2009 the European Parliament offered a conceptual definition of democracy based partially on respective UN resolutions (EP OPPD, 2009). It emphasises eight essential elements of democracy that cover different aspects of socio-political dynamics in any given society:

- Universal human rights;
- Political freedoms: of expression and opinion, association and assembly;
- Separation of powers;
- A strong, functional and accountable parliament;
- The rule of law;
- A variety of alternative policy choices through a pluralistic system of political parties and organisations;
- Transparency and accountability in public administration;
- Free mass media.

These eight elements form the substantive understanding of democracy that is implicitly present in most EU policy documents and declarations such as the crucial Treaty on the European Union and the EU Strategic Framework on Human Rights and Democracy from 2012.

It is possible to distinguish three tiers that constitute the legal and normative foundation of EU democratisation policy abroad. The first tier includes general documents, which define the essence of the EU, set forth its principles and values, and serve as guidance for EU foreign policies. The second tier refers to regional policy documents that define directions of cooperation with certain groups of states, for instance Central Asian countries. Finally, the third tier is constituted by bilateral documents, e.g. cooperation agreements and other documents stipulating country-specific programmes and activities.

The first tier of general documents includes several cornerstones: the Treaty on the EU (hereinafter referred as TEU), the Charter of Fundamental Rights of the EU 2012, and the European Security Strategy. Since the Maastricht Treaty (1992), the TEU emphasises the significance of commitment to democratic principles both in domestic and foreign policies of the European Union. The TEU states that the EU "is founded on the values of respect for human dignity, freedom, democracy, equality, the rule of law and respect for human rights" (European Union, 2012, Art. 2), and puts these principles at the core of EU foreign policy (European Union, 2012, Art. 21). Given that the TEU regulates common EU policies, democratic principles should be incorporated into any domestic or external actions of the EU. The European Security Strategy, another important first-tier document, interprets democracy promotion not only as an objective in itself, but also as an instrument to ensure European security (Council of the European Union, 2003, p. 10). The same logic applies to EU development policy: promotion of democracy and human rights as a priority area can be traced back to the European Council's Resolution of November, 1991, on "Human Rights, Democracy and Development", which defines democracy and human rights promotion as an objective and a condition of development cooperation. These principles form a foundation of the EU, and serve as integral elements of the Union's self-declared global mission. In 2012, the EU adopted the EU Strategic Framework and the Action Plan on Human Rights and Democracy, which specified this EU's global mission to address human rights issues in third countries.

Second-tier legal and normative policy documents governing EU relations with other countries and include region-specific strategies. Given the scope of this chapter, a critical movement in the Kyrgyzstan region is reflected in "The EU and Central Asia: Strategy for a New Partnership" (hereinafter referred to as the Strategy). The adoption of the Strategy in 2007 manifested EU regional approach to relations with post-Soviet Central Asian states and significantly upgraded its efforts to get involved in political and economic developments in the region. The Strategy outlines seven priority areas of EU bilateral and multilateral relations with Central Asia: human rights, rule of law, good governance and democratisation; youth and education; economic development, trade and investment; energy and transport; environmental sustainability and water; common threats and challenges; and intercultural dialogue (Council of the European Union, 2007). The Strategy sets the cooperation framework and declares EU commitment to certain areas of development, thus serving as a reference point for policy-making regarding this region.

Finally, third-tier legal and normative framework documents include bilateral treaties and country-specific programmatic papers and strategies. In the case of EU-Central Asia relations, these are Partnership and Cooperation Agreements (PCAs) negotiated between the EU and individual countries. PCAs set provisions of mutually beneficial cooperation and regulate political, economic, trade, and cultural relations between the EU and third states. While these agreements tend to focus more on trade and economic cooperation, democracy and human rights remain an integral and inevitable element of bilateral cooperation. Nevertheless, the outcomes of such cooperation depend on the balance of normative and non-normative interests, local responsiveness and commitment to democratic principles by both parties.

Democratic principles lie at the core of the normative and legal framework of EU external affairs, and democracy promotion represents a projection and reaffirmation of EU identity beyond its borders. In addition, democracy is an important foreign policy objective, an instrument to ensure security and development, and a part of the European global mission. Extrapolation of values and principles abroad is a legitimate foreign policy objective for the EU. As a regional actor with global ambition but limited concrete power, the EU pursues a soft power approach, i.e. an attempt to influence policies and actions of other countries using non-militaristic means.

The existing research on external democracy promotion distinguishes two major approaches: political and developmental (Carothers, 2009). The difference lies in the way these approaches interpret democracy's value. The political approach views democracy as a value in itself, employing a Dahlian idea of democracy as a universal value serving the interests of the majority (Dahl, 1998). The developmental approach sees the value of democracy in its capacity to facilitate positive social and economic development. This approach understands democratisation as a slow process of societal change, and aims to introduce democratic principles through development aid as it applies less direct democracy promotion mechanisms and rarely confronts the host government (Carothers, 2009, pp. 6–9). EU approach to democracy promotion seems to fit in the latter definition: democracy is both an objective and a means to facilitate development; democratic norms and principles are incorporated into the provision of technical assistance and political dialogue; and EU democracy promotion initiatives require a local government's agreement (Carothers, 2009, p. 14; Del Biondo, 2011). EU developmental approach is characterised with an extensive use of so-called *mainstreaming*: where democratic values and principles are incorporated in all available mechanisms of development assistance. As a result, there might be less direct democracy promotion programmes, but democratic principles are regularly present in EU sources such as official policy documents, speeches by European officials, and project information.

This democracy and development dualism is characteristic of the conventional European mechanisms of democracy promotion. Researchers distinguish between three main channels of norms and values transfers from a socialiser (e.g. democracy promotion agent) to a target of socialisation (e.g. a country targeted by external democracy promotion): strategic calculation, normative suasion, and governance (Lavenex & Schimmelfennig, 2011).

Strategic calculation is based on rationalist thinking and assumes that a target of socialisation calculates costs and benefits associated with adopting norms and principles promoted by a socialiser. If the adaptation cost is higher than ensuing benefits provided by the socialiser, the target of socialisation is reluctant to change. For example, if adopting a free and fair electoral system undermines an authoritarian regime and the ruling elite's grip on power, the leader and the ruling elite should oppose it. However, if the socialiser offers benefits outweighing the costs, the normative transfer might be more successful (Schimmelfennig & Scholtz, 2008). In practical terms, strategic calculation is often associated with technical and financial programmes, which offer assistance with public administration and legislative consolidation.

Normative suasion is a constructivist approach representing a complex yet more effective mechanism to transfer norms and values. Under the framework of normative suasion, a socialiser and a target of socialisation engage in a meaningful argumentation on interpretations of the world. Through the argumentation process, the socialiser persuades the target of socialisation that incorporating democratic values and principles is the right thing to do. In case of successful persuasion, the target of socialisation internalises these values and principles and takes the lead in domestic reforms, policies and actions (Warkotsch, 2008). In practical terms, normative suasion takes the form of political and human rights dialogues, as well as other kinds of interactions that encourage rather than pressure target countries to undertake democratic reforms.

Finally, governance is another mechanism of indirect democracy promotion. Governance refers to the incorporation of democratic norms and principles into various cooperation areas with a target country's government. Instead of directly promoting electoral democracy, a governance mechanism advances administrative and technical requirements for cooperation, thus encouraging a target government to incorporate certain democratic principles into the public administration domain. Governance seeks to mainstream democratic values in other instruments and cooperation areas (Schimmelfennig & Scholtz, 2008). In this regard, development cooperation provides more space for incorporating democratic principles and values. For instance, development projects often require the beneficiaries to ensure transparency and accountability of the state budget management process.

In practice, success of normative transfer processes depends on two major factors: EU power to transform or *push*, and local responsiveness or domestic *pull* (Börzel & Pamuk, 2012, p. 3). An EU push varies from country to country and is often proportionate to the balance of local needs and EU offers. However, a strong push alone is not sufficient to generate significant changes. The domestic disposition to pull a change inward, or local prerequisites for democratisation, often plays a crucial role. If the local stakeholders lack internal motivation to adopt and incorporate democratic principles and values, the EU-generated push might fail (Börzel & Pamuk, 2012).

EU assistance to Kyrgyzstan: Good intentions

External democracy promotion might appear as a straightforward process: a democracy promotion agent generates its push through conditionality and transfer of norms and values (socialisation) and a target country either responds with sufficient domestic pull accepting and adopting the transferred norms and values or rejects them. However, the reality of external democracy promotion is complicated by a broad range of intervening factors. In the Central Asian region, democracy promotion is a challenging task due to the strong authoritarian environment and powerful anti-democratic forces. In addition, sometimes EU normative goals seem less important for its own European constituents due to other, less normative interests (e.g. energy, trade, or security), and the democracy promotion agent fails to generate the push. Normative and non-normative interests are not necessarily incompatible but in certain cases strategic interests might affect EU drive to get involved in democracy promotion policies in a target country.

EU motivation to promote democratic values and principles in Kyrgyzstan reflects its foreign policy narratives and largely stems from the ambition of establishing itself as a normative power with global reach. EU democracy and development assistance to Kyrgyzstan fits well into its normative mission declared in its core treaties and declarations (TEU, the European Security Strategy to name few). The EU has established an ambitious normative and legal basis to engage with democracy promotion in Kyrgyzstan. The Central Asia Indicative Programme[2] explicitly declares that "the EU will contribute to consolidating the values of democracy, the rule of law, good governance, and respect for human rights and fundamental freedoms in the

---

[2] Central Asia Indicative Programme offers more detailed information on the substance and technicalities of the EU assistance to Central Asian countries.

region" (European Commission, 2010, p. 7). The cornerstone bilateral document—Partnership and Cooperation Agreement with Kyrgyzstan, signed in 1995 and in force since 1999, sets an unambiguous partnership objective to support Kyrgyz efforts to consolidate its democracy (European Communities, 1999, Art. 1). The EU projects its normative motivation and identity to the Kyrgyz side stating that "respect for democracy, principles of international law and human rights [...] underpin the internal and external policies of the parties and constitute an essential element of partnership" (European Communities, 1999, Art. 2).

The EU finds itself in a good position to prioritise normative over non-normative interests in Kyrgyzstan because it lacks strong non-normative interests there for example there is no solid European business presence in the country. Kyrgyzstan cannot offer any energy resources nor has it the capacity to engage in significant trade and investment initiatives. Regional security is often mentioned as an EU objective in Central Asia, but Kyrgyzstan does not have enough potential to cause significant troubles or offer and sustain plausible solutions. Kyrgyzstan per se does not represent a security threat; it is relevant to EU security through the medium of other countries. Kyrgyzstan is not a home for transnational extremist or terrorist groups, but it is located in the neighbourhood of large extremist and terrorist hubs in Afghanistan and Pakistan. Kyrgyzstan is not a major source of drug trafficking, but it finds itself on a major drug trafficking route. Afghan opiates are delivered to Europe through the northern route—Central Asia and Russia, in addition to the Balkan and the southern routes (UNODC, 2014). Europe is not a primary destination for both legal and illegal migrants from Kyrgyzstan, as Russia hosts up to 95 per cent of Kyrgyz migrants (IOM, 2015), but a regional crisis might potentially imply an influx of migrants and refugees to Europe. While the importance of these issues should not be disregarded, these worse-case scenarios are less threatening for Europe given the distant geographic location of Kyrgyzstan and the existing strong but undemocratic regional security framework. Lack of strategic interests frees the EU from balancing values with pragmatic interests.

In addition, the EU has some capacity to generate an attractive push for transfer of democratic values. While it cannot offer one of its most attractive "carrots" of prospective membership, the EU has more leverage in Kyrgyzstan than in most of the other Central Asian countries. As a low-income heavily indebted country with regular budget deficit issues, Kyrgyzstan welcomes virtually any assistance and financial injections. Budget support is vital for maintaining social security programmes and preventing social unrest. Local beneficiaries display positive responsiveness and readiness to consider the EU conditions in exchange for providing technical and financial assistance. As a relatively new member of the international community, Kyrgyzstan also needs political support and recognition to find its niche in the international scene. Thus, the EU might have both technical and political push mechanisms to encourage domestic change.

At the same time, there is a potential for good pull on the Kyrgyz side. Against the background of the region hosting some of the world's most oppressive regimes (Uzbekistan and Turkmenistan), Kyrgyzstan is an unusual exception. The Kyrgyz leadership formally accepts democracy and declares its commitment to establishing a parliamentary-presidential republic (Euronews, 2013). Kyrgyzstan is an open and relatively liberal state, where vibrant civil society enjoys freedom of operation and expression unprecedented in Central Asia. These contributing factors make Kyrgyzstan a responsive target country.

In compliance with its general strategy for external democracy promotion, the EU applies a developmental approach to promoting democratic values and principles in Kyrgyzstan. EU assistance to the country aims to ensure poverty reduction and sustainable development, "while not ignoring democracy, good governance, rule of law, and human rights" (Boonstra & Hale, 2010, p. 5). Socio-economic development and democratic political reforms form integral and equally important parts of the EU policy towards Kyrgyzstan. The combination of development and democracy support can be traced in specific EU-funded projects: virtually all projects incorporate development-oriented initiatives with democratic elements.

The EU has a long record of providing democracy and development assistance to Kyrgyzstan. As a fast-track reformer in the early 1990s, Kyrgyzstan went through drastic economic, political and social reforms promoted by international financial institutions (IFIs)—reforms collectively known as "shock therapy" (Steimann, 2011, p. 58). In this period, the EU provided assistance to Kyrgyzstan under the framework of its Technical Assistance to the Commonwealth of Independent States (TACIS) programme. During the lifetime of TACIS from 1991 to 2006, the EU funded more than 500 projects totalling €130 million to support Kyrgyzstan alone, notwithstanding regional assistance to all Central Asian countries (Frenz, 2007).TACIS focused more on transitions to market economies in the former Soviet Union; support to democratisation was not the top priority even though a certain amount of funding and efforts were directed towards this end in Kyrgyzstan (Urdze, 2011, p. 23).

In 2007, the Development Cooperation Instrument (DCI) took over TACIS activities that provided EU assistance to Central Asian states. DCI works in developing countries and focuses on poverty reduction and democratisation. As a low-income nation, Kyrgyzstan is eligible to receive support from the DCI's geographic programmes, which centre on poverty eradication, education, healthcare, governance and democracy, rural development and water management. In addition, Kyrgyzstan benefits from thematic programmes related to human security, environmental management, food security, and non-state actors. The DCI, just like its predecessor TACIS, requires the consent of the local government to be implemented. The European Instrument for Democracy and Human Rights (EIDHR), another EU tool for providing assistance abroad, supports non-state actors and does not require the government's permission to operate. The Central Asian states have become eligible to receive assistance under the EIDHR framework since the early 2000s. The Instrument for Stability (IfS) addresses urgent stability crises and stands out as a quick implementation mechanism as it is not slowed down by the typical bureaucratic procedures.

At the moment, Kyrgyzstan receives funds under both EU regional and bilateral assistance frameworks. During 2007–2010, the EU allocated approximately €314 million in total to support DCI programmes in the Central Asian region (European Commission, 2006). From these, country specific assistance to Kyrgyzstan amounted to €55 million (ibid.). In 2011–2013, DCI budget amounted to €321 million, including bilateral funding for Kyrgyzstan, which amounted to €51 million (European Commission, 2010). In addition, the EU provided assistance through thematic instruments such as the DCI (€21.11 million), EIDHR (€2.7 million), and IfS (€15.13 million). From 2007 to 2013, the EU allocated a total of €146.45 million to Kyrgyzstan (Tsertsvadze & Boonstra, 2013, p. 10). Of the major funds the EU provided to Kyrgyzstan a majority were grants to the government. A large part of the assistance was allocated as conditional assistance; in particular, budget support and food security programmes required Kyrgyzstan to meet certain conditions, often related to anti-corruption policy, and ensuring transparency and accountability.

Social protection programmes tallied up to 31 per cent of the total EU assistance to Kyrgyzstan for the 2007–2013 EU budget cycle period. They aimed to assist in reform of social protection policies, and are vital not only for poverty reduction and improving life standards but also for political stability: Kyrgyzstan's two revolutions in 2005 and 2010 have been significantly fuelled by the frustrations of poverty-stricken people. Good governance is the second largest sector of EU support: it takes up to 24 per cent of the total EU assistance for Kyrgyzstan. Education system reform takes up 17 per cent on average; however, there was a significant increase in education funding between the first and second half of the budget period. In 2007–2010, €5.5 million were allocated to education-related activities. In 2010–2013, this was nearly four times larger at €20 million. For the next budget cycle (2014–2020) the multi-annual financial framework foresees the allocation of €1 billion to assist development in Central Asia.

Challenges for EU democracy assistance to Kyrgyzstan

Despite reasonably favourable conditions for external democracy promotion in Kyrgyzstan, the efficiency and effectiveness of EU democracy assistance faces several important challenges. While it is possible to identify and analyse a broad variety of factors, which might impede democracy promotion, I focus on a few of them here.

As discussed earlier, the EU has capacity to generate a normative push, as it does not have to balance its normative objectives with non-normative considerations (e.g. energy trade) in Kyrgyzstan. This seemingly positive factor might have negative implications for the efficiency of democracy promotion. The EU and Kyrgyzstan managed to establish strong bilateral relations with virtually no tensions. Both parties formally express their interest in regional security, stability, and economic development, and run a variety of joint activities. The EU-Kyrgyz bilateral relations indeed display positive dynamics, but they are missing an important element: vital mutual interests that would drive cooperation. On one side, Kyrgyzstan is undoubtedly interested in getting access to the European market, attracting European investment, socio-cultural and educational exchange, and facilitated visa regulations for its citizens; however, the Kyrgyz Government acknowledges the limits of these aspirations, namely that Europe is socially and geographically less accessible for Kyrgyzstan (interviews with state officials at the Prime Minister's Office, the Presidential Administration and the Parliament of the Kyrgyz Republic, August-September 2012, Bishkek). On another side, the EU has certain normative objectives, but lacks other strategic drivers to engage more with the country.

The lack of mutual strategic interests might have various implications for EU assistance to Kyrgyzstan. Firstly, it might facilitate prioritisation of normative objectives. In the absence of strong non-normative interests, the EU can safely engage in democracy promotion without undermining its collective (EU) and individual interests (those of EU member states) in the country. Secondly, it might impede deeper engagement in Kyrgyzstan because advocating the need for financial support to Kyrgyzstan within the EU might be a challenging task in the absence of clear immediate interests in this country. The financial crisis and strict austerity measures make assistance to third countries difficult to justify to the European public. Thirdly, the lack of interest on the part of the EU is obvious to local stakeholders in Kyrgyzstan and it raises their suspicions about the genuine motivation behind European engagement with Kyrgyzstan and the region (interview with an official at the Presidential Administration, 31/07/2012, Bishkek). The EU activities in the country, especially their normative components, are sometimes seen as a cover for other, more selfish interests. As an interviewee from a Kyrgyz ministry noted, he sees two sets of drivers behind EU activities in Kyrgyzstan. The formal version is that the EU facilitates the democratisation process in Kyrgyzstan by encouraging reforms. The informal version implies deeper geopolitical considerations and involves competition and cooperation dynamics between several powers in the region: Russia, China, and the US engage with Central Asia on different levels, and ensure their political, economic, and sometimes even military presences. The EU, as an emerging power, might feel compelled to be present in the region as well to maintain the status of an international actor with global reach (Interview with an official at the Ministry of Economics, 03/08/2012, Bishkek). Other local actors are concerned about the lack of pragmatism: "While the EU-Kyrgyz relations are good, it is important to note that they lack a solid platform for pragmatic, interests-based cooperation" (Interview with a Kyrgyz foreign policy analyst, 18/08/2012, Bishkek). A Kyrgyz member of parliament compared the EU policies elsewhere, and emphasised that when the EU genuinely wants democracy promotion it devotes much more effort and resources than in Kyrgyzstan. He noted that Georgia, another post-Soviet nation in transit, received far greater assistance and political support than Kyrgyzstan (Interview with a Kyrgyz MP, 22/04/2013, Bishkek). The local narratives on EU democracy promotion represent a combination of gratitude and appreciation coupled with an enduring feeling that more could be done.

Other challenges are deeply rooted in the delivery mechanisms employed to ensure transfer of best practices and democratic norms and principles: technical assistance and budget support. Researchers identify three methods used by the EU to deliver its assistance in Central Asia: sector budget support; technical assistance (project approach); and support to civil society and non-state actors (Tsertsvadze & Boonstra, 2013).

The technical assistance provided to the government relies on the logic of strategic calculation by local actors: rational choice centred research assumes that benefits of adopting externally promoted norms need to be higher than consequential costs of such an adoption for the regime (Warkotsch, 2011, pp. 109–112). However, this calculation can be affected by the presence of alternative sources of development assistance. Kyrgyzstan, as one of the poorer countries in the region, heavily depends on foreign aid. In 1991–2013, Kyrgyzstan received $7.7 billion of international aid provided by 49 donors, including states, transnational NGOs and international financial institutions (Aid Data, 2015). While most of these donors and organisations have Western roots and affiliations and usually promote democracy, or do not mind having democratic component attached to their aid, some donors come from less democratic background (e.g. China and Russia). This kind of donor diversity might affect the efficiency of EU conditionality. If Kyrgyzstan fails to meet EU requirements on enforcing democratic principles in governance, human rights protection, or other areas leading to losses in European support, it might seek to replace the missing assistance with other sources. In other words, it might look to countries such as China and Russia, two authoritarian regional powers, whose assistance comes without normative strings attached. China is a good example in this regard. Unlike the EU, China is a major economic partner and a top investor in Kyrgyzstan. In 2013 alone, China offered much-needed $3 billion in loans for energy and infrastructure projects, including $1.4 billion funding to build an oil pipeline extension through Kyrgyzstan to China. China also offers significant foreign aid, which entails some benefits. Firstly, beneficiaries receive substantial amounts of resources required for social and economic development. Secondly, local governments get an opportunity to lessen their dependence on Western assistance and its political conditionality accompanying virtually every cent donated. Having an alternative to the Western assistance, local rulers feel less constrained in their authoritarian policies.

Chinese assistance is generous, or, at least, so it seems to the local actors. It never fails to impress local stakeholders how China provides its assistance. It is questionable to what extent this aid can actually be viewed as generous, because China has a rather blurred and broad definition of aid: e.g. loans and investment projects are presented as "aid". However, this fact that this aid comes in large amounts and in the form of generous gestures has an impressive subjective impact. In just one voyage around Central Asia in September 2013, President Xi Jinping promised Kyrgyzstan to provide about $3 billion in credits for energy and infrastructure projects. By comparison, in 2007–2013, the EU provided Kyrgyzstan with only €146.45 million (Tsertsvadze & Boonstra, 2013, pp. 8–12). In compliance with the European principles of donor aid, these amounts are usually accompanied with certain conditions and strict requirements of transparency and accountability. As an outcome of such comparisons, local stakeholders become increasingly supportive of China in the region. In an informal conversation, a Kyrgyz MP, who is a member of the Parliamentary Committee on Foreign Affairs, complained about European assistance as unsubstantial when compared to Chinese aid (Interview with a Kyrgyz MP, 22/04/2013, Bishkek):

> We do receive European aid, but not as much as we would like to …[T]he EU assistance is really small, it is not substantial. China provides much more and invests in infrastructure (building roads, bridges and other facilities) and energy sector. Chinese assistance is incomparable to the European, but the Chinese do not make their assistance headline of every newspaper.

Such comparisons clearly do not work in favour of the EU. In the age of donor diversity, democracy promotion agents need to acknowledge that their conditionality mechanisms might have powerful alternatives in the form of financial and other material support from non-democratic countries, who offer assistance with fewer conditions.

Donor diversity is one external factor undermining European conditionality, but the very natures of certain types of assistance have inherently problematic aspects as well. 31 per cent of total EU development aid to Kyrgyzstan is allocated to social protection programmes, with most of it going to budget support (Tsertsvadze & Boonstra, 2013, p. 9). Against the background of continuous budget deficit in Kyrgyzstan, this support is a much needed financial injection into the country's economy and a powerful tool to carry on with social protection programmes. However, in the long-term it entails certain complications. Despite numerous efforts to ensure good governance, transparency and accountability on the beneficiary's side, continuous budget support might imply support of inefficient governance. The budget deficit is partly the fault of the Kyrgyz government, whose development and economic policies are undermined by corruption and financial mismanagement. Providing budget support implies providing a safety net not only for the vulnerable social groups (as originally intended) but also for the corrupt and inefficient government elites. Budget support helps the government get away with its policies, which otherwise would have failed. Having this safety net induces the government's reluctance to make structural changes and drastic amendments.

Local stakeholders express mixed feelings about financial support. A Kyrgyz civil servant involved in the programme on the beneficiary's side notes that EU budget assistance is both timely and useful as it allows paying social benefits to the population. However, it also contributes to Kyrgyzstan's dependence on foreign assistance. Within the first twenty-two years since its independence (1991–2013), Kyrgyzstan received $7.7 billion (Aid Data, 2015). In total, 50 various funding organisations have been providing and still provide donor assistance through more than 6,000 projects to the country (Aid Data, 2015). While donor aid is a matter of necessity in the short-term perspective, in the long-term donor dependence and a shrinking role of the state might imply gradual transfer of state functions to external actors.

Mixed results: Democracy, the Kyrgyz way

It is difficult to measure the impact of EU assistance to democratic reforms in Kyrgyzstan based on the quantities of support. Certainly the EU, along with other democratically orientated international donors, contributed to the development of a "democracy infused" discourse among the local political elites. In an attempt to fit into the donors' expectations and meet the requirements of international socialisation processes, state officials, as well as politicians, have mastered the art of mimicking: "We (the Kyrgyz) are quickly adaptable. Our people know how to shape proposals and rhetoric to get funding" (Interview with Dr. Elmira Nogoibaeva, August 2012, Bishkek). At some point, this discourse should turn into action. But in the case of the Kyrgyz Republic, the discourse of democratic freedoms, human rights and citizen engagement has been distorted by a variety of reality factors and resulted in a hybrid regime termed "street democracy" (Artemyev, 2006)

Two violent changes of power in 2005 and 2010 gave Kyrgyzstan an ambiguous reputation as an unstable democracy where changes occur only under the extreme pressure of public protest. The public protest practices have not disappeared with the most recent violent change of power in 2010.

On October 3rd, 2012, a group of protesters headed by several members of parliament undertook a failed attempt to take over the House of Government. The protest action initially started with the demand to reconsider the agreement between the Kyrgyz Government and Kumtor Operating Company, the leading gold mining company in the country. The anti-gold mining protest quickly turned violent, and protesters attempted to climb the fence of the Government House (RFE/RL Kyrgyz Service, 2012). One of the protest leaders, MP Kamchibek Tashiev was video-recorded encouraging his fellow protestors:

> Why should we bring 10,000 people here to gain power? Why should we bring 20,000 people here to gain power? We don't have to. If necessary, we can go now and take the power! We must take it! We must take it! We must! (RFE/RL, 2012).

The rally was dispersed by the police, organisers were detained, and the key leader Tashiev was tried and convicted to a year and five months in prison (Begalieva, 2014). But an important value of this rather short and awkward incident is that it illustrates what is called "street democracy".

Street democracy is not an academic term in Kyrgyzstan; it is rather a handy way for local people to explain the chaotic freedom in this small country. Street democracy is often used by locals with reference to protest actions outside the House of Government, also known as the White House, in Bishkek, and other important administrative buildings both in the capital of Kyrgyzstan and in provinces. Another feature of this incident is that it reinforces what I call a "White House Fence Phenomenon". Both in 2005 and 2010, as well as on other, less successful attempts to overthrow the government, the White House was the ultimate destination for protestors, who sometimes would walk miles from provinces to reach the physical location of the President and his administration in Bishkek. While demands and slogans vary from time to time, and from one protest action to another, the task stays the same: reach the White House, cross the fence, enter the Presidential Hall, and declare a new leader. The President and the White House have become symbols of power under two strong presidential regimes. Nowadays, Kyrgyzstan labels itself as a parliamentary democracy, but the Parliament and the President are located in the White House making it again a target for popular discontent. As an NGO leader notes, the street democracy might be reaching excess and turning into a commercial activity: "Nowadays, people with any issues go protesting to the parliament. Protest actions are turning into a kind of business; politicians use protest action for their benefits, while people use it as a means to make money" (Interview with the head of an NGO, 15/08/2012, Bishkek).

In the immediate aftermath of the October 3rd, 2012 fence exercise, Parliament's Speaker Asylbek Jeenbekov stressed at the plenary meeting that Kyrgyzstan needs to move from street democracy to parliamentary democracy: "Peaceful meetings are not prohibited, but the law does not permit violent overthrow of the government" (Moldalieva, 2012). However, doing so might be a challenging task given the political culture that formed over the last twenty years in Kyrgyzstan

In addition to street democracy, or chaotic exercise of popular will, there are other phenomena, which might affect democracy promotion and democratisation. Poor performance of the state administration represents a human resources challenge for carrying out activities targeted at state institutions. Ongoing lack of public trust in government institutions impedes establishment of stable and reliable connections between the public and the government, which are an essential component of a functional political system. In addition, the clear domination of informal politics over the formal political arrangements complicates both the understanding of local politics by the Europeans and the implementation of democracy related projects. Turbulent political developments in Kyrgyzstan might be instrumental for Central Asian authoritarian regimes in their own domestic propaganda. The political regime in Bishkek, the only regime in the region resembling democracy, has been so far characterised with continuous instability, regular security crises, and poor economic performance. While these negative dynamics owe to a range of various factors, the recent Kyrgyz experience is a convenient example for local dictators to demonstrate fragility and instability of the democratic development path, and justify their own authoritarian positions.

Street democracy together with the vulnerable state represents both an outcome of flawed democratisation process and an impeding factor for successful democratisation. On one hand, the very concept of street democracy is an awkward child of democratic aspirations and rhetoric, and corrupt realities on the ground. On the other hand, the frequent protest actions of street democracy undermine and distort the idea of the rule of law and non-violent lawful citizen engagement. In addition, the unstable Kyrgyz democracy has become an exemplary case of how things could go wrong if you promote democratic principles within an illiberal society. References to the Kyrgyzstan's continuous state of instability have become a powerful argument in the rhetoric of authoritarian leaders in Central Asia, who equal democracy to catastrophe when addressing their domestic audiences:

> When our neighbours in Kyrgyzstan tried to establish complete freedom of democracy, it led to such cataclysms that they still can't recover. We see this in Ukraine, we see this in Georgia. Our people see it. We say the economy first, then politics. We need to move gradually (Nazarbayev, 2010).

Conclusion

In the last twenty years, the EU has been regularly providing assistance to Kyrgyzstan with the intention to encourage democratic reforms and promote liberal values. In this empirical study, I examined some issues that challenge EU external democracy promotion in the country, where the EU has neither experience of democracy promotion prior to 1991 nor socio-cultural similarities. I argued that EU democracy support to Kyrgyzstan faces several challenges, which impede the promotion of liberal democratic norms and values in the country and distort the ostensible outcomes.

Firstly, the EU does not have vital strategic interests in Kyrgyzstan. This fact in itself is not yet an impediment to democracy promotion. On the contrary, the lack of pragmatic interests might enhance the prioritisation of normative objectives in EU engagement. However, in the case of the EU-Kyrgyzstan relations, the lack of vested interests downscales EU democracy promotion efforts. EU interests in the country are sufficient to carry on with certain activities to ensure some degree of presence and visibility in Kyrgyzstan. But as the EU lacks strategic interests in the country, other more prioritised regions push Kyrgyzstan off EU foreign policy agenda, minimising EU commitment to the bilateral engagement with Bishkek.

Secondly, the delivery methods of assistance might entail unintended reactions or results. In this regard, budget support, technical assistance and the use of conditionality present interesting cases, which could be investigated further. Poor economic performance of Kyrgyzstan makes it more responsive to conditionality-based mechanisms of socialisation into democratic norms if the socialiser (in this case the EU) offers sufficient financial and other material rewards. However, the dynamic nature of Kyrgyzstan's donors might make this leverage mechanism less efficient: the Kyrgyz government relies on a combination of externally produced rents and does not depend too much on a single external assistance source. As a result, Kyrgyzstan can be selective in adapting the democratic principles, practices and values promoted by the EU in favour of less democratically-oriented providers.

Finally, the democratisation process in the Kyrgyz Republic took unintended roots despite (or perhaps, because of) the involvement of various international actors, including the European Union. The distortion of good intentions through the prism of local idiosyncrasies resulted in the birth of street democracy. The case of street democracy in Kyrgyzstan poses a considerable threat to EU intentions to promote good governance, citizen engagement and the rule of law because the very existence of regular mass protest actions that are allegedly fuelled by clientele loyalties, and individual ambitions of politicians and their money are threats to the fledgling Kyrgyz state. Unstable street democracy and the images of chaos and lack of control that it entails impede the democracy promotion efforts in the wider region as well: in the eyes of the regional governments and respective societies the continuous political instability and uncertainty of the Kyrgyz democracy is a strong case against democracy.

As the chapter argues, the transfer of norms and values is a complex process, which can be undermined by a variety of factors. However, this does neither imply that norm transfer is impossible and democracy promotion is a futile effort do not necessarily nor it indicates the EU's lack of capacity to promote democracy. Much the opposite, the issues raised in this paper reflect the complexity of external democracy promotion and will hopefully stimulate the reader to think of possible solutions. Democracy promotion initiatives might bring some results in the long run, but it is important to take into account the existing and potential challenges.

References

Aid Data. (2015). Open data for international development. *Aid Data Portal*, College of William and Mary, Development Gateway and Brigham Young University. Retrieved from http://aiddata.org.

Artemyev, M. (2006). Ulichnaya demokratiya po-kirgizski. *Central Asia News,* November 9, online edition. Retrieved from https://ca-news.info/2006/11/09/61.

Begalieva, N. (2014). Tashiev: Ya nameren nastaivat' na snyatii sudimosti. *Vecherniy Bishkek Newspaper,* October 20, online edition. Retrieved from http://vb.kg:80 80/290357.

Boonstra, J. & Hale, J. (2010). EU assistance to Central Asia: Back to the drawing board? *EUCAM Working Paper,* No. 8. Brussels: FRIDE.

Börzel, T. A. & Pamuk, Y. (2012). Pathologies of Europeanisation: Fighting corruption in the Southern Caucasus. *West European Politics*, 35(1), 79–97.

Carothers, T. (2009). Democracy assistance: Political versus developmental? *Journal of Democracy,* 20(1), 5–19.

Council of the European Union. (2003). *A Secure Europe in a Better World: European Security Strategy.* Brussels: EU.

Council of the European Union. (2007). *The European Union and Central Asia: Strategy for a New Partnership*, Brussels: EU.

Dahl, R. A. (1998). *On democracy.* London: Yale University Press.

Del Biondo, K. (2011). Democracy promotion meets development cooperation: The EU as a promoter of democratic governance in Sub-Saharan Africa. *European Foreign Affairs Review,* 16(5), 659–672.

EP OPPD. (2009). *Democracy revisited: Which notion of democracy for the EU's external relations?* European Parliament's Office for Promotion of Parliamentary Democracy (EP OPPD). Retrieved from http://www.europarl.europa.eu.

Euronews. (2013). Kyrgyzstan turns to EU for advice on democracy. *Euronews,* September 18. Retrieved from http://www.euronews.com, last accessed on April 1, 2015.

European Commission. (2006). Central Asia DCI Indicative Programme 2007–2010. Brussels: European Commission. Retrieved from http://eeas.europa.eu/central_asia/rsp/nip_07_10_en.pdf.

European Commission. (2010). Central Asia DCI Indicative Programme 2011–2013. Brussels: European Commission. Retrieved from http://www.eeas.europa.eu/central_asia/docs/2010_ca_mtr_en.pdf.

European Communities. (1999). Partnership and Cooperation Agreement (PCA) establishing a partnership between the European Communities and their Member States, of the one part, and the Kyrgyz Republic, of the other part. *Official Journal of the European Union,* No. L196, July 28, 48–89.

European Union. (2012). Treaty on the European Union. *Official Journal of the European Union,* C 326, October 26.

Frenz, A. (2007). *The European Commission's TACIS programme 1991–2006: A success story.* Retrieved from http://www.osce.org/eea/34459?download=true.

IOM. (2015). *World Data. International Organisation on Migration.* Retrieved from http://iom.int.

Lavenex, S. & Schimmelfennig, F. (2011). EU democracy promotion in the neighbourhood: From leverage to governance? *Democratization,* 18(4), 885–909.

Moldalieva, A. (2012). Neudavshiysya perevorot. *Slovo Kyrgyzstana Newspaper,* October 5. Retrieved from http://slovo.kg/?p=13264.

Nazarbayev, N. (2010). Economy first, then politics. *Euronews,* January 15. Retrieved from http://www.euronews.com.

RFE/RL Kyrgyz Service. (2012). Hundreds rally in Bishkek against Kumtor Gold Mine. *Radio Free Europe/Radio Liberty Kyrgyz Service,* October 3. Retrieved from http://www.rferl.org.

Schimmelfennig, F. & Scholtz, H. (2008). EU democracy promotion in the European neighbourhood: Political conditionality, economic development and transnational exchange. *European Union Politics,* 9(2), 187–215.

Steimann, B. (2011). *Pastoralism and farming in Central Asia's mountains: A research review.* Bishkek, Kyrgyzstan: University of Central Asia Press.

Tsertsvadze, T. & Boonstra, J. (2013). Mapping EU development aid to Central Asia. *EUCAM Factsheet,* No. 1. Brussels: FRIDE.

UNODC. (2014). *World Drug Report 2014.* Retrieved from http://www.unodc.org/wdr2014/.

Urdze, S. (2011). The toolkit of EU-Central Asian cooperation. In A. Warkotsch (Ed.), *The European Union and Central Asia* (pp. 22–33). Oxon, UK: Routledge.

Warkotsch, A. (2008). Normative suasion and political change in Central Asia. *Caucasian Review of International Affairs*, 2(4), 62–71.

Warkotsch, A. (2011). Human rights, democratization and good governance. In A. Warkotsch (Ed.), *The European Union and Central Asia* (pp. 102–115). Oxon, UK: Routledge.

Poland's democracy promotion in Belarus—closer to the US' or the EU's approach?

Tsveta Petrova

Introduction

Democracy promotion has become an important element of the work of many governmental and non-governmental actors in international affairs (Diamond, 1995; Burnell, 2000). Most studies of democracy promotion focus on the activities of a few Western countries, yet some of the new democracies in Eastern Europe have also actively engaged in democracy promotion. How is the support they provide similar to and different from the support supplied by established democracies?

To answer this question this chapter examines Polish democracy promotion in Belarus in the first twenty years after Poland's democratic revolution (1989–2009), and compares this to the democracy promotion efforts of the United States (US) and the European Union (EU) in the same context. Poland has been among the most active democracy promoters within the group of new Eastern European democracies (Jonavicius, 2008; Kucharchyk & Lovitt, 2008; Petrova, 2014) and is thus an empirically important case to study. The US and the EU are the two most prominent and successful democracy promoters in the world today but they have very different approaches to supporting democracy abroad (Magen, Risse, & McFaul, 2009). The US tends to use more interventionist policy instruments and to follow a more political approach, that is, to support civil and political society in the process of political liberalisation and democratisation abroad, whereas the EU tends to employ less intrusive policy instruments and to follow a more developmental approach, namely to focus on governance and the more technical aspects of consolidating democracy. On the recipient side, Belarus is a priority recipient for Poland. Belarus also features a repressive regime, which has generated a heated debate within the international democracy promotion community as to the best approach on the continuum from engagement to sanctions and isolation.

This chapter finds that Poland's approach to democracy promotion has been political and minimally intrusive. Warsaw used diplomacy, assistance, and at times positive conditionality to convince and prepare the political elites and especially the civic actors and citizenry in Belarus to implement democratisation reforms. In its political nature, Poland's approach has been similar to the US' strategy; however, in its non-intrusiveness, Poland's efforts have been closer to the EU. Still, unlike both the EU and the US, Poland has preferred to persuade and pressure through quiet diplomacy and to choose engagement over sanctions.

This chapter contributes to the literature on democracy promotion by examining the activities of one country among a new generation of democracy promoters. Although often overlooked (for some important exceptions see Petrova, 2014; Pospieszna, 2014; Mikulova & Simecka, 2013), the category of new democracies working as democracy promoters is important to study because their recent transitions give them first-hand experience with democratisation and therefore credibility with recipients as well as valuable expertise that other donors lack. Therefore, understanding how these democracy promoters fit in the international democracy promotion community informs our understanding of the ways in which they are influencing this community and the liberal international order more generally.

After defining the key concepts of interest of *democracy promotion* and *democracy promotion approaches* in the next section, the chapter proceeds by briefly discussing the democratisation trajectory of Belarus. It then provides an overview of the democracy promotion efforts of the US, the EU, and Poland, in this order. The chapter concludes with a comparison of the approaches of these three democracy promoters.

Research agenda

Democracy promotion is defined in this chapter as purposeful actions—diplomatic, financial, or technical assistance—meant to support a transition to democracy and to enhance the quality or prevent the retrenchment of regimes that have already moved towards democratic government. Most democracy-promotion efforts target three different categories (or sectors) of the domestic political order of the recipient:

1) political process, including elections and parties;
2) governing institutions, including national and local institutions and rule of law;
3) civil society, including formal and informal groups and non-state actors with important democratic functions (after Carothers, 2000).

These sectors can be targeted through different policy instruments, most frequently through:

1) diplomacy: persuasion, socialisation and pressure;
2) assistance: technical or financial;
3) conditionality: incentives or sanctions;
4) intervention: military or administrative/political.

This chapter examines which of these sectors are prioritised and which instruments are preferred by different democracy promoters.

There is somewhat of a consensus in the democracy promotion literature that the US has mostly shied away from the socio-economic dimensions of democracy aid and has instead supported primarily procedural, election-related aspects of democracy and secondarily, at least since the 1990s, the development of civil society and especially advocacy groups (Cox, Ikenberry, & Inoguchi, 2000; Kopstein, 2006; Crawford, 2001). Scholars also agree that the EU focused mostly on aiding good governance and political modernisation and that democracy has been supported as part of a package of principles that also include fundamental rights, the rule of law, good neighbourliness, and respect for international law (Young, 2008; Wetzel, Orbie, & Bossuyt, 2015). Some have juxtaposed American democracy promotion favouring civil and political society in the process of political liberalisation and democratisation with EU democracy promotion focused on governance and the state and generally the more technical aspects of consolidation of democracy (Kopstein, 2006). Others have similarly suggested that US donors are more likely to focus on the political aspects of democracy assistance, that is, to support pro-democratic societal and political actors and key institutions that level the political playing field (such as independent electoral commissions and independent media). On the other hand, the EU is more likely to prioritise the developmental elements of democracy assistance and to pursue incremental, long-term change in a wide range of political and socioeconomic sectors, frequently by emphasising governance and the building of a well-functioning state (Carothers, 2009).

In addition, some argue that the US is known for its "hard-ball" intrusive tactics, whereas the EU has a preference for a "softer" and more non-intrusive approach (Magen et al, 2009, pp. 16–17). These authors find that when it comes to autocratic regimes, the EU and its member states have in general tended to rely more on dialogue and "engagement" than the US, which has favoured "an uncompromising approach, including diplomatic and trade isolation, economic sanctions and direct assistance to opposition movements" seeking to overthrow their regime (ibid.).

How does Poland compare to the two most prominent democracy promoters—the US and the EU? This chapter follows the consensus in the field of democracy promotion studies on the importance of detailed scrutiny of individual cases (Hook, 1998). The case studies are based on secondary sources, on more than 250 in-depth interviews conducted between 2007 and 2013 with the Polish, EU and US foreign policymakers, and their Belarusian counterparts;[1] and on archives of relevant Polish, EU and US state institutions.

The Belarusian post-communist transition

Aleksander Lukashenko won the country's first presidential elections in 1994, promising to re-establish the social protection of the Soviet era. He instead marginalised the opposition and established direct presidential control over all institutions, including the electoral process, the various state institutions, the independent press, and the economy and society. He was re-elected in 2001 amid criticism surrounding the disappearance of key opposition figures. A 2004 referendum removed limits on the presidential term and Lukashenko was again re-elected in 2006 and 2010 amidst widespread electoral irregularities and violence. Although the opposition attempted to organise an electoral breakthrough in 2001, 2006, and 2010, they were un-

---

[1] All interviews were conducted in confidentiality and the names of the interviewees are withheld by mutual agreement. The interviews were often conducted in informal settings. They were semi-structured and included open-ended questions. The interviewees were blind to the research question of interest to the author.

successful and Lukashenko continues to enjoy the support of a majority of the population in the country (Bunce & Wolchik, 2011; Korosteleva, 2012).

Since the early 2000s, the government system in Belarus has been based on the principle of unlimited presidential authority (Marples, 2009; Beichelt, 2004; di Quirico, 2011). The constitution severely restricts the legislative powers of the Belarusian parliament. Belarusian NGOs operate in a hostile legal environment, structured to de-legitimise and even criminalise most forms of independent civic activity. The constitutional guarantee on the freedom of speech is routinely disregarded by the government, which harasses and silences journalists. Meaningful electoral contestation is also unlikely.

US involvement in Belarus

The most important instrument of US democracy promotion in Belarus has been the use of sanctions (Jarabik & Silitski, 2008; Wilson & Kramer, 2010; Potocki, 2011). Two years after coming to power in 1994, Lukashenko manipulated a constitutional revision referendum to consolidate power in the presidency, after which the US downgraded government-to-government contacts. And after four prominent opposition figures disappeared in 1999, the US (and the EU) imposed a travel ban on officials implicated in the event. Sanctions were expanded in 2002 following a manipulated presidential election in 2001 and the closure of a human rights monitoring mission of the Organisation for Security and Cooperation in Europe by Minsk in 2002. In 2003, Belarus allowed the office to re-open, so the ban was lifted and the US (and the EU) proposed to normalise relations with Belarus if it made improvements with respect to human rights and democratic principles. The next year, however, the travel ban was reinstated after another manipulated referendum allowed Luskashenko to run for president after serving his otherwise constitutionally limited two terms. Following a rigged presidential election and a violent crackdown on peaceful demonstrators in 2006, the US (and the EU) imposed both a visa ban and an asset freeze against several dozen top Belarusian officials. They offered to move toward more positive engagement if the regime eased up on repression and freed political prisoners. Initially, the regime did not respond, so in 2007, the US (alone) imposed additional sanctions by freezing the assets of Belneftekhim, the state-run Belarusian oil-refining enterprise, which is Belarus' top hard currency earner and in which Lukashenko himself reportedly had a stake. This provoked a heated reaction from Minsk, which expelled all but six diplomats from the US embassy. By the fall of 2008, however, Minks had released some political prisoners and taken some steps towards media liberalisation. In 2009, the US Assistant Secretary of State travelled to Belarus to discuss improved relations on the basis of further improvements in respect for human rights and democratic principles.

Additionally, the US has been providing democracy aid to Belarus since 1992.[2] The so-called Freedom for Russian and Emerging Eurasian Democracies and Open Markets Support Act of 1992 offered assistance to Belarus in a number of policy areas, including democratisation. However, after the 1996 referendum, Washington reduced its aid to the Belarusian authorities but maintained its assistance to the Belarusian opposition and especially to civil society in general. Moreover, when Minsk failed to respond to the US' (and EU)'s offers for conditional normalisation of relations by 2004, the US Congress passed the Belarus Democracy Act which provided for increased assistance to civil society organisations, democratic political groups, and independent media. The US became the largest democracy donor in Belarus.[3] Washington's assistance, which steadily increased from 2004 to 2009, focused on building the capacity of NGOs in Belarus to increase public participation and act as agents for change, on strengthening independent media inside and outside of Belarus to increase access to independent information, and on building the capacity of democratic parties to unify, strategise, organise, and connect with constituents (US DOS, Bureau of European and Eurasian Affairs, 2009).

Diplomatically, the US protested the violations of human rights and democratic principles in Belarus throughout the 1990s and 2000s. Moreover, while government-to-government ties have been downgraded since 1996, in the mid- and late 2000s, the US president and the US Secretary of State met several times with Belarusian pro-democracy political and civic activists to underscore US support for the pro-democratic development of Belarus.

---

[2] Interview with K. S., August 18, 2011, interview with R. P., August 10, 2011, interview with D. K., August 8, 2011.
[3] In 2008, the Belarus Democracy Act was extended for two more years.

EU involvement in Belarus

Much like the US, the EU responded to political developments in Belarus with mostly negative conditionality (Jarabik & Silitski, 2008; Wilson & Kramer, 2010; Potocki, 2011). After the 1996 referendum in Belarus, the EU suspended the 1995 EU-Belarus Partnership and Cooperation Agreement, downgraded ties with Minsk, and withdrew its aid to Belarus except for some democracy assistance programs. Brussels also joined the US in its 1999 travel ban on top Belarusian officials and initiated the ban's 2002 expansion and 2003 suspension. In 2004, Brussels offered Belarus improved relations and access to loans and aid tied to "reforms" in the context of European Neighbourhood Policy. Minsk, however, did not respond to the basic democratic requirements of the Policy, so the EU denied it the full benefits of participation. Moreover, after the manipulated referendum in 2004 the EU imposed again a travel ban on responsible officials, and then after the manipulated 2006 presidential elections the EU joined the US in imposing additional visa bans and asset freezes against senior Belarusian politicians. The EU also withdrew its Generalized System of Preferences for Belarusian goods. In 2008, the EU chose to accept the release of political prisoners and some steps towards media liberalisation and suspended the sanctions against the regime.

Until the mid-2000s, most of the assistance provided by Brussels was offered to the Belarusian state for social and humanitarian projects (Jarabik & Silitski, 2008). However, after gaining EU membership, some Central and Eastern European countries and especially Poland, joined some Western European states in arguing for an increase in EU assistance to Belarus and for channelling it through Belarusian non-state actors (Kucharczyk & Lovitt, 2008). Soon thereafter, the EU began supporting independent media, students punished by the regime, and to a lesser extent civic groups in Belarus (Jarabik & Silitski, 2008). The EU funded the European Radio for Belarus and Belarus-Live.tv. The EU also supported the Belarusian European Humanities University, which was closed down in 2004 and resumed work in Vilnius, Lithuania. In 2006, the EU launched a scholarship program for 350 Belarusian students wishing to study abroad because they were denied access to local universities for political reasons. In 2007, the EU established an additional program for 300 more students, victims of political persecution in Belarus, to continue their studies at European Humanities University and in Ukraine. Since 2007, Brussels also provided scholarships for Belarusian students to study within the EU through the Erasmus Mundus Programme. At the same time, the EU addressed the Belarusian citizenry in a campaign called "What the European Union could bring to Belarus", which again offered to improve relations with Belarus, if certain political liberalisation conditions were met. And finally since 2006, the EU used the European Instrument for Democracy and Human Rights and the EU's Decentralized Cooperation Budget Line to offer some support to Belarusian civil society organisations in the promotion of human rights, political pluralism, and democratic participation and representation.

The EU also continuously expressed concern about democracy and human right violations in Belarus.[4] After the 2006 presidential elections, Brussels moved to diplomatically engage more meaningfully with the regime in Minsk. The EU worked with the Belarusian bureaucracy through an ongoing financial aid programme within the European Neighbourhood Policy and maintained frequent contact with the regime through the European embassies in Minsk, a small Technical Assistance to the Commonwealth of Independent States office in Minsk, a chargé d'affaires for Belarus working from Kiev, the Belarus embassy in Brussels, and since 2008 through a small European Commission delegation in Minsk (Jarabik & Silitski, 2008; Potocki, 2011). Moreover, Belarus was included in the EU's Eastern Partnership—a cooperation policy that was launched in 2009 and includes democracy support for the immediate eastern EU neighbours through bilateral and regional political dialogue and assistance. At the same time, in part thanks to some Central and Eastern European member states and especially Poland, opposition leaders began to receive a warm welcome from top EU officials and were given support from the EU's Head of Missions around the 2004 referendum and the 2006 elections.[5] The European Parliament has twice awarded its prestigious Sakharov (Human Rights) Prize to Belarusian nationals: in 2004 to the Belarusian Association of Journalists and in 2006 to the opposition candidate in the presidential elections.

---

[4] Interview with J. K., November 27, 2008, interview with J. P., February 27, 2009, and interview with J. M., March 6, 2009.

[5] Interview with J. K., November 27, 2008 and Interview with J.S.-W., February 25, 2009.

Poland's involvement in Belarus

The Polish democracy promotion approach to Belarus relied primarily on assistance and diplomatic support to the opposition. Initially, Warsaw focused on creating a network of bilateral and multilateral ties that would exercise a democratisation pull on Belarus (Balmaceda, Clem, & Tarlow, 2002). However, Poland's policies changed after Alexander Lukashenko was re-elected. Like most other Eastern and Western European countries, Poland downgraded its ties with Belarus in 1996. Warsaw also went along with the sanctions imposed by the EU and the US in 1999, 2002, 2004, and 2006.[6] In addition, in 2005, the Polish ambassador to Belarus was recalled for two years in protest to Lukashenko's efforts to subordinate the organisation of the Polish minority in Belarus.[7] However, throughout most of the 2000s, Warsaw also expressed concern that while the isolation of Belarus had not harmed Lukashenko's regime, it had slowed down the development of pro-democratic forces in the country.[8] Polish diplomats advocated that the West should "build a dialogue with Belarus so as to overcome its isolation in the European arena and thereby stimulate the development of democracy and the civil society in that country."[9] What is more, Warsaw insisted that Belarus be given strong incentives to liberalise through inclusion in the group of countries offered prospective EU membership (Gromadzki, Lopata, & Raik, 2005).

Much more prominent than the use of conditionality has been Warsaw's practice of "critical dialogue" with Minsk. Poland supported the pro-democratic forces and protested the violations of democracy and human rights in Belarus while also engaging the Lukashenko regime in limited, unofficial, and often non-political ways. Warsaw spoke against repression and election manipulation in Belarus but preferred that criticism of Minsk come from regional international organisations such as the EU.[10] Moreover, dur-

---

[6] However, Poland opposed the 2008 EU decision to withdraw its Generalized System of Preferences for Belarusian goods.
[7] Interview with R. D., October 19, 2008.
[8] Interview with J.S.-W., February 25, 2009.
[9] Aleksander Kwasniewski, President of the Republic of Poland, *Vision of a United Europe in the 21st Century: The Polish Point of View*, lecture at the Accademia Nazionale dei Lincei, Rome, February 27, 2002.
[10] Interview with M. M., October 13, 2008.

ing bilateral meetings and inter-parliamentary visits, Polish elites also worked to convince political elites in Belarus that "democracy is well worthwhile."[11] Warsaw further made efforts to point out to Minsk that there are many benefits of closer EU-Belarus relations and that there are "forms and areas of co-operation [with the EU such as economy and culture] that can be developed in the present political reality in Belarus."[12] At the same time, Poland unambiguously and publicly supported the Belarusian pro-democratic forces. Polish state leaders and parliamentarians provided moral and political support to the embattled opposition in Belarus after the 1996 and 2004 referenda (Balmaceda et al, 2002). In the late 1990s, Poland also made several attempts to organise a roundtable in Belarus with the assistance of Polish mediators (Herman and Piccone, 2000). And in the 2000s, Warsaw welcomed Lukashenko's challengers before the 2001 and 2006 presidential elections.[13]

Moreover, Poland advocated that the EU practice a policy of critical dialogue towards Belarus. In part thanks to the Polish efforts, the EU increased its support for the Belarusian opposition and the European Parliament passed more resolutions condemning democratic violations in Belarus than in any other country in the late 2000s, in addition to bestowal of the aforementioned Sakharov Prize to Belarusian nationals twice.[14] Poland also worked to convince the EU to accept the few signs of liberalisation in Belarus and to admit it into the Eastern Partnership.

Most importantly, Warsaw provided democracy assistance to Belarusian civil society and citizenry in general. Initially, Warsaw sponsored informal contacts between the Belarusian opposition and Polish NGOs led by former Polish dissidents (Snyder, 2003). Also, a number of Polish politicians joined Polish NGOs working in Belarus in training pro-democratic political leaders, civil society organisations, and journalists (Balmaceda et al, 2002). And when Lukashenko continued consolidating his power in the early and mid-2000s, Warsaw stepped up its assistance to the Belarusian opposition and especially its political and civic leaders, by leveraging its development aid

---

[11] Donald Tusk. *Expose.* Warsaw, November 23, 2007.
[12] Wlodzimierz Cimoszewicz and Mikhail Khvastov, *Declaration after an Unofficial Meeting Held in Bialystok*, March 10, 2002.
[13] Interview with M. M., October 13, 2008.
[14] Interview with J.S.-W., February 25, 2009.

system. Moreover, before the 2006 elections, the Polish government set up a Kalinowski Scholarship programme to annually fund up to 300 Belarusian students expelled for political reasons to attend Polish universities as well as a traineeship program for young working Belarusians to learn "how democracy functions in action" (Gromadzki Kononczuk, & Vesely, 2006). The Polish government further decided to "temporarily employ" some people who had lost their jobs in Belarus for political reasons (ibid.).

After the opposition was once again unsuccessful in defeating Lukashenko, Warsaw refashioned and reinforced its assistance to target not just Belarusian NGOs but also to reach out to Belarusian society more systematically.[15] Warsaw launched two state-run media projects—Radio Racyja and the Belsat TV channel for Belarus—to provide alternatives to the official media line in Belarus. Moreover, PolishAid continued to fund Polish NGOs developing the capacity of Belarusian civic groups and independent media, and socialising and mobilising the Belarusian youth. Poland increased its bilateral assistance and in 2007 Belarus became the single largest recipient of its democracy assistance projects (Kucharczyk & Lovitt, 2008). Aid became the most important instrument of Polish democracy promotion in Belarus. Lastly, Warsaw also advocated for increased EU aid for civil society in, and people-to-people contacts with, Belarus, through the "What the European Union Could Bring to Belarus" campaign and by successfully steering the reforms of the European Instrument for Democracy and Human Rights to include support for the Belarusian opposition and to slightly increase aid to Belarus.[16]

Discussion: Polish democracy promotion in comparative perspective

To take stock: The US and the EU both relied primarily on conditionality with the Belarusian regime and only secondarily on social and oppositional assistance. As expected by the literature, the EU emphasised positive conditionality more than the US. Similarly, in terms of diplomacy, Brussels prioritised engagement with the regime much more than Washington, which only provided political and moral support to the opposition. In terms of sectorial priorities, the EU focused on supporting the Belarusian youth, media,

---

[15] Interview with M. M., October 13, 2008.
[16] Interview with K. P., March 27, 2008

and civic groups, and the US focused on civic groups, the political process, and media in Belarus (in this order of priority).

Poland's approach to democracy promotion, on the other hand, has been political and minimally intrusive. Poland supported the media, civic groups, and youth (again in this order of priority). Warsaw preferred to use even "softer" democracy promotion measures than the EU but has leveraged them in a much more political than developmental manner, much like the US. Warsaw distinctively favoured criticism of Minsk but preferred engagement over penalties by targeting the Belarusian civil society and pro-democratic opposition political elites.[17]

Even in a repressive regime such as Belarus, Warsaw preferred to provide democracy assistance and diplomatic support and to deploy positive conditionality. Warsaw tended to persuade and pressure albeit behind closed doors, choosing engagement over sanctions. Moreover, Warsaw does not appear to understand democracy promotion as a part of an investment in a larger and longer-term process of national development of recipients. Instead, Poland worked with political and civic elites abroad to convince them to implement democratisation reforms and to provide them with know-how based on the Polish transition. Poland has not invested in meaningful ways in capacity-building programmes for Belarusian state institutions as a means to contributing to a gradual process of socio-economic and state capacity development that would eventually lead to political liberalisation.

In its political nature, Poland's approach has been similar to the US's approach. Warsaw, much like Washington, has not shied away from providing assistance to civil society, including opposition groups; though Poland has targeted political parties less than the US. Moreover, while it has provided assistance to the Belarusian youth like the EU, Warsaw also encouraged civic and political participation more directly (instead of just relying on scholarships to expose them to life in a democratic state). In general, and in contrast to the EU, democracy promotion efforts targeting primarily the recipient's state institutions (despite their autocratic nature), both the US and Poland preferred to work with civic and political elites, thus engaging with a range of non-state/ non-regime actors. However, if the US focused more on

---

[17] For a summary of the approaches of these three donors see a table below.

such actors involved in a recipient's political process, Poland has almost exclusively focused on civic activism or the policy process.

In its non-intrusiveness, Poland's approach has been closer to the EU's than to the US's efforts. Much like the EU, Poland has emphasised engagement, even if it has been critical engagement, with Belarus. However, Warsaw has been less willing to condemn the regime and has, in fact, preferred that such criticism come from a regional multilateral forum, such as the EU, and thus in the name of all of democratic Europe. Moreover, unlike the EU and US, which have embraced conditionality as their primary democracy promotion instrument in autocratic Belarus, Poland argued against isolating Belarus although going along with the lead of these larger democracy promoters. Warsaw has lobbied for some cooperation with and the inclusion of the country in the Euro-Atlantic structures, thus providing Minsk with powerful incentives for reform.

Table 1: Polish, EU, and US democracy promotion initiatives in Belarus by policy instrument and targeted sector in order of priority

Poland	United States	European Union
Assistance: Civil society > Political process	Conditionality (negative): Governing institutions	Conditionality (negative > positive): Governing institutions
Diplomacy: Political process > Governing institutions	Assistance: Civil society Political process	Assistance: Civil society
Conditionality (positive > negative): Governing institutions	Diplomacy: Political process	Diplomacy: Governing institutions Political process

Source: Own compilation

Conclusion: Democracy promotion made in Poland?

So what are the implications of Warsaw's political and minimally intrusive approach to democracy promotion for Poland's role in the international democracy promotion community? The political nature of Poland's efforts build on and reinforce US democracy promotion. Similarly, in its non-intrusiveness, Poland's efforts complement and add to the EU's democracy support. These asymmetrical complementarities allow for fruitful cooperation combining the capacity, power, and democratic standing of the EU and the US with Polish transition expertise, thus giving Warsaw credibility as a democracy promoter and tester of best democratisation practices. At the same time, next to the US whose "hard-ball" intrusive tactics make it a "bad cop" within the international democracy promotion community, Poland stands out as the "good cop" who relies on cautious and quiet diplomacy. Similarly, given its "civil-society centred" approach, Poland has sought to politicise the EU's developmental approach, ensuring that Brussels not only invests in the political modernisation of the recipient country but also helps it create windows of democratic opportunity by empowering pro-democratic civic and political actors.

Understanding how emerging democracy promoters like Poland fit in the international democracy promotion community has important implications for the ways in which they influence not only this community but also the liberal international order more generally. For example, this chapter finds that Polish democracy promotion is very much in line with the Euro-Atlantic model of promoting "liberal democracy" as opposed to some kind of non-Western approach. As a result, Polish democracy promotion serves to reinforce the current liberal international order.

This conclusion invites further research into the democracy promotion approaches of other new democracies around the globe, especially since these countries are seeking new roles and more influence within this order and since some authoritarian states that are hostile to this order have risen to prominence (Kupchan, 2003; Kagan, 2008; Zakaria, 2009; Gat, 2009). Future research might ask: In what ways do (other) new democracies constitute a new coalition of states interested in global transformation and in what ways do they embrace the political and economic principles of the Western world, including in terms of their democracy promotion models? And how successful have these new democracies been in promoting "liberal democracy" or alternative to it models? Answering these questions would shed light on the ways in which democracy is "translated" at the regional and global levels to reinforce and challenge the liberal international order.

References

Balmaceda, M. M., Clem, J. I., & Tarlow, L. L. (2002). *Independent Belarus: Domestic determinants, regional dynamics, and implications for the West*. Cambridge, Mass.: Distributed by Harvard University Press for the Ukrainian Research Institute and Davis Center for Russian Studies, Harvard University.

Beichelt, T. (2004). Autocracy and democracy in Belarus, Russia and Ukraine. *Democratization*, 11(5), 113–132.

Bunce, V. & Wolchik, S. L. (2011). *Defeating authoritarian leaders in postcommunist countries*. Cambridge: Cambridge University Press.

Burnell, P. J. (2000). *Democracy assistance: International co-operation for democratization*. London: F. Cass.

Carothers, T. (2000). Taking stock of US democracy assistance. In M. Cox, J. Ikenberry, & T. Inoguchi (Eds.), *American democracy promotion: Impulses, strategies, and impacts* (pp. 181–99). Oxford: Oxford University Press.

Carothers, T. (2009). Democracy assistance: Political vs. developmental? *Journal of Democracy*, 20(1), 5–19.

Cox, M., Ikenberry, J., & Inoguchi, T. (Eds.) (2000). *American democracy promotion: Impulses, strategies, and impacts*. Oxford: Oxford University Press.

Crawford, G. (2001). *Foreign aid and political reform: A comparative analysis of democracy assistance and political conditionality*. New York: Palgrave.

Diamond, L. (1995). *Promoting democracy in the 1990s: Actors and instruments, issues and imperatives*. New York: Carnegie Corporation.

Gat, A. (2009). *Victorious and vulnerable: Why democracy won in the 20th century and how it is still imperiled*. New York: Rowman & Littlefield.

Gromadzki, G., Kononczuk, W., & Vesely, L. (2006). *Belarus after the 'election'. What future for the Lukashenko regime?* Warsaw: Stefan Batory Foundation.

Gromadzki, G., Lopata, R., & Raik, K. (2005). Friends or family?: Finnish, Lithuanian and Polish perspectives on the EU's policy towards Ukraine, Belarus and Moldova. *FIIA Report*, No. 12. Helsinki: Finnish Institute of International Affairs.

Herman, R. G. & Piccone, T. J. (2002). *Defending democracy: A global survey of foreign policy trends, 1992–2002*. Washington, DC: Democracy Coalition Project.

Hook, S. (1998). Building democracy through foreign aid: The limitations of United States political conditionalities, 1992–96. *Democratization*, 5(3), 156–80.

Jarabik, B. & Silitski, V. (2008). Belarus. In R. Youngs (Ed.), *Is the European Union supporting democracy in it neighbourhood?* (pp. 101–120). Madrid: FRIDE.

Jonavicius, L. (2008). *The democracy promotion policies of Central and Eastern European states. FRIDE Working Paper*, No. 55. Retrieved from http://fride.org/descarga/WP55_Central_Estearn_EU_ENG_mar08.pdf.

Kagan, R. (2008). *The return of history and the end of dreams*. New York: Knopf.

Kopstein, J. (2006). The transatlantic divide over democracy promotion. *Washington Quarterly,* 29(2), 85–98.

Korosteleva, E. (2012). Questioning democracy promotion: Belarus' response to the 'colour revolutions'. *Democratization,* 19(1), 37–59.

Kucharczyk, J. & Lovitt, J. (2008). *Democracy's new champions: European democracy assistance after EU enlargement.* Prague: PASOS.

Kupchan, C. (2003). *The end of the American era: US foreign policy and the geopolitics of the twenty-first century.* New York: Knopf.

Magen, A., Risse, T., & McFaul, M. A. (2009). *Promoting democracy and the rule of law: American and European strategies.* New York: Palgrave Macmillan.

Marples, D. (2009). Outpost of tyranny? The failure of democratization in Belarus. *Democratization,* 16(4), 756–776.

Mikulova, K. & Simecka, M. (2013). Norm entrepreneurs and Atlanticist foreign policy in Central and Eastern Europe: The missionary zeal of recent converts. *Europe-Asia Studies,* 65(6), 1192–1216.

Petrova, T. (2014). *From solidarity to geopolitics: Support for democracy among post-communist states.* Cambridge: Cambridge University Press.

Pospieszna, P. (2014). *Democracy assistance from the third wave: Polish engagement in Belarus and Ukraine.* Pittsburgh, Pa.: University of Pittsburgh Press.

Potocki, R. (2011). Belarus: A tale of two elections. *Journal of Democracy,* 22(3), 49–63.

Quirico di, R. (2011). The prospects for democratization in the European Union post-Soviet neighbours: An overview. *Comparative European Politics,* 9, 432–447.

Snyder, T. (2003). *The reconstruction of nations: Poland, Ukraine, Lithuania, Belarus, 1569–1999.* New Haven, Conn.: Yale University Press.

US DOS, Bureau of European and Eurasian Affairs. (2009). *Foreign operations appropriated assistance factsheet. Belarus,* December. Retrieved from http://www.state.gov/documents/organization/140526.pdf.

Wetzel, A., Orbie, J., & Bossuyt, F. (2015). One-of-what-kind? Comparative perspectives on the substance of EU democracy promotion. *Cambridge Review of International Affairs,* 28(1), 21–34.

Wilson, D. & Kramer, D. J. (2010). When sanctions work: The Belarus Buckle. *The American Interest,* 6(2). Retrieved from http://www.the-american-interest.com/2010/11/01/when-sanctions-work-the-belarus-buckle/.

Youngs, R. (2008). *Is the European Union supporting democracy in its neighborhood?* Madrid: FRIDE.

Zakaria, F. (2009). *The post-American world.* New York: Norton.

Academic cooperation with Russian higher education institutions: German organisations as transfer agents?

René Lenz

Introduction

Cooperation in science and academia is bound to activities of organisations and individual actors in academic structures. Different levels of cooperation are a part of slowly developing networks between societies. Cooperation with academic partners and political engagements with international and transnational organisations create awareness of alternative higher education systems and the potential for change.

After the breakdown of the Soviet Union a restructuring process started in Russia. The re-orientation from a communist to a more democratic and capitalist system implied the adaptation of a "world model". Within the field of higher education institutions (HEI), the world model is based on European and US-American models and practices. While the French and German ideas of university studies were influential before World War II, several aspects of the US and British higher education systems have been copied by European countries later on, including the introduction of a two-level university system.

The European Higher Education Area (EHEA) represents the internationalisation and integration of higher education policies throughout Europe. Since Russia signed the Bologna Declaration in 2003, it became a part of the Bologna Process (BP) and further EHEA integration.[1] The BP led to reforms of

---

[1] The EHEA was launched in 1999 with the beginning of the BP. Quickly the BP extended beyond the member states of the European Union. Today, with the exception of Belarus, all countries in Europe are taking part. All signatory states have implemented the recommended two-study system, which is why the BP is often credited with the introduction of a two-tier system of study with degrees such as bachelor and master. Furthermore, all participating countries agreed to implement a system of "easily readable and comparable degrees" (Bologna Follow-Up Group, 2010a) which means the introduction of the European Credit Transfer System (ECTS) and diploma supplements. Diploma supplements list all the courses and grades of a student. As an ongoing process, the BP was intensified and prolonged until 2020 (see Bologna Follow-Up Group, 2010b).

curricula and studies in most of the countries that joined. By creating convergence between different systems of higher education it aims to eliminate obstacles to the free mobility of students and the scientific community. Cooperation takes place not only in the area of study and research but also in quality assurance.

The adaptation and spread of institutional models to different countries—also on a global scale—can be explained in reference to the sociological Neo-Institutional approach (see Schofer & Meyer, 2005). Due to "transnational standardization processes" (Meyer, Ramirez, Frank, & Schofer, 2006, p. 36) previous path dependencies of various higher education systems are losing their importance. The diffusion of models and practices depends on organisations, states, and individuals. While the BP is surely not a global phenomenon, it has initiated a further process of creating transnational standards beyond European borders and provides an example of transnational convergence. Here the interplay of German and Russian organisational changes and quality assessment will be discussed as a specific part of the BP example.

While being both subjects and objects of the BP, German academic organisations are active in almost every region in Russia. But why do they cooperate with Russian HEI and do they act as "transfer agents" in the diffusion process of Western educational models and practices (cf. Stone, 2004)? These are the guiding questions of this study.

This chapter is based on structured interview data from over 30 interviews with representatives of German and Russian organisations and HEI, who have been or are involved in academic cooperation projects. Documents and published statements from German institutions and organisations were also analysed.

Isomorphism and diffusion

The reason for Russia's participation in the BP surely has its source in inner-Russian political structure and discourse. However, Russia is part of the development of globalised transnational standardisation. The reforms of HEI are taking place in the context of global processes and are influenced by specific European developments. The term "institutional isomorphism" describes the spreading of organisational models and stems from an article by Paul DiMaggio and Walter Powell (1983).[2] The term was developed to explain organisational change "in a competitive marketplace" (DiMaggio & Powell, 1983, p. 147) but quickly became used for other societal areas and global diffusion of models. Authors of the "world polity approach" suggest that this is a global phenomenon, and practices and models spread across borders so that national systems resemble each other on the basis of similar structures (Meyer, 2007; Drori & Meyer, 2006; Meyer, Ramirez, Frank, & Schofer, 2006; Schofer & Meyer, 2005; Schofer, 1999). These authors are associated with the Neo-Institutional approach in Sociology, which seeks to explain why organisations and institutions resemble each other all over the world. This made it possible to observe diffusion—meaning the spread of certain practices, models of organisational structures and behaviours or ideas—in organisational fields such as the higher education system.

Isomorphism describes recent global developments especially within the field of higher education. Universities provide an important source for normative isomorphism. Universities and their networks as well as other "professional training institutions are important centers for the development of organizational norms and their staff" (DiMaggio & Powell, 1983, p. 152). From this perspective, individuals and organisations within the academic system can be perceived as transfer agents who diffuse certain ideas, practices, and models. They support isomorphic processes beyond nation states, as in the case of the German-Russian academic cooperation discussed in this study.

Changing Russian HEI

Following the breakup of the Soviet Union, most of the HEI and the scientific facilities in the territory of the former Russian Socialist Federal Soviet Republic came under the administrative sovereignty of the newly founded

---

[2] The implementation of uniform models, ideas and practices is defined as institutional isomorphism. It emphasises the possibility of organisational change but it also includes a notion of harmonisation. Together with actors in their direct environment, organisations constitute an organisational field. This is not only created by increased information between the participants: the participants are also mutually aware of each other and their common issues. They need to interact and require "interorganizational structures of domination and patterns of coalition" (DiMaggio & Powell, 1983, p.148).

Russian Federation and its constituent members. The Russian Federation thus inherited a Soviet legacy in its education sector. Reforms began to take place in the 1990s, but they did not have a strong financial backing, similar to other reforms in the public sector. The HEI were given the authority to manage their own relations with other institutions and universities from abroad. They could now independently cooperate with foreign universities and foundations as outlined in Article 57 of the Law on Education from 1992. This strengthened the autonomy of the HEI (Meister, 2009a, p. 59; see also Bain, 2003). The law further included the possible introduction of degrees focussed on professional education called "Bakalavriat" in Article 9, clearly mirroring the bachelor degrees in the Anglo-American system. The HEI could decide by themselves whether or not to introduce the new degrees of Baccalaureate and Magister. The reform encountered public objection, as it was perceived as alien to the Russian higher education system (Mühle, 1995, p. 98).

The first private HEI were already founded in the last years of the Soviet Union. Until today, their dominant areas are the social sciences, economics and law. Adaptation to and integration into the international scientific community happened especially in those areas that had previously been neglected or avoided for ideological reasons in the former Soviet Union. However, the first decade in the new Russia was dominated by crises. The state budget for science and education decreased in spite of official commitments. Its nadir was reached in 2000 when only 2.9 per cent of the official GDP was spent on education (Meister 2007, p. 7). As a result, academic positions lost most of their former prestige. Another side-effect was the exodus of young scientists. This "brain drain" did not happen only towards the West, which became the destination of approximately 800,000 migrating scientists and engineers, but it also occurred inside the country (Pogorel'skaja, 2008, p. 38). The highly skilled labour force often left universities and research facilities to work in new enterprises, in the oil and gas industry or in the state apparatus. At the same time, cooperation with HEI and research collaborations with partners in other countries became common. A considerable amount of immaterial and financial support came from external sources such as EU programmes, the German DAAD or the Open Society Foundation sponsored by George Soros. The diverse cooperation schemes supported the conditions for joining the international arena of competing HEI. It also laid the basis for an active participation of Russian institutions in the EHEA. Over the last two decades, Russia has been adapting to a world model of higher education. Science, education and knowledge are the basis for modern societies that take part in "a worldwide wave of scientization" (Drori & Meyer, 2006, p. 31) and establish models which dominate a globalised world. In Russia, the "emerging global model" (Mohrman, Ma, & Baker, 2008; also Altbach & Knight, 2007) of HEI can be observed as a new phenomenon.

Towards the end of the Yeltsin era, the economic and political situation in Russia stabilised. Since 1999, tax revenues increased. The Russian state profited from its state apparatus, rising tax incomes and increased revenues from raw materials like oil and nickel. This allowed the state to again invest in its own infrastructure and social sector. It is hardly a surprise that the share of the GDP spent on education increased as well. However, until today the salaries of academic personnel are comparatively low (see Endovitskij & Fedchenko, 2009).

Modernisation became one of the big projects of the Putin administration, and education was one of the four "national projects" at which the main efforts were to be directed. It was seen as crucial in enabling innovative developments in the economy and in technology (Ministry of Education and Science of the Russian Federation, 2009, p. 24). The Putin and Medvedev administrations increased the budgets for universities, but they also emphasised the accountability of individual universities.[3] In any case, students were expected to be ready to pay their shares for their own educations.

When Russia joined the BP in 2003 it thereby declared its willingness to not only cooperate on a European level but furthermore implement the required changes to its own national higher education system. The federal law dating from October 24, 2007 eventually obliged all HEI to introduce bachelor and master degrees. The bachelor degree is granted after the completion of a four year study programme and the master is awarded after two further years of study. However, the Russian Diploma Specialist is supposed to remain the main degree in such crucial areas as law, medicine and engineering (Fedorov, Korshunov, & Karavaeva, 2009).

---

[3] As state universities are not private enterprises, accountability remains fictional as success cannot be measured via market gains.

The Russian higher education system also witnessed the establishment of a two-tier system of international orientated research universities and more regional based institutions (see Meister, 2009b; Kiroj, 2010, Lenz, 2011). The Russian government established a group of research universities and thereby adapted its university landscape to the "emerging global model". The introduction of federal and national universities started after 2006 with a few selected to gain global recognition and compete with elite institutions like Harvard or Oxford. The Moscow State University (MGU) and the St. Petersburg State University (SPBGU) were the first institutions to receive the status of national universities in 2007, meaning an increase in state funding and organisational autonomy as an entrepreneurial university.

Russian relations with the international academic community

German-Russian relations are of particular interest here because German-Russian academic ties have a special historical legacy. With the inauguration of the Academy of Sciences in 1725, Russia became part of the emerging international science community. German influence was of particular importance (see Gavrilov, Kolesniko, Olesyeyuk, & Shulus, 2009; Pfrepper, 2009; Pfrepper, 2012). The links to the West were only interrupted with the introduction of Stalinist science policies. The Iron Curtain was fractionally lifted for the scientific community when the Soviet Union joined the International Council of Scientific Unions (ICSU) in 1954 (see Niederhut, 2009).

With the end of the Second World War the Soviet Union and its university system gained dominance in Central and Eastern Europe (see Connelly, 2000). In these regions it was considered highly prestigious to study or to conduct research at Soviet universities. The Sputnik shock demonstrated to the world that a formidable science system was operating in the Soviet Union. Despite the Cold War, research collaboration with Western countries continued after 1953, if on a limited scale. This was the case even in highly sensitive areas like computer science (see Dittmann, 2009). Knowledge flowed East and West, for example developments in biomechanics in the Soviet Union were widely received in the United States (Rohdewald, 2009, p. 187). However, by the late 1980s it was obvious that Russia could no longer compete with the advances in computing and other high-tech innovation in the West (Trautmann, 1989, p. 92). Gorbachev's reforms encouraged beneficial knowledge exchange through research collaborations including with Germany. Thus, in response the German Academic Exchange Service (DAAD) started its first programme geared exclusively at the Soviet Union in 1987.

During the crisis in the 1990s foreign aid gained importance in the Russian higher education system. Western foundations and universities provided help to the under-funded Russian institutions. Western science became particularly influential in the field of social sciences and economics. After the signature of the *Partnership and Cooperation Agreement* with the *European Community* in 1994, the Russian HEI system profited directly from EU programmes, such as TACIS and Tempus.[4] Under these frameworks, more than 250 projects assisted the development at universities and institutes throughout Russia (Meister, 2008, p. 159). The new Russian state explicitly opened its education sector to develop international experiences as outlined in the "First Temporary Order of the Higher Education System" from March 1992 (documented in: Hochschulrektorenkonferenz, 1995, pp. 127–149). Foreign support came especially from Germany (see e.g. Eimermacher & Justus, 2002).

Education and science remain the top priority area in Russia for aid from and cooperation with the EU. Thus, of the four common spaces of reinforced cooperation defined in the September 2003 formal agreement, the knowledge domain was the first mapped out by precise aims (see Adomeit & Lindner, 2005; Entin, 2005). The Russian Federation was admitted to the Erasmus Mundus Programme of the European Union in 2004. EU countries, Germany in particular, are the preferred exchange location for students from Russia (Prahl, 2009, p. 301). There is continued support of increasing mobility and exchanges between Germany and Eastern Europe by the German state. Bilateral partnerships, research projects, seminars and sessions offered via scientific collaborations aim for active engagement from both sides. International conferences are regularly organised and

---

[4] TACIS stands for Technical Assistance to the Commonwealth of Independent States. According to the Tempus website, the programme "supports the modernisation of higher education in the Partner Countries of Eastern Europe, Central Asia, the Western Balkans and the Mediterranean region, mainly through university cooperation projects". See: http://eacea.ec.europa.eu/tempus/funding/higher_education_institutions_en.php.

Russian HEI and research facilities participate in research networks. However, the internationalisation of teaching staff remains wishful thinking for academic life in Russia. Few foreign academics are working at Russian universities and the majority of them are teaching foreign languages.

The international mobility of Russian researchers and students also remains relatively low. In 2008, only 0.4 per cent of the latter were studying abroad (Prahl, 2009, p. 301). The number of visiting foreign students is similarly insignificant, and even with the inclusion of students from the CIS countries[5], the total barely exceeds one per cent. In 2008, foreign students constituted only 1.3 per cent in total, the majority of them coming from developing African countries and states in Russia's so called "near abroad", republics of the former Soviet Union.[6]

German foreign policy as a framework

Today, academic exchange and mobility are part of a modern foreign policy approach that is especially important for states relying on the use of "soft power" in international relations (see Nye, 2004). The case of Germany is exemplary in this sense. In the following sections the role of German organisations in the Russian HEI system is analysed.

The area of the Central and Eastern European countries became a major interest for Germany's foreign policy with the fall of the so called Iron Curtain. These countries were defined as a core area of the foreign policy *Außenkulturpolitik* (AKP), encompassing all cultural aspects (Auswärtiges Amt, 1999, p. 4). In addition to security and economic issues, the area of cultural cooperation is an important part of the German foreign policy concept, as mentioned in the guidelines for the cultural foreign policy in 1970 (*"Leitsätze für die Auswärtige Kulturpolitik"*).[7] The support of academic and cultural exchange with other countries, including Russia, is one of the key elements of the AKP.

---

[5] The Commonwealth of Independent States that emerged following the break-up of the Soviet Union.

[6] These numbers are provided by the Federal State Statistic Service, http://www.gks.ru/bgd/regl/b10_12/IssWWW.exe/stg/d01/08-12.htm.

[7] The paper can be downloaded from the Institute for Foreign Relations, http://www.ifa.de/pdf/aa/akbp_leitsaetze1974.pdf.

The AKP became the "third pillar" of Germany's foreign policy with the goal of increasing the country's political and economic influence. It is an officially declared "instrument for supporting a positive image of Germany abroad" (Deutscher Bundestag, 2010, p. 4). The German Foreign Office (Auswärtiges Amt) finances a diverse set of organisations, the so-called *Mittlerorganisationen*, which work as agencies in the area of cultural and educational exchange. Officially, these organisations work independently and the government cannot give any orders, but at the same time they almost entirely depend on the state budget.[8] Their common aim is to improve Germany's reputation in the international sphere and to promote German as a foreign language abroad.

Academic exchange is also connected to Germany's internal political debates and objectives. Heavily influenced by the discourse that saw Germany as "Europe's sick man" after reunification, the higher education system was under pressure. The degree of internationalisation of German HEI and research facilities was perceived as too low. Officially, the government stated that there was a decreased attractiveness of German academic institutions in contrast to increased global competition (Deutscher Bundestag, 1997, p. 2). Support for internationalisation measures became a common feature of the foreign policy debate. The area of higher education was declared a key sector in the foreign policy guidelines "Konzeption 2000". These demanded an intensified promotion of study and research in Germany from abroad and a further development of bachelor and master degrees (ibid., p. 14). The number of foreign students was supposed to increase from 10 to 20 per cent. In addition, several "Centres for German Studies" were to be established in important partner countries (ibid.). These suggestions mark a reaction to the debate about Germany's presumed weak competitiveness on a global scale in the 1990s. The introduction of bachelor and master degrees is an instrument in the HEI system to deal with this issue and to further internationalise German universities. Supporting student grants and scholarships were already a major instrument of the AKP for a long time, especially for HEI and science (Auswärtiges Amt, 1999, p. 13).

---

[8] The *Goethe-Institut* is important for language teachers as the agency that provides teaching materials and language courses. The DAAD is the main academic exchange agency and the *Alexander von Humboldt-Stiftung* supports outstanding research on an individual basis.

There is no altruistic illusion, instead the AKP academic exchange with other countries "is an essential element for such a high technology country as Germany" to gain economically and politically (ibid., author's translation). The support for the German language in education systems abroad is perceived as a main instrument to enhance economic ties. In the "*Konzeption 2000*" the *Auswärtige Amt* frankly acknowledges its keen interest to support the current and future elites in politics, economy, culture and media in Central and Eastern Europe with the expectation that this will help develop "personal relations between the future elites of Germany and the partner countries" (ibid., p. 12).

This foreign policy approach is evident in formal academic linkages with Russia. One of the most important pillars of German-Russian academic cooperation is the Treaty on Scientific-Technical Cooperation (WTZ), signed in 1987 with the Soviet Union. A second treaty on cultural cooperation was concluded with the new Russian Federation on December 16, 1992. A supplement concerning the teaching of Russian and German as foreign languages was signed in 2003. The German government also created the post of Coordinator for Intersocietal Cooperation. Two years earlier, both governments added a so-called civil society forum to the existing communication forums, which became known as the *Petersburger Dialog*.[9] The forum includes high-ranking officials from the higher education systems. The positive relations between the two states manifested in a "Joint Declaration on a Strategic Partnership in Education, Research and Innovation" in 2005.[10] Official statements also made direct reference to the implementation of the Bologna Process.

Despite geographical distances and the German responsibility for crimes in WWII, Russia has relatively close and diverse links to the German higher education and research systems. Students from the Russian Federation at German HEI are the second largest group of foreign students, yet Russia on the other hand is hardly a destination for German students. The academic year 2011–12 was declared by both governments as the "German-

---

[9] For a critical assessment see Pörzgen (2010).
[10] A "Modernisation for Partnership" agreement was also signed between the Russian Federation and the EU in 2010.

Russian Year of Education, Science and Innovation", with the aim of strengthening the existing relations.[11]

German organisations and Russian HEI

Three types of actors involved in cooperation with academic organisations or universities in Russia can be identified: organisations of the academic community that may also work as agencies within the context of German foreign policy; German universities with an ongoing cooperation based on partnership agreements; and finally, private foundations that provide funding for exchange and teaching programmes aiming to impact Russian HEI.

All significant German academic and scientific organisations are active in Russia. The German Research Foundation (*Deutsche Forschungsgemeinschaft*; DFG)[12] runs an office in Moscow, as does the DAAD, the biggest organisation, which did much pioneering work in establishing contacts between German and Russian HEI. The German Rectors' Conference, the HRK, was an important actor in the 1990s but currently has no permanent representative working in Russia.

German HEI are the second type of organisations active in Russia. The number of institutional cooperation activities between German and Russian HEI increased from over 500 in 2005 to 870 in 2014.[13] They exist on all levels as agreements between institutions, faculties, departments, and universities. There is a noteworthy rise in double-degree study opportunities. This is the case for the four universities which are part of the research sample in this study: *Freie Universität Berlin*, *Universität Leipzig*, *Justus-Liebig-Universität Gießen* and the *Universität Bielefeld*.

---

[11] While the German Federal Ministry for Education and Research (BMBF) was responsible for organising this project and for the coordination of the ongoing WTZ-activities with its Russian counterpart, this does not imply any activities with HEI in particular. See: http://www.deutsch-russisches-wissenschaftsjahr.de/ru/wissenschaftsjahr.php.

[12] The DFG describes itself as "the self-governing organisation for science and research in Germany". It is mainly state-funded, which makes it a main funding institution for scientific research in Germany. See: http://www.dfg.de/en/dfg_profile/mission/index.html.

[13] These numbers are provided by the Association of All Chancellors of German HEI, the *Hochschulrektorenkonferenz*, http://www.hochschulkompass.de/internationale-kooperationen.html.

Philanthropic organisations can also play an important role. The *Robert Bosch Foundation* is an interesting example as it runs a programme for young graduates who teach at HEI in Central and Eastern Europe. Until recently the "Lektorate", as these teaching positions are called, at Russian HEI were among the biggest group in the so called *Boschlektorenprogramm*.

In addition to the larger foundations, there are a few existing private initiatives, such as the association of German graduates of the Moscow MGU (DAMU e.V.). These initiatives are part of a transnational civic engagement.

In the following, the three types of organisations and their activities are examined in more detail. The focus is on the organisations that are exemplary for each type, namely the DAAD, selected German universities, and the Robert Bosch Foundation.

The German Academic Exchange Service (DAAD)

Officially, the Bonn-based DAAD is the organisation working to support all German HEI and their activities abroad. It is mainly dependent on funding by two governmental departments: the *Auswärtige Amt*, as the dominant source of income, and the *BMZ* (the Ministry of Economic Cooperation and Development). The DAAD works as an agency for the German government. Its Russian representation is based in Moscow where since 1993 it shares the former embassy building of the GDR with the *Goethe-Institut*. Both institutions state the mission to promote German as a foreign language, with the DAAD focusing on HEI. Another DAAD objective is to support internationalisation processes of German HEI. At the same time HEI activities often rely on financial support provided by the DAAD. The main practical instrument on a local level is to send German specialists to teach their subjects or give language classes at foreign universities. In 2008, 43 so-called *Lektoren* were teaching at Russian universities. Some of them teach specific subjects, such as law or sociology. In addition, a total of 11 long–term professors have been employed in Russia. For Russia, Germany is a major partner for academic exchange. More than 1,600 German citizens have received support for an academic stay in Russia in 2012 (Berghorn, 2013, p.

154). Furthermore, over 3,700 Russian citizens were supported to come to Germany by the DAAD alone in 2012 (ibid.).[14]

The orientation towards the AKP goals in creating ties to future Russian elites is an important feature of the DAAD activities, as was emphasised during the interviews. In Russia, its task is to promote partnership programmes and the Bologna Process. In general, its work is highly appreciated in Russia. In institutional terms, the DAAD is the main financier of the Centre for German and European Studies (ZDES), which is attached to the prestigious State University of St. Petersburg (SPbGU).It was established in 2004 and represents a major AKP effort to connect to the "future elite", at least in the field of social sciences. More importantly, it also aims to impact the development of social sciences in Russia. In this process, the *Universität Bielefeld* represents the academic pillar of Germany, with the SPbGU acting as its counterpart in Russia. There are just two so-called *Fachlektoren* for social sciences operating in the Russian Federation: one lecturer for sociology is based at the ZDES since its beginnings; another is working at the Moscow Higher School of Economics since 2010. In addition, there are short- and long-term lecturers from various German universities teaching sociology, in particular at the ZDES.

Universities: Twinning programmes and global activities

A few privileged universities benefit from the "Exzellenzinitative" launched by the German government in 2007. This programme provides special funding for research as well as internationalisation activities. The *Freie Universität Berlin* is one of these universities. The special funding allows the university to send a representative to Russia who works at the Moscow State Institute for International Relations (MGIMO) with one task of supporting the search for a strategic partner in connection with the global activities of the university. In 2012, this partner was the SPbGU. One reason for the choice was its status as a classic full university; another was its status as an "elite" institution in Russia. Furthermore, it was also involved in several ongoing cooperation programmes. In addition, it can be noted that Moscow HEI did not have the required potentials or, as with the case of the MGU, turned out

---

[14] This number remained steady in the last decade (see Prahl, 2006; Prahl, 2009; Berghorn, 2010; Berghorn, 2013).

to be too difficult to cooperate with as partners. Cooperation with Russian universities is a way to increase the degree of internationalisation and the reputation of German universities in a national and global context.

Officially, about 870 cooperation projects exist between German and Russian HEI.[15] Collaboration is taking place on different levels and with different degrees of engagement. The so called *Hochschulpartnerschaften* is an instrument to help internationalise the German part of the cooperation in particular, and this is actively supported by the *DAAD* through a programme called *Ostpartnerschaften*, established in 1987. This funding scheme allows a regional focus which can go beyond Russia.

The cooperation of the *Justus-Liebig-Universität Gießen* (JLU) with the Federal and former State University Kazan (KGU, today KFU) can be taken as an example in this context. Their mutual relationship is a significant one for both universities. The partnership between the two universities was established in 1989 and its 20th anniversary was celebrated by both institutions. The focus on Central and Eastern Europe and the cooperation with the KGU/KFU is an important pillar of the *JLU* internationalisation strategy. With its funding schemes the *DAAD* is an important source of finances in this context.

The Teaching Programme of the Robert Bosch Foundation

Philanthropic foundations and their activities are perceived as one pillar of a vital civil society (see Anheier & Daly, 2007). The Robert Bosch Stiftung (RBS), based in Stuttgart, is a good example of such a foundation. In 1993 the foundation began the *Boschlektorenprgramm* which funds special teaching initiatives in Central and Eastern Europe. This programme has been coordinated by the *Osteuropazentrum*, the Centre for Eastern Europe at the *Universität Hohenheim* since 1999.[16] Graduates or young professionals are sent as teaching staff (*Lektoren*) to HEI in Central and Eastern Europe to offer seminar courses in German. As part of the reconciliation pro-

---

[15] Hochschulrektorenkonferenz, http://www.hochschulkompass.de/internationale-kooperationen/statistik/kooperationen-nach-staat-und-ausl-hochschultyp.html.

[16] It should be mentioned that the Bosch Foundation is also co-financing the Europe Institute "Klaus Mehnert" in Kaliningrad which focuses on European Studies with nearly a dozen master students. See: http://www.europastudien-kaliningrad.de.

cess with these countries, the main objective is to enable mutual understanding, or *Völkerverständigung* as it is known in German. In addition to teaching, the programme aims to involve students in projects ranging from film and theatre clubs to political debates and election monitoring. The programme initiated a Russian segment starting in the academic year 1999–2000. A few years later, *Fachlektoren* in the social sciences arrived at certain Russian faculties, e.g. the SPbGU, the KGU and the more Western oriented departments in Yekaterinburg and Tyumen.

The programme benefits from special agreements between Russia and Germany. For instance, *Boschlektoren* can receive entry visas without fees. Their activities, like the ones of the DAAD, are generally supported by the host institutions. The young lecturers create a network consisting of German colleagues and their Russian counterparts. Furthermore, they support other organisations and initiatives such as the *Theodor Heuss Kolleg*, which was established as an organisation by alumni of the *Boschlektorenprogramm* in the 1990s aiming to support the transformation process in Central and Eastern Europe. It is mainly funded by the RBS which also established its first Russian centre in Perm in 2009.

Organisations and individuals as transfer agents

Each organisation creates structures that enable their agents to generate cooperation possibilities. Germans and Russians are establishing communication networks allowing for the exchange of ideas and concepts. Different types of actors directly contribute to the formation and strengthening of these networks: *Academic staff* is involved in direct activities in Russia during joint seminars, symposia and conferences, and their focus is on the development of the Russian institutions and academic mobility between Russia and Germany. *Foundations* and *academic organisations* realise mobility through student grants and scholarships. Applications for research grants or for support of organisational change require adaptation to a certain organisational language used by donors from Western countries. Project partners from these countries help to translate the wording. Partnership programmes and cooperation schemes on all levels are an essential framework. The *individual members* of the organisations are another binding factor. The individuals establish the networks on behalf of their organisations and decide which academic issues they want to focus on. In doing so, they create or otherwise enhance organisational fields in which ideas and practices can spread. For example agents such as professors diffuse ideas, literature, concepts and working methods. They create bilateral cross-border networks that are bound to local, regional and international contacts which in turn allow them to engage in transnational networks. The German organisations help by providing a communicative structure in which it becomes possible to take action and to develop the transnational higher education area.

As external actors, German organisations have a comparatively good position within the Russian academic field. They have been working there for over 20 years and some can even trace their cooperation back to the establishment of the Russian academic system. Internationalisation and academic reforms are issues that are debated not only in Germany, but in Russia as well. The Bologna Process has been an important topic ever since Russia joined. Reforms concerning the BP are used to find a common basis for institutional cooperation. Cooperation schemes between HEI provide an important framework for the transfer of models and practices.

Organisational change and the practice of model transfer

The German HEI system is an organisational field which influences the conceptual and strategic planning of German academia. The German HEI system went through a slow process of reform driven by the Bologna Process and the push for internationalisation as a way to increase Germany's competitiveness. The cooperation schemes with Russia are a result of these processes. At the same time German organisations and HEI are influenced by a global model of higher education. The discourse on excellence and elite institutions and the resulting policies are re-shaping the higher education system (see Gläser & Lange, 2009; Gläser & Weingart, 2009; Interdisziplinäre Arbeitsgruppe "Exzellenzinitiative" der Berlin-Brandenburgischen Akademie der Wissenschaften, 2010). The German organisations discuss and implement organisational models not only during their work at home but also abroad thus spreading ideas and practices in Russia.

The German state and its external cultural policy (AKP) provide financial means for organisations like the DAAD and for internationalisation activities of German HEI. Joint projects can be easily implemented and put to work if the motives and objectives of them fit into the internationalisation and disciplinary concepts of Germans and Russians. For example, the DAAD cooperation includes its network of over 41 *Lektoren*, teaching staff who provide and diffuse knowledge about the German academic system at their host universities in Russia and at countless presentations throughout the country (Berghorn, 2013, p. 154). As an organisation the DAAD supports the Bologna Process and promotes it in Russia. German universities also play an important role on the local level. They can finance their cooperation with Russian counterparts with money provided by the DAAD through the *Ostpartnerschaften* programme as the cooperation schemes towards the Eastern European countries are called by the DAAD. Twinning programmes provide the opportunities to develop joint degree programmes and organisational coherence according to the BP.

Since the academic year 2006–07, the *Boschlektorenprogramm* has aimed to give *Lektoren* special work experience while supporting institutional changes, reforms and adaptation processes. The *Lektoren* are expected to find the areas of reform on which they would like to focus at the host universities. They receive special training for such activities and can thus be seen as agents working on behalf of the German organisation in this context. The BP is considered as ambivalent by the majority of such individual actors. Some are highly critical but the majority refers to it as unavoidable.

German organisations have been engaged in the Russian higher education system since the late 1980s, some East German universities have been active even longer. The academic exchange between German and Russian scientists takes place in all disciplines. The scale of it differs; it ranges from an exchange across all faculties to student mobility. In case of the Justus-Liebig-Universität Gießen nearly all important disciplines are involved in the cooperation with Kazan. The cooperation between the *Universität Bielefeld* and the SpbGU in St. Petersburg resulted in a master programme in "Studies in European Societies" at ZDES. The amount of international conferences with Western participants can be interpreted as a direct result of experienced transnational cooperation. However, representatives of both German and Russian universities doubt that these cooperation schemes have had a profound impact on the development of social sciences in Russia.

Joint degrees can be seen as a sign of successful collaboration, for instance in the case of Gießen and Kazan in economics. However, the implementation of the Bologna Process as a reform of curricula, the use of credit points, and diploma supplements have barely materialised in Kazan. A few years ago, the DAAD provided funding for the major part of the ongoing cooperation. Today, the Russian state and the Republic of Tatarstan are co-financing all programmes, an important and welcome change for the Germans involved. The research and teaching staff in Kazan is far from internationalised, although the few exchanges marginally broaden their horizons. Concerning the disciplines, none of the German participants mentioned a particular German influence in the social sciences. Instead, the German impact is seen as part of a broader Western influence dominated by Anglo-American patterns. There is a general appreciation of the fundamental sciences in Kazan by the German counterparts, while economy, law and social sciences are still seen as developing fields where Germany intends to support adaptation to Western standards.

Internationalisation is an objective mentioned by both sides. It is clear that partnerships are used to strengthen university statuses, mainly in the German and Russian contexts, but partially on a transnational level. Cooperation is seen as a win-win situation. It helps to both secure funding and promote successfully functioning of HEI. This might be helpful in extending the HEI network. International partnerships sometimes merely exist as agreements on paper and lack productivity. This is certainly not the case for the twinning programme of the two universities in Gießen and Kazan or at the ZDES in St. Petersburg.

Despite a few notable problems, none of the three types of actors stopped their activities because of political circumstances or arguments. Even while pretending to be in line with expected behaviour, norms and routines, some alternative action patterns can cause offence. These offences can even be part of the official policy when a new law did not become a norm or is just one more law alongside other similar regulations. This is particularly the case with the expected implementation of the BP in Russian universities. Concerning German-Russian relations, Germans are at times confronted with situations where bilateral agreements are not fully implemented because local circumstances hinder them or because the national educational policy lags behind.

The cooperation resulting in joint degree programmes has an effect on the organisational development in Russia; however, further research is necessary to measure its impact on Russian HEI.

Transfer of political ideas

While the interviewed representative of the RBS denied any impact of German foreign policy on the foundation's programmes, this influence can clearly be observed in the activities of the DAAD and even the twinning programmes of German and Russian universities as they benefit from special funding provided by the German state.

There is no programme by German organisations working in the Russian higher education system that aims to explicitly influence political processes in Russian society. However, teaching activities are a priori an act of transferring knowledge, ideas and methods. This also implies political issues and debates which reflect current processes and motivate involvement in societal developments.

In the German-Russian cooperation, critical questions are generally avoided or debated on more abstract levels. For instance, in the partnership between Gießen and Kazan, difficult political issues, such as democratic setbacks in Russia, are barely touched upon in joint seminars. The courses tend to focus more on such questions as the role of water shortages in internal and external conflicts, or on Europe and its relations with Russia. At the same time, the ties in the area of social sciences are rather weak, while the cooperation in the field of economics is comparatively strong. Nevertheless, the *Universität Gießen* supports institutional changes in curricula and in teaching techniques. These efforts further the diffusion of alternative methods which imply active participation. They help to create an open atmosphere and an open-minded academic culture.

The *Boschlektorenprogramm* grants scholarships to German graduates and young scientists in order to teach and bring people together on a local level. Another aspect of the programme is to organise projects with young people outside the framework of university curricula. This includes cinema clubs, environmental activities or even election monitoring. One result of this project-orientated work is the so-called *Theodor Heuss Kolleg*. It diffuses German knowledge on how to organise projects and how to support civil society activities among young people in Central and Eastern Europe. The aim of the *Theodor Heuss Kolleg* is to foster individual commitment by the young participants and studentship holders.

Only few interviewed persons mentioned general problems while working with or in the Russian higher education context. However, there are complicated situations in relation to state officials such as the office for registration and migration. Some occur if individual actors from the German organisations start to deal with issues that must be considered delicate due to the political situation in Russia. Problems occurred for instance when the *Lektoren* gave seminar courses on election monitoring, as happened in Kazan and St. Petersburg, and were threatened with visa termination if they continued such seminars (see Peters, 2005). Political topics such as the promotion of democracy are at times taken up by individual *Lektoren* within the Lektorenproramm of the RBS. While this activity is not an objective of the foundation it is nevertheless compliant with general policy.

The Western model is not transferred by German organisations working within the field of Russian HEI. They support the idea of free academia and help to provide an example of how civil society works in Germany. Nevertheless, foundations such as Robert Bosch encourage individual activism through organisational networks. Furthermore, academic mobility provides the possibility for selected individuals to study abroad and therefore increases the likelihood that ideas are taken home and are in a long-term perspective implemented in Russia.

Conclusion

This chapter debated whether external actors, such as professors, universities or academic organisations diffuse organisational models and practices. It showed that German academic organisations on an individual and organisational level use their ideas and practices within cooperation projects with Russian partners. These projects are guided by the German foreign policy and by strive for internationalisation, and are implemented with funding support for HEI cooperation from the German government and private foundations.

Organisations and individual academics transfer ideas and ways of teaching and organising or improving the academic systems while working in

Russia. Academic activities always include an organisational agenda. While the Western model of the Bologna Process is far from dominating this agenda, it is used as a frame of reference for organising joint projects such as double degree programmes. To this end, Germany has a strong position based on its continuous activities since the end of the Soviet Union. German organisations support internationalisation projects. However, this is done because of their own intrinsic interests: supporting German foreign policy and internationalisation strategies of German HEI as a way to increase their competitiveness. The activities of individuals and institutions from Germany can be perceived as part of a diffusion process in which ideas, models and concepts are transferred into the Russian context. At the same time, German organisations are mediators between the two nations in Europe. The transfer agents are the individual actors on site. In this context the Bologna Process is a framework that provides the instruments, rhetoric means and models which help to orient the Russian HEI administration experts.

The bilateral academic relations are embedded in a diplomatic framework. The German state is the main source of funding that supports such organisations as the DAAD and cross-border university partnerships. These institutions use these means to increase their national and international reputation while cooperating with Russian partner organisations. The German external cultural policy focuses on HEI as the future elites are educated there. This is also the case for transnational activities of foundations. The ongoing German cooperation schemes lack financial resources to have a real impact on an entire national higher education system in Russia. Nevertheless, they still have the potential to strengthen the ties between the Russian and the German academic communities and thus to enhance the internationalisation of the Russian system. As part of the external cultural policy, the internationalisation efforts of German HEI and academic organisations support a positive image of Germany and foster German-Russian relations.

The study was carried out and concluded before the current crisis in the Western-Russian relations. It is difficult to predict whether the confrontation over the annexation of the Crimea by Russia and the conflict in Ukraine will have a strong impact on German-Russian academic relations. The deep rooted ongoing cooperation schemes can lead to the assumption that the academic organisations will overcome this diplomatic crisis as long as it does not go much further.

References

Adomeit, H. & Lindner, R. (2005). *Die "Gemeinsamen Räume" Russlands und der EU. Wunschbild oder Wirklichkeit?* Berlin: Stiftung Wissenschaft und Politik.

Altbach, P. G. & Knight, J. (2007). The internationalization of higher education: Motivations and realities. *Journal of Studies in International Education*, 11 (3–4), 290–305.

Anheiner, H. & Daly, S. (2007). Philanthropic foundations in modern society. In H. K. Anheiner & S. Daly (Eds.), *The politics of foundations. A comparative analysis* (pp. 3–26). London/New York: Routledge.

Auswärtiges Amt. (1999). *Auswärtige Kulturpolitik – Konzeption 2000*. Retrieved from http://www.ifa.de/pdf/aa/akbp_leitsaetze1974.pdf.

Bain, O. B. (2003). *University autonomy in the Russian Federation since Perestroika*. New York/London: Routledge/Falmer.

Berghorn, G. (2010). Moskau. In DAAD, *Berichte der Außenstellen 2009* (pp. 296–315). Bonn: DAAD.

Berghorn, G. (2013). Moskau. In DAAD, *Berichte der Außenstellen 2012* (pp. 144–154). Bonn: DAAD.

Bologna Follow-Up Group. (2010a). *Bologna Declaration*. Retrieved from http://www.ehea.info/Uploads/about/BOLOGNA_DECLARATION1.pdf.

Bologna Follow-Up Group. (2010b). *Vienna-Budapest Declaration*. Retrieved from http://www.ehea.info/Uploads/Declarations/Budapest-Vienna_Declaration.pdf.

Connelly, J. (2000). *Captive university. The Sovietization of East German, Czech, and Polish higher education, 1945–1956*. Chapel Hill/London: The University of North Carolina Press.

Deutscher Bundestag. (1997). Antwort der Bundesregierung auf die Große Anfrage der Abgeordneten Armin Laschet, Hermann Gröhe, Helmut Jawurek, Andreas Krautscheid, Thomas Rachel, Norbert Röttgen und der Fraktion der CDU/CSU sowie der Abgeordneten Roland Kohn, Dr.-Ing. Karl-Hans Laermann, Dr. Karlheinz Guttmacher und der Fraktion der F.D.P, Drucksache 13/8165. *Internationale Attraktivität und Wettbewerbsfähigkeit des Hochschulstandortes Deutschland als Aufgabe deutscher Politik*. Drucksache 13/9372. Retrieved from http://dip21.bundestag.de/dip21/btd/13/093/1309372.pdf.

Deutscher Bundestag. (2010). *Unterrichtung durch die Bundesregierung. Bericht der Bundesregierung zur Auswärtigen Kulturpolitik 2008/2009*. Drucksache 17/970 17. Retrieved from http://dip21.bundestag.de/dip21/btd/17/009/1700970.pdf.

DiMaggio, P. J. & Powell, W. W. (1983). The iron cage revisited: Institutional isomorphism and collective rationality in organizational fields. *American Sociological Review*, 48, 147–160.

Dittmann, F. (2009). Technik versus Konflikt. Wie Datennetze den Eisernen Vorhang durchdrangen. *Osteuropa*, 59, 101–119.

Drori, G. S. & Meyer, J. W. (2006). Scientization: Making a world safe for organizing. In M.-L. Djelic & K. Sahlin-Anderson (Eds.), *Transnational governance, institutional dynamics of regulation* (pp. 31–52). Cambridge, Mass./London: Harvard University Press.

Eimermacher, K. & Justus, U. (Eds.) (2002). *Vom Sinn und Unsinn westlicher Förderung in Rußland*. Bochum: Lotman-Institut für Russische und Sowjetische Kultur, Ruhr-Universität Bochum.

Endovitskij, D. A. & Fedchenko, A. A. (2009). Oplata truda rabotnikov vuza: realnost' i perspektivy. *Vysshee obrazovanie v Rossii*, 3, 12–21.

Entin, M. L. (2005). On the prospects for the establishment of the Common Space of Education between the Russian Federation and the European Union. In C. Pursiainen & S. A. Medvedev (Eds.), *The Bologna Process and its implications for Russia. The European integration of higher education* (pp. 52–61). Moscow: Russian-European Centre for Economic Policy.

Fedorov, I. B., Korshunov, S. V., & Karavaeva, E. V. (2009). Struktura podgotovki v vysshei shkole: analiz izmenenii v zakonodatel'stve Rossiiskoi Federazii. *Vysshee obrazovanie v Rossii*, 5, 3–14.

Gavrilov, V. S., Kolesnikov, V. I., Olesyeyuk, E. V., & Shulus, A. A. (2009). K voprosu o natsionalnyh modelyah obrazovaniya. *Vysshee obrazovanie v Rossii*, 3, 137–149.

Gläser, J. & Lange, S. (2009). Governance-Reformen nationaler Hochschulsysteme. Deutschland in internationaler Perspektive. In J. Bogumil & R. G. Heinze (Eds.), *Neue Steuerung von Hochschulen. Eine Zwischenbilanz* (pp. 123–137). Berlin: edition sigma.

Gläser, J. & Weingart, P. (2010). Die Exzellenzinitiative im internationalen Kontext. In S. Leibfried (Ed.), *Die Exzellenzinitiative. Zwischenbilanz und Perspektiven* (pp. 233–258). Frankfurt am Main/New York: Campus Verlag.

Hochschulrektorenkonferenz. (1995). *Die "Entsowjetisierung" der russischen Hochschule. Historische Voraussetzungen, Anliegen und Verlauf der Hochschulreform in Rußland seit 1985. Dokumente zur Hochschulreform,* 103. Bonn.

Interdisziplinäre Arbeitsgruppe "Exzellenzinitiative" der Berlin-Brandenburgischen Akademie der Wissenschaften. (2010). Bedingungen und Folgen der Exzellenzinitiative. In S. Leibfried (Ed.), *Die Exzellenzinitiative. Zwischenbilanz und Perspektiven* (pp. 35–50). Frankfurt am Main/New York: Campus Verlag.

Kiroj, V. N. (2010). Novye universitety Rossii: problemy i puti ih resheniya. *Vysshee obrazovanie v Rossii*, 3, 7–23.

Lenz, R. (2011). Russlands Hochschulen im Modernisierungsprozess. Zur Frage einer Integration in den Europäischen Hochschulraum. *Die Hochschule*, 2, 146–160.

Meister, S. (2007). Russlands Hochschulpolitik zwischen Wettbewerb und staatlicher Kontrolle. *Russlandanalysen,* 132/07, 4–13.

Meister, S. (2008). *Das postsowjetische Universitätswesen zwischen nationalem und internationalem Wandel: Die Entwicklung der regionalen Hochschule in Russland als Gradmesser der Systemtransformation.* Stuttgart: Ibidem-Verlag.

Meister, S. (2009a). Bologna po russkij. Internationalisierung der Hochschulbildung. *Osteuropa*, 59(5), 59–71.

Meister, S. (2009b). Föderale Hochschulen – Russlands neue Kaderschmieden? *Russland-Analysen,* 185/09, 2–5.

Meyer, J. W. (2007). Globalization. Theory and trends. *International Journal of Comparative Sociology*, 48, 261–273.

Meyer, J. W., Ramirez, F., Frank, D. J., & Schofer, E. (2006). Higher education as an institution. *CDDRL Working Papers*, No. 57. Stanford University. Retrieved from http://iis-db.stanford.edu/pubs/21108/Meyer_No_57.pdf.

Ministry of Education and Science of the Russian Federation. (2009). National innovation system and state innovation policy of the Russian Federation. *Background report to the OECD Country Review of the Russian innovation policy.* Moscow. Retrieved from http://he.ntf.ru/DswMedia/091111_dokladonis_eng.pdf.

Mohrman, K., Ma, W., & Baker, D. (2008). The research university in transition: The emerging global model. *Higher Education Policy,* 21, 5–27.

Mühle, E. (1995). Darstellung. In Hochschulrektorenkonferenz, *Die "Entsowjetisierung" der russischen Hochschule. Historische Voraussetzungen, Anliegen und Verlauf der Hochschulreform in Rußland seit 1985. Dokumente zur Hochschulreform*, 103 (pp. 11–116). Bonn.

Niederhut, J. (2009). Grenzenlose Gemeinschaft? Die scientific community im Kalten Krieg. *Osteuropa,* 59(10), 57–68.

Nye, J. S. Jr. (2004). *Soft power. The means to success in world politics.* New York: Public Affairs.

Peters, T. (2005). Wahlbeobachtung in Tatarstan: Möglichkeiten und Grenzen politischer Projektarbeit im heutigen Russland. In A. Umland (Ed.), *Geistes- und sozialwissenschaftliche Hochschullehre in Osteuropa I: Eindrücke, Erfahrungen und Analysen deutscher Gastlektoren. Ein Projekt des Lektorenprogramms der Robert Bosch Stiftung in Mittel- und Osteuropa* (pp. 151–160). Frankfurt am Main et. al.: Peter Lang.

Pfrepper, R. (2009). *Lebensvorgänge. Deutsch-russische Wechselbeziehungen in der Physiologie des 19.Jahrhunderts.* Aachen: Shaker Verlag.

Pfrepper, R. (2012). *Wirksubstanzen. Deutsch-russische Beziehungen in der Pharmakologie des 19.Jahrhunderts.* Aachen: Shaker Verlag.

Pogorel'skaja, S. (2008). Gleichschaltung oder Modernisierung? Russlands Akademie der Wissenschaften. *Osteuropa,* 53(1), 35–48.

Pörzgen, G. (2010). Dringend reformbedürftig. Der Petersburger Dialog auf dem Prüfstand. *Osteuropa,* 60(10), 59–81.

Prahl, T. (2006). Moskau. *Berichte der Außenstellen 2005* (pp. 143–159). Bonn: DAAD.

Prahl, T. (2009). Moskau. In DAAD, *Berichte der Außenstellen 2008* (pp. 282–302). Bonn: DAAD.

Rohdewald, S. (2009). Schneller, höher, weiter. Biomechanik zwischen Ost und West. *Osteuropa*, 59(10), 185–195.

Schofer, E. (1999). Science associations in the international sphere. 1875–1990: The rationalization of science and the scientization of society. In J. Boli & G. M. Thomas (Eds.), *Constructing world culture. International nongovernmental organizations since 1875* (pp. 249–266). Stanford: Stanford University Press.

Schofer, E. & Meyer, J. W. (2005). The worldwide expansion of higher education in the twentieth century. *American Sociological Review*, 70(12), 898–920.

Stone, D. (2004). Transfer agents and global networks in the 'transnationalization' of policy. *Journal of European Public Policy,* 11(3), 545–566.

Trautmann, G. (1989). *Sowjetunion im Wandel. Wirtschaft, Politik und Kultur seit 1985.* Darmstadt: Wissenschaftliche Buchgesellschaft.

That's what friends are for—
external migration management of the European Union in its eastern neighbourhood

Bettina Bruns and Helga Zichner

Introduction

For some time now, the European Union (EU) tried to involve third countries into its migration management policy area, in particular asylum policies and refugee matters. The involvement of neighbouring (non-EU) countries is of central relevance to the overall approach developed by the EU in this field over the last decades. This approach is in line with a general tendency of restricting immigration, a path the EU followed long before its enlargements to the East in 2004 and 2007. What is the aim of the EU's policy of making third countries adapt their migration management according to EU and other international standards? Which instruments does the EU use to motivate countries to comply? And what can we say about the outcome of these efforts in terms of standardisation of refugee protection? We will approach these questions by analysing policy and legislative documents, as well as interview data we gathered in Ukraine, Moldova and Belarus in 2012 and 2014 from stakeholders of the EU-funded Regional Protection Programme (RPP) aimed at building the countries' capacities in matters of refuge and asylum.

By developing an external migration policy, the EU seeks improvement to asylum systems and refugee protection in neighbouring countries. In the first place, this serves the EU's own interests, because improving the conditions in third countries presumably lowers the migration pressure towards the EU through these countries. In addition, external migration policy should benefit refugees and asylum seekers and their host states because the latter get funding for building up capacities that enable them to live up to their international obligations.[1] Furthermore, the host states are rewarded with increased opportunities of mobility into the EU for their own citizens.

---
[1] In line with the 1951 Geneva Convention relating to the Status of Refugees and its 1967 New York Protocol.

We will start by giving an overview of some of the most important aspects of the EU's approach towards its neighbours focusing on Belarus, Ukraine and Moldova, and draw attention to the inherent ambiguities in the EU's policy. The latter combines divergent protection goals. On the one hand, it aims at safeguarding internal security in the EU, an interest that is used to legitimate restriction and increased control in migration issues. On the other hand, as the numbers of refugees rise globally, so does the need to protect them, given the EU's commitment to international standards of refugee protection. The position of the EU's migration policy between home affairs and external affairs reflects these potentially countervailing goals. We will describe how third countries are simultaneously integrated into the immigration policy of the EU and treated as threats to its internal security.

We will proceed by introducing the RPP as one of the EU's instruments to support third countries in their efforts to implement international standards in this field, before briefly discussing the national legislation that forms the immediate context in which the RPP is carried out. By analysing the RPP as an instrument of standards transfer in refugee and asylum matters, we will shed light on one of the measures through which the EU tries to enhance its own security interests with the help of third countries. Turning finally to the case of Moldova, and to a lesser extent to Ukraine and Belarus, we will show that not only legislative arrangements play a role in implementing new standards, but also the overall situation in a country influences the level of protection it can offer.

The EU and its neighbour states

The Treaty of Amsterdam (European Union, 1997, p. 8) introduced the political concept of "the area of freedom, security and justice" as an official aim of the EU. It provided a definition of the guidelines for EU common home affairs and security policies. The "area of freedom, security and justice" covers the EU's former third pillar, which was largely communitarised in order to enable closer cooperation in the field. This includes the EU's policy on migration and asylum and presents a first step towards the realisation of a common asylum system, envisaged by the EU's 2004 Hague Programme[2] and its follower, the 2009 Stockholm Programme.

To establish and guarantee internal security within the "area of freedom, security and justice", the EU quickly started influencing its direct and indirect neighbour states. The 2003 European Security Strategy (ESS), launched right before the first eastern enlargement round, defined potential threats (European Council, 2003, p. 8), drawing the conclusion that "a ring of friends" needs to be created (Prodi, 2002, no page number). The European Neighbourhood Policy (ENP), introduced in 2004, is one element in the production of these friends and a more secure Europe as made clear by the Commission of the European Communities (2004, p. 2):

> We have acquired new neighbours and have come closer to old ones. These circumstances have created both opportunities and challenges. The European Neighbourhood Policy is a response to this new situation. It will also support efforts to realise the objectives of the European Security Strategy.

Thus, the ENP is clearly an instrument of the mentioned security strategy of the EU, "since internal security is interlinked with the external dimension of the threats" (European Council, 2010, pp. 115–118) and needs a "reinforced external dimension", according to the Stockholm Programme (Ibid., p. 33).

Consequently, the EU considers actions outside its borders as necessary in order to produce external security around its own territory. The EU legitimatises its increasing external engagement by delivering two contradictory arguments, which focus on differentiation as well as integration. Firstly, there is an increasing geographical proximity to third states resulting from the enlargement process: "The integration of acceding states increases our security but also brings the EU closer to troubled areas" (European Council, 2003, p. 8). From this perspective, the EU keeps its character as a secure area in contrast to the external environment, perceived as troubled and insecure. This also means that the EU upholds a clear distinction between

---

[2] The Hague Programme defines ten priorities for strengthening freedom, security and justice in the European Union within the period 2004-2009. It includes, *inter alia*, anti-terrorist measures, a balanced approach to migration, an integrated management of the Union's external borders and the setting up of a common asylum procedure (see Council of the European Union, 2004).

states inside (EU) and outside (non-EU), yet the buffer between the EU and "troubled" areas threatens to shrink without the construction of "a ring of well governed countries" (ibid.)—in other words secure third states—around the EU. According to the second argument, it is this border between inside and outside, respectively secure and insecure, which is increasingly under pressure because of the process of globalisation: "The post Cold War environment is one of increasingly open borders in which the internal and external aspects of security are indissolubly linked" (European Council, 2003, p. 2).

This paradox is reflected in the EU's interaction with its neighbours. They are confronted with efforts of inclusion and exclusion at the same time. On the one hand, they face a sharper delimitation of the EU towards its neighbourhood. The status of non-membership in the EU results for neighbouring countries in a rigid EU visa system and an impermeable border with respect to certain categories of persons and products. On the other hand, the neighbour states are treated as a transition zone, in which they are attached to the EU by certain EU-driven measures and programmes. The neighbour countries become part of the EU's security policy and are expected to adopt relevant EU and international standards.

We argue that the EU tries to bind these countries to its space. This binding happens in two different ways. One is by means of externalising certain political tasks for which the EU holds the third countries responsible. This presupposes the above mentioned approximation to EU standards because otherwise the delegated tasks cannot be accomplished in the intended way. When having a look at the Action Plan for Moldova, the terms "adopt", "align", "converge", "implement" or "streamline" are found on almost every page and represent expressions that aim at changing something in a certain way according to a pre-established standard set by the EU (European Commission, 2004). The EU tries to expand the validity of certain rules that make it a safe place, which consequently should lead to the transformation of the external environment into a safe place. From this perspective, certain tasks could be delegated to these newly secure third states, especially in migration issues.

Another way of binding is to provide rewards to third countries making an effort to adopt EU standards by offering them roles as partners (taking over some tasks) and prospects of inclusion into the space of the EU. This is encapsulated in the famous formulas of "moving beyond cooperation" (European Commission, 2004, p. 2, see also Sasse 2008, p. 301) or "sharing everything but institutions" (Prodi, 2002, no page number).

Thus, it is not only externalisation of certain tasks that blurs the border between internal and external security but also granting of a certain degree of participation in the EU, especially in its market, to the neighbour countries. Present in both binding strategies is the policy of conditionality, a mechanism which is well illustrated in the EU's visa/readmission policy, a standard instrument in the ENP (Trauner & Kruse, 2008, p. 14). The EU's incentive is visa facilitation for a third country's citizens, given that this country agrees on a readmission agreement with the EU (Barbé & Johansson-Nogués, 2008, p. 10). Altogether, the different strategies of binding aim to streamline adoption of EU standards by the countries in question.

The external aspects of home affairs

The task the EU ascribes to its neighbour countries in matters of migration was characterised by one of our interviewees in Moldova as "installing filters in order to prevent migration into the EU" (Interview person in charge of RPP Moldova, 15.05.2012). This section looks at reasons for involving third countries as "filters" and in other dimensions of migration management. Furthermore, we present mobility partnerships as EU's central instrument that transfers responsibility in matters of asylum and refugee protection to third countries. We show that asylum and refugee protection is structured strongly by international and national norms. Respect for these norms is partly subordinated to security concerns of the EU.

In many EU documents, migration policy is wrapped in rhetoric of opportunities and challenges (e.g. European Commission, 2013). Opportunities are associated, *inter alia,* with the potential that arises from people coming to the EU as part of the workforce and potentially creative minds, as well as with filling the demographic gap. The challenges refer to what is termed illegal or irregular migration; keywords are e.g. visa-over-stayers or human trafficking. Common to both narratives of migration is the focus on people who want to come from non-EU into EU countries. This is criticised as a Eurocentric view. Regional migration challenges are "seen from the viewpoint of how much they eventually affect Europe, while South-South migration has always remained limited", stated the European Council on Refugees and Exiles (ECRE, 2012, p. 2).

Many immigration policy matters are in the competence of the European Commission's Directorate General (DG) Justice and Home Affairs, whose key objective is preserving the "area of freedom, justice and security". With the creation of the Schengen area, internal border controls were reorganised and border checkpoints dismantled. At the same time, efforts directed at the control of the external borders were intensified and the standards for these controls were defined in the Schengen implementation agreement. External border regulation restrictions are often referred to as "flanking" or "compensatory" measures for the process of internal liberalisation of the movement of people. The measures guarantee security inside the EU by installing stricter and more intelligent control mechanisms for those desiring to enter the EU (Andreas, 2003), but also by keeping an eye on irregular movements inside the EU (Boswell, 2003, p. 622). Treating immigration and asylum as a predominant responsibility of the DG Justice and Home Affairs "... places the regulation of migration in an institutional framework that deals with the protection of internal security" (Huysmans, 2006, p. 68). Thus, throwing regular and irregular as well as refuge and asylum issues together in one pot places all migration matters into the realm of potential criminality. This becomes especially obvious in the sphere of asylum. While refugees and asylum-seekers are presumably in need of protection, the common framing under justice and home affairs increases a connotation of security for immigration and asylum matters (Huysmans, 2006, p. 69). Several authors point out, however, that this is not a development of the last 15 years, but that this kind of politicisation and limited perspectives on migration date back to the 1970s (Boswell, 2003, p. 619; Huysmans, 2006, p. 65).

Currently, the EU aspires to a "comprehensive migration policy", in which the management of legal migration, the tackling of irregular migration and the link between migration and development shall be integrated into the EU's overall external relations (European Commission, 2011a). This applies also to more recent approaches, whereby the EU puts "wanted" and "unwanted" forms of migration together (Carling, 2011), trying to hand over a part of the channelling of migration to third countries.

The integration of non-EU countries into the common migration management is not new; certain components of this approach were applied as early as 1991 (Boswell, 2003, pp. 620–621; Lavenex, 2006, pp. 333, 335). The external dimension of migration affairs gained momentum in the aftermath of the events of 1989/1990, which led to a rise of migration flows and provoked "fears about a mass influx of immigrants" (Boswell, 2003, p. 621; similarly Byrne, Noll, & Vedsted-Hansen, 2002, p. 5). Lavenex (2006, p. 329) stressed that it was difficult to achieve a common understanding of what should be done and especially to what extent migration matters should lie in the competences of the European Community. The orientation towards third countries thus may be seen as motivated in the first place by the search for a resolution of EU internal blockades, which emerged because of sensitivities in relation to migration matters (Ibid., p. 330).

A second motivation for stronger engagement with third countries is rooted in the growing frustration about the outcomes of internal migration policies that fail to limit or control immigration (Boswell, 2003, p. 621). Frustration mounted due to the ruling practice of European courts, whose decrees stated that the increasingly restrictive practices of states were not in line with national and international legal norms (ibid.).

Altogether, the inclusion of third countries in controlling migration to "Europe" can be interpreted as a double solution or double bypass: as a way to get around the internal blockades due to sensitivities in domestic politics and as a way to get around binding international and national norms (Rijpma & Cremona, 2007, p. 17; Jakob, 2013). Against the background of internal blockades, the idea of an external dimension of migration policy quickly became a central point in co-operation with non-member states (Lavenex, 2006, p. 330). The basic idea was to engage non-EU countries in the control of migration flows into the EU in exchange for certain concessions concerning opportunities for legal migration for the citizens of cooperating third countries. From the EU's perspective, this is a form of "burden sharing" between EU and non-EU states. Critical voices see this arrangement as part of building a "buffer zone" around the EU (Rijpma & Cremona, 2007, p. 16). At any rate, the role of third countries for the EU's migration management cannot be underestimated, as the EU just recently restated that a successful migration policy depends largely on its cooperation with third countries (European Commission, 2014).

Designing migration cooperation along the principle of conditionality

In the following, we illustrate how the instruments by which the EU tries to involve third countries in its migration policy are connected with the logic of conditionality mentioned above. In 2005, the EU came up with the idea of a Global Approach to Migration (GAM), initially comprising three dimensions, and later renewed to be the Global Approach to Migration and Mobility (GAMM) comprising four dimensions in this field, also known as pillars; the new pillar being the one on international protection:

1) Organising and facilitating legal migration and mobility;
2) Preventing and reducing irregular migration and trafficking in human beings;
3) Promoting international protection and enhancing the external dimension of asylum policy;
4) Maximising the development impact of migration and mobility (European Commission, 2011b, p. 7).

As proposed in the GAMM (European Commission, 2011b, p. 10), mobility partnerships should become the "principal framework" for cooperation in the area of migration and mobility. This means that all the pillars shall be included in the design of cooperation agreements with third states. Thus, before entering negotiations on mobility partnerships, third countries must prove that they have put an effort for the solution of migration matters across the pillars two, three and four and that they are engaged in taking their share in the burden of migration management. This is often done through signing of a readmission agreement, by which a state is obliged to take back people who entered the EU irregularly from its territory (see Coleman, 2009), including citizens of other countries transiting through this state. Such agreements are usually signed before negotiations on mobility partnerships or visa facilitation can even start. In fact, there is a heavy asymmetry at play, as the commitments on the part of the third countries in the framework of readmission agreements are legally *binding* while the mobility partnerships are legally *non-binding* political declarations (Martin, 2012, p. 3).

Thus, establishing a mobility partnership requires "certain commitments" (Reslow, 2012, p. 394) on the part of the neighbour states. Besides taking back irregular migrants in the framework of binding readmission agreements, other commitments consist of strengthening the countries' asylum capacities. A document on the mobility partnership with Moldova helps illustrate how commitments of third countries fit into the third pillar of the GAMM "Promoting international protection and enhancing the external dimension of asylum". It is stated that the purpose of the mobility partnership is the facilitation of legal migration (of Moldovans into the EU). "To this end, they [the signatories, the authors] will ENDEAVOUR to develop further their dialogue and cooperation on migration issues" (Council of the European Union, 2008, p. 2, emphasis in the original). Part of this architecture is also found in the RPP, by which the countries shall strengthen their protection capacities and asylum systems (Commission of the European Communities, 2005). In reference to the pillar on asylum and international protection, these are also woven into mobility partnerships. In the case of the Moldovan partnership agreement the mentioned endeavours "include strengthening the institutional capacity to manage migration in accordance with the Regional Protection Programme" (Council of the European Union, 2008, p. 3).

It seems, the EU's principal aim is not to contribute to a better asylum and refugee system in these countries but to increase control of migration into the EU, be it regular or irregular migration. Mobility is thus conditioned upon cooperation in controlling migration (Martin, 2012, p. 2). It is thus part of the "more for more" approach of the EU towards neighbouring countries (ECRE, 2012, pp. 3–4). On paper, however, the implementation of standards is part of the third pillar of the GAMM:

> The EU should increase cooperation with relevant non-EU countries in order to **strengthen** their **asylum systems and national asylum legislation** and to ensure compliance with international standards (European Commission, 2011b, p. 17, emphasis in original).

In general, the issue of international norms and standards is present in the field of asylum more than in other areas of migration policy, due to its international standardisation in the aftermath of the World War II (Loescher & Milner, 2011, p. 189). However, with respect to standards, a strange mechanism seems to repeat itself: increased efforts in strengthening the uniform application of standards leads to a lowering of these standards despite the existence of international human rights and refugee norms. This was the case already in the early 1990s, when access to the EU was increasingly restricted and the share of asylum seekers whose refuge was deemed legitimate went down symptomatically to below 10 per cent (Diederich, 2009, pp. 53–54).[3] At that time, efforts to improve standards by harmonising existing variation across EU countries led to this opposite result. According to several authors, this happened because the harmonisation was reached only on the basis of the lowest possible denominator (DeJong, 1997, p. 177, for a similar analysis see Loescher & Milner, 2011). A repetition of this effect can be seen in the approximation of the states in Central Europe and the Baltics to the EU asylum policy, shortly before the EU enlargement in 2004. Again, efforts to raise the standards of protection by harmonising them produced the opposite effect. Petersen (2002, p. 361) explains this in the following way: "States maintaining higher standards may feel obliged to revise them downwards with a view to becoming less attractive asylum countries". Given that standards tend to become lower in the harmonisation process, the following question arises: what will happen to the level of standards, if a policy aims at transferring a part of the responsibility for asylum and refugee issues to countries whose capacity to integrate vulnerable populations is questionable from the very start (Martin, 2012, p. 4)? Before approaching this question on the basis of empirical material in the last section, we turn to one of the EU's main frameworks for the migration policy implementation, the RPP.

The RPP as an instrument of standards transfer

Following the distinction made by Benedetti (2012, p. 23), differentiating between the externalisation of EU migration control tools and measures to prevent migration into the EU in the countries of origin, the RPP is a child of the former. The externalisation of EU migration tools into neighbouring countries has different facets, including measures of border control, combatting illegal migration and smuggling, and the development of asylum capacities (Benedetti, 2012, pp. 23–24). In short, it is an instrument used to

---

[3] By comparison, it used to be around 80 per cent in the 1970s (Diederich, 2009, pp. 53-54).

transfer EU standards to third states when it comes to the management of asylum and refugee migration.

The RPP originated between 2003–2005 in light of the eastern enlargement of the EU, the establishment of the European Neighbourhood Policy and the ESS. It was during these years that the external dimension of Justice and Home Affairs became further communitarised and the Hague Programme on a common migration and asylum system of the EU was elaborated.

These developments meant, on the one hand, that the EU fully respected the right of protection and asylum, as stated in the Hague Programme (Council of the European Union, 2004). On the other hand, the EU perceived (illegal) migration as a security threat close to organised crime, which needed an efficient management system:

> Europe is a prime target for organised crime. This internal threat to our security has an important external dimension: cross-border trafficking in drugs, women, illegal migrants and weapons accounts for a large part of the activities of criminal gangs (European Council, 2003, p. 4).

The EU's migration policy has to cope with the tension between the need of migrant protection and the protection of its internal security. From the EU's point of view, the internal security is threatened by certain forms of migration reaching the EU through the neighbouring countries. Therefore, third states are more and more involved in the EU's ambivalent migration policy and expected themselves to fulfil tasks of protection and border security:

> EU policy should aim at assisting third countries, in full partnership, using existing Community funds where appropriate, in their efforts to improve their capacity for migration management and refugee protection, prevent and combat illegal immigration, inform on legal channels for migration, resolve refugee situations by providing better access to durable solutions, build border-control capacity, enhance document security and tackle the problem of return (Council of the European Union, 2004, p. 11).

The initiative for the RPP is exactly in line with the quoted suggestions aiming principally at protecting refugees **outside** EU borders (ECRE, 2008, own accentuation).

The RPP was launched as a pilot project in two regions: the Western Newly Independent States (WNIS) comprising Belarus, Moldova and Ukraine, as a transit region, and Sub-Saharan Africa, as a region of origin. The project's official first phase started in 2009 and ran for two years.[4] From October 2011 to the end of 2013 the second phase of the RPP took place. The choice of the WNIS countries is not self-evident when looking at the small numbers of refugees and asylum seekers staying in these countries. In 2005, Belarus counted 725 refugees and 56 asylum-seekers in its territory (UNHCR, 2005). In 2009, when the RPP officially started, the numbers remained small with 580 refugees and 90 asylum-seekers (UNHCR, 2009). In the same year, Moldova received only 141 refugees and 52 asylum-seekers (Ibid.). Numbers for Ukraine are different. In 2009, the country hosted 2,334 refugees and 2,059 asylum-seekers (Ibid.), making it "the most important transit migration country in the East of the EU" (Benedetti, 2012, p. 78). In comparison with the numbers of refugees approaching the EU from the South, however, these figures are modest,[5] and even Frontex admits that there are no hotspots of irregular migration at this section of the border (Frontex, 2012, p. 10).

Thus, the manageability of migration flows might have been an asset for this region when it came to the decision to carry out the RPP, because of the EU's intention "to select a region which will allow for rapid and measurable results" (Commission of the European Communities, 2005, p. 5). Furthermore, the region was previously a target of financial support by the EU and was embedded in various cooperation frameworks, which meant that no extra funding streams were necessary. Moreover, since the beginning of the 1990s, United Nations High Commissioner for Refugees (UNHCR) cooperated with governments and authorities to work on asylum legislation and infrastructure in that region. This allowed the RPP to focus on the strengthening of existing protection capacities, such as registration, case consideration, reception, and integration (Commission of the European Communities, 2005, p. 6).

In general, the RPP's main objectives are assistance to enhanced protection capacities and provision of better protection for refugees in third coun-

---

[4] During the first phase, it was implemented only in Ukraine and Moldova. In Belarus, a similar project "Strengthening the Protection Capacity in the Republic of Belarus" was carried out at the same time with comparable funding.

[5] In 2009, Algeria, for example, had to cope with 94,137 refugees and 1,153 asylum-seekers (UNHCR, 2009).

tries (Commission of the European Communities, 2005). A precondition for this is assurance that asylum seekers have access to territory and fair national asylum procedures in accordance with EU standards. This includes improvements in registration and integration. In order to achieve efficiency in this, cross-border and in-country cooperation between border, interior and migration authorities, civil societies and international organisations are necessary in third countries (UNHCR, 2011a). The improvement of local infrastructure and management of migration movement are additional aims of the programme. The UNHCR (2011a) states that further concrete measures such as detention monitoring, legal assistance, interpretation, monitoring of readmission agreements, legal training for government officials, and information activities are also required.

Also, under the Geneva Convention relating to the status of refugees, assistance is required to create conditions for three durable solutions for refugees, namely repatriation, local integration, and resettlement. An example of realising an obligation stemming from the Geneva Convention gives the second implementation phase of the RPP. Therein, a new element was introduced in the programme: measures on strengthening the self-reliance of the asylum seekers. This included vocational training and employment support in order to grant asylum seekers the means to achieve their own socio-economic protections and financial sustainability (UNHCR, 2011c). As the Geneva Convention obliges states to provide refugees with the right to employment (UNHCR, 2010, pp. 22–23), this measure also represents a standards transfer into the practices of third countries.

To sum up, the RPP developed out of a stimulus of a walls-up-policy rather than out of humanitarian ideals on how to support asylum seekers and refugees on their way towards the EU. Real direct support for migrants was only implemented in the last phase of the project with the focus on self-reliance. This priority list is resembled in the funding structure of the RPP. No new funds were provided in order to carry out the programme, rather it was embedded in existing programmes and their funding lines and was financed first by Aeneas and TACIS (Technical Assistance to the Commonwealth of Independent States), two instruments which were transformed in 2007 into the ENPI (European Neighbourhood and Partnership Instrument). In the first pilot round during 2005, the RPP was financed by 2 million EUR from Aeneas for asylum and protection in the region (ECRE, 2008). UN-

HCR's hopes for more substantive funding for 2007–2013 (ECRE, 2008) did not materialise. On the contrary, from April 2009 until September 2011, the budget for Ukraine and Moldova was only 1 million EUR; phase II was covered by a budget of 1.5 million EUR for all three countries (UNHCR, 2011a). The shortcomings of these figures come to light when comparing them to EU expenditures in the field of strengthening detention capacities and border control of third countries. Just for Ukraine, the EU provided 35 million EUR in funding for a programme intended to enhance Ukraine's capacity to receive returnees under the EU-Ukraine readmission agreement (Human Rights Watch, 2010, pp. 2–3, 27–28; see also ECRE, 2008, p. 16).

Due to the RPP's meagre financial equipment, compared to measures of border strengthening, coupled with its ambitious objectives, there is a gap between stated intentions and project reality. According to observations by UNHCR (2011a), national stakeholders often follow different priorities than supranational actors and relevant international organisations. In this case, national governments often perceive refugee and asylum issues as part of their national security agenda, which makes them approach the topic more from a perspective of law enforcement. The idea of building an adequate asylum system in line with international standards, which are promoted by the EU and the UNHCR, seems to be less important for national governments.

Elements of migration policies and the transfer of standards on the legislative level

The likelihood of successful standards transfer and other effects of the RPP depend on both the financial means of the project and the context in which the project is carried out. As shown in this section, the national migration policies of Belarus, Ukraine and Moldova and the ways they are implemented directly affect the effectiveness of the RPP.

The EU transfers its migration management tasks to international organisations like UNHCR in order to implement, control and legitimise its migration policy in third states (Geiger, 2011, pp. 141–149). Since the mid-1990s, all three countries cooperated with UNHCR. The Regional UNHCR office in Ukraine is located in Kiev, and the concomitant offices in Chişinău, Moldova, and Minsk, Belarus. Assistance in the development of national legislation on asylum and refugee issues and the implementation of projects in this field are two main areas of cooperation between the international organisation and the countries. The UNHCR assisted in the development of the new refugee law of Belarus enacted in 2008, counselled the Ukrainian government in setting up the latest refugee law in 2011, and was involved in the formation of the law on asylum in the Republic of Moldova in 2008.[6]

How does the legislation on migration in the mentioned three countries look like? Belarus has had a very low number of asylum-seekers, which might be connected with the circumstance that it considers all its neighbours safe third countries whose citizens are not in need of refuge and asylum protection (ENPI, 2007). By law, refugees have the same rights to social benefits as Belarusian citizens but currently not all provisions are fully complied with (ECRE, 2009, p. 7). Several endeavours were undertaken to assure better monitoring of the overall situation of refugee protection (Ministry of Foreign Affairs of the Republic of Belarus, 2015). Yet, despite summits with EU and UNHCR representatives, the asylum and refugee protection system remains weak (ENPI, 2007), *inter alia,* due to very limited state funding (Andrysek & Rantala, 2008, pp. 13, 23).

Concerning Moldova, UNHCR attests that the current law on refugee protection of 2008 is "largely in line [...] with international standards" (UNHCR, 2011b, p. 1). Moldova does not use the safe third country notion at all in its law. It adopted the long-term National Strategy in the Field of Migration and Asylum for 2011–2020 (Mosneaga, 2013, p. 3). In 2011, Moldova, in contrast to Belarus and Ukraine, adopted an additional law on the integration of foreigners (Mosneaga, 2013, p. 2), following a UNHCR recommendation (UNHCR, 2011b, p. 4). However, due to the difficult economic situation Moldova faces, asylum seekers are very much dependent on UNHCR assistance (UNHCR, 2011b, p. 3).

---

[6] The relevant law in Belarus is called "On the granting of refugee status, complementary and temporary protection to foreign citizens and stateless persons within the Republic of Belarus", see: http://unhcr.org.ua/img/uploads/docs/Law%20on%20granting%20refugee%20status_Belarus.pdf; in Ukraine: "On refugees and persons in need of complementary or temporary protection in Ukraine", see: http://unhcr.org.ua/attachments/article/400/Refugee%20law%202011%20ENG_final.pdf; in Moldova: "On asylum in the Republic of Moldova", see: http://www.refworld.org/docid/4a27c07b2.html.

In 2009, UNHCR signed a Memorandum of Understanding with the border service of Moldova, the Migration and Asylum Bureau of the Moldovan Ministry of Interior, and a non-governmental organisation. The memorandum stipulates that joint monitoring of protection will be regularly carried out in border areas in order to ensure the entry of asylum seekers into the country, and their access to asylum procedures (Mosneaga, 2013, p. 6).

Ukraine implemented its first refugee law in 1993, which was several times modified before the latest version was adopted in 2011. In the same year, for the first time, the comprehensive "Concept of the State Migration Strategy" was developed. UNHCR severely criticises this law, as it would not provide asylum-seekers with adequate reception conditions or equal socio-economic rights, which prevents them from becoming self-reliant (UNHCR, 2013). In theory, Ukrainian law guarantees refugees the same rights and benefits as Ukrainian citizens, similar to Belarus, but the practice falls far short of equality. Provisions and by-laws are not implemented. Furthermore, refugees often do not have access to basic information concerning their rights (ECRE, 2009, pp. 70–71; Andrysek & Rantala, 2008, pp. 54–55). Given this poor legislative background, it is not surprising that, apart from laws, EU standards are not found in other relevant fields such as access to and quality of asylum procedures, accommodation and reception assistance, and detention of asylum-seekers in Ukraine. These deficient conditions are also associated with the inefficiently working State Migration Service, founded in 2010, which is characterised as highly corrupt and having unclear responsibilities and competences (UNHCR, 2013, pp. 7–9; see also Andrysek & Rantala, 2008, p. 54). The domestic conditions in Ukraine prompted UNHCR to state that it "should not be considered as a safe third country" (UNHCR, 2013, p. 20).

To summarise, in all three countries new relevant legislation was established, which aligns more (in the case of Moldova) or less (in the case of Belarus and Ukraine) with EU and international standards. In order to be fully effective, these countries' laws need to be harmonised with national social and labour legislation (Andrysek & Rantala, 2008, p. 74). Furthermore, government officials could play more vital roles in assisting refugees in practice (ibid.). The very modest budgets allocated for asylum and refugee issues in these countries make it hard to implement legislation and demonstrate how low these issues are on the countries' agendas.

How does the RPP contribute to enhancing third states' capacities to receive asylum seekers and refugees?

The strategy to "outsource" (Gammeltoft-Hansen, 2011, p. 129) the reception of asylum seekers by the RPP may be viewed from different perspectives. From the EU's point of view, strengthening asylum capacities in other states represents a form of burden-sharing (Noll, 2002). The EU stipulates that every country should offer protection depending on its economic capacity (Commission of the European Communities, 2004, p. 13). UNHCR also welcomes the EU's initiative of RPP, since it generally increases the possibility for refugees to seek protection in different parts of the world (Petersen, 2002, p. 361). However, there is one reservation: the countries in question here are categorised as in "a region where conditions for the local integration of refugees remain virtually inexistent and where basic standards of national protections are not available" (UNHCR, 2011a, p. 2).

Given the comparative economic weaknesses of the three countries considered in this chapter[7] and the pessimistic estimations of UNHCR concerning them, it is difficult to understand why they should be implicated in a scheme of burden-sharing at all. Especially prominent is the example of Moldova, featuring a combination of socio-economic challenges with the most-advanced legislative framework related to migration. There are contradicting perceptions of how the RPP worked out in Moldova. Several of our interviewees stressed that, even with small numbers of refugees, there is a huge challenge for the country, namely in organisational, financial and social terms. Yet, in most documents on the RPP available on the UNHCR's homepage, Moldova appears to be a country where the RPP performed well.

We stress that, even if important legislative requirements have been implemented (accommodation centres for asylum seekers are available, information concerning the modalities to seek asylum for potential asylum seekers installed at international border crossing points, and training for border guards and other officials carried out), this does not mean that the capacity is durable or that standards are met. Two concrete examples, where the Moldovan state has not yet applied international standards completely is the

---

[7] The GDP in these countries is less than a tenth of the EU average. See Levy, 2011, p. 157.

availability of interpreters and translators for refugees during their court procedures and the issuance of travel documents for refugees. Both issues concern the scope of protection offered by the Moldovan state and represent a shortfall in practice to meet the range of rights which refugees and asylum seekers are entitled to (Gammeltoft-Hansen, 2011, p. 132).

The first example in this sense refers to the application of Article 16 of the 1951 Convention, the free access to the courts of law which includes the right to free assistance of an interpreter,[8] anchored well in Moldovan legislation: "An asylum seeker shall enjoy the following rights: to be provided for free with an interpreter (translator) at any stage of the asylum procedure" (UNHCR, 2008, p. 121). As state budgets however "do not contain financial provisions for interpretation in the migration/refugee context" (UNHCR, 2011a), there is a serious lack of interpretation services at the border and detention centres, as well as during administrative and judicial proceedings of refugee claims (UNHCR, 2011a; for Ukraine see UNHCR, 2013, p. 12). In case there is an interpreter, often his/her skill level is very poor (Human Rights Watch, 2010, p. 7). One of our interviewees working with an NGO in charge of integrating refugees is asked time and again to work as an interpreter with irregular migrants without remuneration. The reason for this is partly that there are languages for which there is not a single interpreter in the entire country of Moldova. Also, appointing them from neighbouring countries is not possible because the state cannot afford it. Consequently, the degree of institutionalisation for the right to language assistance is very low. The international right in this case cannot be guaranteed in an efficient and reliable way, potentially hindering the access to the procedure altogether due to language barriers.

The second example refers to the right of refugees to get travel documents from their host states, in accordance with Article 28 of the Geneva Refugee Convention (UNHCR, 2010). As of spring 2014, Moldova did not issue any travel documents to refugees, with which they would be able to travel outside Moldova:

---

[8] Commentary on the refugee convention 1951. Articles 2-11, 13-37. Published by the Division of International Protection of the UNHCR 1997, see: www.unhcr.org/3d4ab5fb9.pdf, especially pages 38-40.

> [...] we have one major problem: persons with recognised refugee status are locked up in the territory of Moldova, they do not have travel documents (Interview with person in charge of RPP Moldova, 29.05.2012).

This problem was reported by several interview partners, some of them have also reported it to officials from the EU, but for several years, nothing has changed. Unsurprisingly therefore, many refugees apply for citizenship as soon as they are entitled to do so (after eight years of residence in Moldova). This in turn is interpreted on the official level as a proof of the high degree of integration of them into the Moldovan society, meanwhile the reality is that it is the only option left for refugees to gain the right to travel.

Summing up, we can state that from the point of view of travel documents and translators, refugees in Moldova are worse off than in a country where refugees get travel documents and language assistance during court procedures, to which they are entitled according to Article 28 and 16 of the Geneva Refugee Convention. Practically speaking, the rights of refugees are constrained, contributing to an uneven quality of protection in this region:

> The result is what could be termed 'protection lite', understood as the presence of formal protection, though with a lower certainty, scope and/or level of rights afforded (Gammeltoft-Hansen, 2011, p. 133).

The last aspect concerns the degree of autonomy and reliability of local actors to help people claim and enjoy refugee and asylum rights. For example, one of the interviewees estimates that it would be too early to stop the regular monitoring at border crossing points in order to see whether border authorities are still working according to international law, even if before he had said that the procedure in general is working quite well:

> [...] the presence of the UNHCR at the border, the presence of monitoring should be felt by the border staff. Because if not, we don't know what will be (Interview with person in charge of RPP Moldova, 29.05.2012).

He assumes that, if the monitoring stopped at that point in time, more infringements would occur. Of course, non-respect for legislation is omnipresent and nothing specific to Moldova. Rather, it is a product of a high degree of fluctuation in these kinds of institutions due to ongoing restructurings, emigration due to the economic situation, and a high degree of corruption. All of this leads to the need for constant training and monitoring of border guards. Adding to these uncertain circumstances is the existence of only one juridical NGO specialised in refugee and asylum issues offering the only perceptible organisation a refugee could seek for help. This organisation is heavily dependent on international funding. All this makes clear that the protection a country like Moldova is able to offer is fragile. Almost all forms of assistance to refugees and asylum seekers are provided by UNHCR (from pencils and paper to hygiene or food packages, clothing, pocket money and medical assistance) (Interview with person in charge of RPP Moldova, 26.2.2014). Members of one of the few NGOs in charge of distributing this assistance see this financial non-implication of the state (as the one who should actually build its capacities in refugee and asylum matters) as highly problematic. It is an indicator that in practice, the whole system is completely dependent on the presence and the work of UNHCR, which is not sustainable and likely to leave Moldova sooner or later. Interestingly, the role of the EU is estimated as rather marginal:

> We did the same work years before the EU started these projects, we did it together with EU funding, and we continue it as best as we can; without it now the project has ended (Interview with person in charge of RPP Moldova, 12.02.2014).

The pessimistic outlook that interviewees gave was that as soon as UNHCR leaves Moldova, the system will break down completely. Several interview partners expressed their desire for some more years of assistance on part of UNHCR and also the EU in accompanying the process of implementation.

Altogether, these insights hint to the long process that it takes before one can speak of enhanced capacities of third states. Moldova is one of the weak states (Levy, 2011, p. 155) the EU tries to employ for the management of migration towards the EU. The country is confronted with serious economic, societal and political problems, e.g. strong migration, dependence on remittances and defective public services, not to mention the unresolved territorial conflict in the eastern part of the country. In informal talks, one colleague of the project responded that it is difficult to understand why Moldova must receive refugees at all, given the extremely difficult situation of the country and its financial inability to provide for the refugees' basic needs.

Conclusion

What is the outcome of the third countries' involvements in EU migration management regarding the standardisation of refugee protection? We scrutinised the RPP as an EU-run project that aimed at transfer of standards in migration and asylum policies. The project is supported with only marginal funding, leaving the initiative "limited in scale", as admitted by the European Commission itself (Commission of the European Communities, 2005, p. 8). Our findings suggest that external transfer of standards in migration and asylum management is not taken seriously by the EU, as the process of standards harmonisation leads to a lowering of precisely these standards.

Additionally, standards transfer is not easy to measure. The pure legislative adjustment and the inclusion of EU and international norms into national law appears to represent progress, but this lacks significance when it comes to the evaluation of concrete realisations of the adopted standards into practice in third states. If protection does not work even in Moldova, where legislation is mostly in line with EU and international norms and standards, one can only imagine the current situation in Belarus and Ukraine with respect to the implementation of protection tools into daily practices.

There is strong evidence that a project like the RPP, designed to support and protect refugees and asylum-seekers, actually serves merely as eye-candy concealing the one-sidedness of the EU's politics on asylum and refugee issues: nearly a complete focus on border securing and detention facilities. To reiterate, the EU's involvement in regulating migration and refugee flows in the neighbouring countries draws first and foremost on domestic interests and concerns of the EU Members States. The original target groups of the concrete measures carried out, namely refugees and asylum-seekers in Belarus, Moldova and Ukraine, certainly do not profit sustainably from the half-hearted EU engagement.

References

Andreas, P. (2003). Redrawing the line: Borders and security in the twenty-first century. *International Security*, 28(2), 78–111.

Andrysek, O. & Rantala, T. (2008). *The local integration of refugees in the Republic of Belarus, the Republic of Moldova and Ukraine. "A Strategy for Action"*. Retrieved from http://www.refworld.org/pdfid/47ce77f72.pdf.

Barbé, E. & Johansson-Nogués, E. (2008). The EU as a modest 'force for good': The European Neighbourhood Policy. *International Affairs*, 84(1), 81–96.

Benedetti, E. (2012). EU migration policy and its relations with third countries: Russia, Ukraine, Belarus and Moldova. In S. Devetak & S. Olesea (Eds.), *EU migration policy and its reflection in third countries: Belarus, Moldova, Russia* (pp. 7–75). Maribor: Iscomet.

Boswell, C. (2003). The 'external dimension' of EU immigration and asylum policy. *International Affairs*, 79(3), 619–638.

Byrne, R., Noll, G., & Vedstet-Hansen, J. (2002). Western European asylum policies for export: The transfer of protection and deflection formulas to Central Europe and the Baltics. In R. Byrne, G. Noll, & J. Vedstad-Hansen (Eds.), *New asylum countries?* (pp. 5–28). The Hague: Kluwer.

Carling, J. (2011). The European paradox of unwanted migration. In J. P. Burgess and S. Gutwirth (Eds.), *A threat against Europe? Security, migration and integration* (pp. 33–46). Brussels: Brussels University Press.

Coleman, N. (2009). *European readmission policy. Third country interests and refugee rights*. Leiden: Nijhoff.

Commission of the European Communities. (2004). *European Neighbourhood Policy Strategy Paper*. COM (2004) 373 Final. Brussels: Commission of the European Communities. Retrieved from http://www.iemed.org/docs_oficials_migracio/regionals/COM_2004_373_ENP_Strategy_paper/ENP_COM_2004_373_strategy_paper_en1.pdf.

Commission of the European Communities. (2005). *Communication from the Commission to the Council and the European Parliament on Regional Protection Programmes*. COM (2005) 388. Brussels: Commission of the European Communities. Retrieved from http://www.refworld.org/pdfid/43e203ed4.pdf.

Council of the European Union. (2004). *The Hague Programme. Strengthening freedom, security and justice in the European Union*. Document 16054/04. JAI 559. Brussels: Council of the European Union. Retrieved from http://ec.europa.eu/home-affairs/doc_centre/docs/hague_programme_en.pdf.

Council of the European Union. (2008). *Addendum to "I/A" item note (9460/08 ADD I)*. Brussels: Council of the European Union. Retrieved from http://eeas.europa.eu/delegations/moldova/documents/eu_moldova/joint_declaration_2008_en.pdf.

DeJong, C. D. (1997). Europäische Integration und internationale Migration: Herausforderungen und Handlungsmöglichkeiten. In S. Angenendt (Ed.), *Migration und Flucht. Aufgaben und Strategien für Deutschland, Europa und die internationale Gemeinschaft* (pp. 173–189). Bonn: BPA.

Diederich, H. (2009). *Melilla: Transit oder Endstation. Europäische Abschottungspolitik und ihre Folgen für die Flüchtlinge*. Frankfurt am Main: Brandes & Apsel.

ECRE. (2008). *The European Union funding priorities for refugee protection, migration management and border reinforcement*. Brussels: ECRE. Retrieved from http://www.refworld.org/docid/49997ae71a.html.

ECRE. (2009). *Here to stay? Refugee voices in Belarus, Moldova, the Russian Federation and Ukraine*. Brussels: ECRE. Retrieved from http://www.refworld.org/docid/49b11be53a7.html.

ECRE. (2012). *ECRE comments to the Commission Communication on the Global Approach to Migration and Mobility*. COM (2011) 743 Final. Brussels: ECRE. Retrieved from http://www.ecre.org/topics/areas-of-work/protection-in-third-countries/277.html.

ENPI. (2007). *Annex. Belarus. Country Strategy Paper 2007–2013 and National Indicative Programme 2007–2011*. Brussels: ENPI. Retrieved from http://eeas.europa.eu/enp/pdf/pdf/country/enpi_csp_nip_belarus_en.pdf.

European Commission. (2004). *EU-Moldova Action Plan*. Brussels: European Commission. Retrieved from http://ec.europa.eu/world/enp/pdf/action_plans/moldova_enp_ap_final_en.pdf.

European Commission. (2011a). *Communication from the Commission to the European Parliament, the Council, the Economic and Social Committee and the Committee of the Regions. Communication on migration*. COM (2011)248 Final. Brussels: European Commission. Retrieved from http://ec.europa.eu/home-affairs/news/intro/docs/1_EN_ACT_part1_v11.pdf.

European Commission. (2011b). *Communication from the Commission to the European Parliament, the Council, the European Economic and Social Committee and the Committee of the Regions. The global approach to migration and mobility*. COM (2011)743 Final. Brussels: European Commission. Retrieved from http://ec.europa.eu/dgs/home-affairs/what-we-do/policies/pdf/1_en_act_part1_v9_com2011-743_en.pdf.

European Commission. (2013). *The European Union explained: Migration and asylum*. Brussels: European Commission. Retrieved from http://europa.eu/pol/justice/flipbook/migration/en/files/migration-and-asylum_en.pdf.

European Commission. (2014). Die auswärtige Migrationspolitik der EU: ein ambitioniertes Konzept. *Pressemitteilung*, IP/14/167. Brussels: European Commission. Retrieved from http://europa.eu/rapid/press-release_IP-14-167_de.htm.

European Council. (2003). *A secure Europe in a better world. European security strategy*. Brussels: European Council. Retrieved from https://www.consilium.europa.eu/uedocs/cmsUpload/78367.pdf

European Council. (2010). Notices from European Union institutions, bodies, offices and agencies. European Council. The Stockholm Programme—an open and secure Europe serving and protecting citizens. *Official Journal of the European Union*, C 115. Retrieved from http://www.eurojust.europa.eu/doclibrary/EU-framework/EU frameworkgeneral/The%20Stockholm%20Programme%202010/Stockholm-Progr amme-2010-EN.pdf.

European Union. (1997). *The Treaty of Amsterdam. Amending the Treaty on European Union, the treaties establishing the European Communities and certain related acts. Amsterdam (2 October 1997).* Luxembourg: Office for official Publications of the European Communities.

Frontex. (2012). *Eastern borders. Annual overview 2012.* Warsaw: Frontex.

Gammeltoft-Hansen, T. (2011). Outsourcing asylum: The advent of protection lite. In L. Bialasiewicz (Ed.), *Europe in the world. EU geopolitics and the making of European space* (pp. 129–152). Surrey: Ashgate.

Geiger, M. (2011). *Europäische Migrationspolitik und Raumproduktion. Internationale Regierungsorganisationen im Management von Migration in Albanien, Bosnien-Herzegowina und der Ukraine.* Baden-Baden: Nomos.

Human Rights Watch. (2010). *Ukraine. Buffeted in the borderland. The treatment of migrants and asylum seekers in Ukraine.* Retrieved from http://www.hrw.org/de/re ports/2010/12/16/buffeted-borderland-0.

Huysmans, J. (2006). *The politics of insecurity. Fear, migration and asylum in the EU.* New York: Routledge.

Jakob, C. (2013). Imagepflege der Grenzschützer. *Die Tageszeitung*, February 11. Retrieved from http://www.taz.de/!5073508/.

Lavenex, S. (2006). Shifting up and out: The foreign policy of European immigration control. *West European Politics,* 29(2), 329–350.

Levy, A. (2011). The European Union Border Assistance Mission (EUBAM) and the remote control border: Managing Moldova. In L. Bialasiewicz, (Ed.), *Europe in the world. EU geopolitics and the making of European space* (pp. 153–183). Surrey: Ashgate.

Loescher, G. & Milner, J. (2011). UNHCR and the global governance of refugees. In A. Betts (Ed.), *Global migration governance* (pp. 189–209). Oxford: Oxford University Press.

Martin, M. (2012). Analysis. The global approach to migration and mobility: The state of play. *Statewatch Journal*, 22(2/3), 1–7.

Ministry of Foreign Affairs of the Republic of Belarus. (2015). *Office of the United Nations High Commissioner for Refugees.* Minsk: Ministry of Foreign Affairs of the Republic of Belarus. Retrieved from http://mfa.gov.by/en/organizations/member ship/list/e95ffd653b58149c.html.

Mosneaga, V. (2013). Asylum-seekers, refugees and displaced persons in Moldova: Problems of recognition, social protection and integration. *Carim East: Explanatory Note*, 13/103. Retrieved from http://www.carim-east.eu/media/exno/Explanatory%20Note_2013-103.pdf.

Noll, G. (2002). Protection in a spirit of solidarity? In R. Byrne, G. Noll, & J. Vedsted-Hansen (Eds.), *New asylum countries* (pp. 305–324). Leiden: Kluwer.

Petersen, M. (2002). Recent developments in Central Europe and the Baltic states in the asylum field: A view from UNHCR and the strategies of the High Commissioner for enhancing the asylum systems of the region. In R. Byrne, G. Noll, & J. Vedstet-Hansen (Eds.), *New asylum countries?* (pp. 351–372). The Hague: Kluwer.

Prodi, R. (2002). A proximity policy as the key to stability. "Peace, security and stability international dialogue and the role of the EU". Sixth ECSA-World Conference. Jean Monnet Project. Brussels, 5–6 December 2002. *European Commission - SPEECH/02/619 06/12/2002.* Retrieved from http://europa.eu/rapid/press-release_SPEECH-02-619_en.htm.

Reslow, N. (2012). The role of third countries in EU migration policy: The mobility partnerships. *European Journal of Migration and Law,* 14(4), 393–415.

Rijpma, J. J. & Cremona, M. (2007). The extra-territorialisation of EU migration policies and the rule of law. *EUI Working Papers,* Law 2007/01. Retrieved from http://cadmus.eui.eu/bitstream/handle/1814/6690/LAW_2007_01.pdf?sequence=1.

Sasse, G. (2008). The European Neighbourhood Policy: Conditionality revisited for the EU's eastern neighbours. *Europe-Asia Studies*, 60(2), 295–316.

Trauner, F. & Kruse, I. (2008). EC visa facilitation and readmission agreements. Implementing a new EU security approach in the neighbourhood. *CEPS Working Document*, No. 290.

UNHCR. (2005). *Statistical Yearbook 2005. Belarus.* Retrieved from http://www.unhcr.org/cgi-bin/texis/vtx/page?docid=464183670.

UNHCR. (2008). *Information brochure for asylum seekers, refugees, beneficiaries of humanitarian and temporary protection in the Republic of Moldova.* Chişinău: UNHCR.

UNHCR. (2009). *Statistical Yearbook 2009.* Retrieved from http://www.unhcr.org/4ce532ff9.html.

UNHCR. (2010). *Convention and protocol relating to the status of refugees.* Retrieved from http://www.unhcr.org/3b66c2aa10.html.

UNHCR. (2011a). *Regional Protection Programme. Support to UNHCR's activities in Belarus, Moldova and Ukraine. April 2009–September 2011.* Retrieved from http://unhcr.org.ua/en/publications-3/regional-protection-programme-m.

UNHCR. (2011b). *Submission by the United Nations High Commissioner for Refugees for the Office of the High Commissioner for Human Rights' Compilation Report - Universal Periodic Review: Moldova.* Retrieved from http://www.refworld.org/pdfid/4d806f9ec.pdf.

UNHCR. (2011c). *Support to UNHCR activities in Eastern Europe (Belarus, Moldova and Ukraine) in the context of Regional Protection Programmes – Phase II (MIGR/2011/272-415). Concept Note on Implementation of the Self-reliance Component.* Retrieved from http://unhcr.org.ua/attachments/article/398/Concept%20Note%20on%20Self-reliance%20-%20RPP%20Phase%202.pdf.

UNHCR. (2013). *Ukraine as a country of asylum. Observations on the situation of asylum-seekers and refugees in Ukraine.* Retrieved from http://www.refworld.org/docid/51ee97344.html.

Inescapable partners: The European Union and the Council of Europe as rule of law promoters in Ukraine

Olga Burlyuk

Introduction

The dissolution of the Soviet Union changed the political landscape in Europe and transformed the membership and role of Europe's two major organisations—the European Union (EU) and the Council of Europe (CoE). The nature of these organisations' relationships with post-Soviet states and with each other received considerable scholarly interest in the 1990s and early 2000s. Originally founded as alternatives, the EU and the CoE "have run in parallel for most of the time, each within its very own field of activity" (Kolb, 2010, p. 2). Following the decades of transformation, however, the two found themselves pursuing similar tasks in similar fields: promoting the triptych of European values –democracy, human rights and the rule of law—in post-Soviet states. Scholars examined transforming networks of "interlocking" European organisations and concluded that there are increasing overlaps of their memberships and competences, with elements of both cooperation and competition (see Baracani, 2008; Bartole, 2000; Dimitrova & Pridham, 2004; Guetzkow, 1998; Merlingen & Ostrauskaite, 2004; Peters, 1996; Strohal, 2005). In the last decade, the political and developmental context in Europe altered once again, due to the maturing of the EU as an actor and the new quality of EU relations with post-Soviet states after the 2004 and 2007 EU enlargements. The EU value promotion discourse solidified, development assistance funds grew, and interest, presence and engagement in the region intensified. Post-Soviet states themselves developed an interest in EU, all the way to membership aspirations for some, giving the EU greater political weight. The CoE also expanded its membership and competences in the last decade, but not as dramatically as the EU.

Acknowledging these changes, this study revisits the relationship between the EU and the CoE as promoters of European values in post-Soviet states. To provide empirical detail and analytical depth, the study examines a single case: rule of law promotion efforts of the two organisations in Ukraine.[1] The rule of law is extracted from the basket of shared European values for two reasons. First, the rule of law has been visibly mainstreamed inside both the EU[2] and the CoE[3] over the last twenty years. Second, rule of law compliance, or rather drastic rule of law incompliance, in post-Soviet states constitutes a great challenge for domestic reformers and a major concern for external actors. Ukraine is selected among post-Soviet states for its elaborate relationships with both the EU and the CoE, which have engaged in extensive rule of law promotion efforts in this country. Moreover, Ukraine's formal aspirations of EU membership give the EU additional political leverage, affecting the EU-CoE relationship.[4] It should be emphasised that this case study research strategy is used instrumentally to investigate in-depth the general phenomenon, the relationship between the EU and the CoE as promoters of European values in post-Soviet states, inasmuch as it examines rule of law promotion in the Ukrainian case in particular.

---

[1] Rule of law promotion efforts of the OSCE, the UN, the OECD, International Financial Institutions and individual states (in particular, USA and EU Member States), as well as the relationship between them and the EU/the CoE are not addressed by this study due to scope limitations, without prejudice to their effect on developments in post-Soviet states and Ukraine in particular.

[2] Rule of law clauses occupy a solid place in the Treaty on the European Union (TEU) and permeate EU internal and external policies, including relevant framework policies (the European Neighbourhood Policy and the Eastern Partnership) and policies specifically towards Ukraine (Burlyuk, 2014b).

[3] In 2005, the CoE, the OSCE and the UN adopted a "Multilateral organizations rule of law pledge"; in 2007, the Parliamentary Assembly of the Council of Europe (PACE) adopted a resolution "The principle of the rule of law" (1594/2007); in 2008, Rapporteur Group on Legal Co-operation issued a report "The Council of Europe and the rule of law: an overview" (GR-J(2008)11); in 2011, Venice Commission adopted a "Report on the rule of law" (2011-003.rev); and due to the latest restructuring, the rule of law now is featured not only in the titles of CoE programmes, but also in the title of Directorate General I – Human Rights and Rule of Law.

[4] For the first time, Ukraine declared its intention to develop relations with the EU based on the principles of integration leading to full membership in the Decision of the Parliament of Ukraine "On key directions of the foreign policy of Ukraine" on July 2nd, 1993. At the same time, formal aspirations most of the time do not match the attitude and performance behind them, which made scholars speak of "integration by declaration" (Sherr, 1998, p. 12) and "integration without Europeanisation" (Wolczuk, 2004, p. 2) as strategies of the Ukrainian political elites.

The main objective of this study is to explore and conceptualise the complex nature of the EU-CoE relationship. The existing scholarship on the subject revolves around the competition-cooperation dichotomy[5] and concludes that the EU and the CoE are simultaneously involved in a conflictive and cooperative relationship (Kolb, 2013). Recognising that "relations between international organizations are, as a rule, based on both co-operation and competition" (Rotfeld, 2000, p. 377), this study aims to enrich the debate empirically and analytically by revealing and conceptualising the relationship's nuances in the studied case. The investigation focuses on the substance and process of EU and CoE rule of law promotion.[6] The elements of comparison notwithstanding, this is not a comparative study as such: the main objective is to analyse how and why the two actors interact in the shared field of rule of law promotion. The analysis draws on original empirical data collected through document analysis; semi-structured interviews with EU and CoE officials (working on rule of law promotion in the region or cooperation between the two organisations) and experts (working for these and other development actors) in Ukraine; and participant observation at policy events, panel discussions and EU/CoE project conferences. Data collected through expert interviews and participant observation are especially valuable for exposing informal details, attitudes and perceptions that add nuance to understanding the relationship between the EU and the CoE.

The findings reaffirm that the EU and the CoE as rule of law promoters in Ukraine are in a complex interactive relationship, with elements of both co-operation and competition. In addition to this, the findings reveal three important details (or tendencies) in their relationship: first, cooperation prevails over competition at substantive, political and operational levels, while competition is concentrated at the institutional level; second, cooperation at the

---

[5] Many contributions include the dichotomy in the very title (e.g. De Schutter, 2007; Kolb, 2010, 2011; Polakiewicz, 2009).

[6] That is to say, this study does not investigate actors' motivations to promote the rule of law. It assumes the aspiration of the EU and the CoE to make a positive impact, but does not imply altruism behind such an aspiration and allows for their engagement to be driven by "enlightened self-interest" (Whitman & Wolff, 2010, p. 7). This study also does not investigate the impact of their efforts as such. The impact is a feature in the analysis only in so far as concerns about impact inform actors' decisions on the substance and process of their engagement.

political and operational levels precedes and even triggers cooperation at the institutional level, bending the reluctant institutional structures of the two organisations; and, third, the growing political, financial and normative leadership of the EU does not cancel out the traditional and special relevance of the CoE in this region and policy area.

The chapter proceeds as follows. The first section examines the quest for normative leadership given substantive overlap in the value agendas of the two actors. The second section explores how this substantive overlap in value agendas leads to operational overlap in actors' areas of actual engagement. The third section analyses why, despite such substantive and operational overlap, there is more cooperation than competition between the two actors, concluding on a determinant role of the unity of their "civilising mission", or political overlap. The fourth section examines how the limitedness of resources and the complementarity of comparative advantages of the two organisations make them natural key partners for each other. Finally, the fifth section addresses an observation that the inevitability of cooperation at political and operational levels triggers cooperation at the institutional level. The findings' implications for future research and policy are stipulated in the concluding section.

Value agenda, substantive overlap and the quest for normative leadership

First of all, the obvious: the EU is a latecomer in the field of rule of law promotion, in Ukraine and globally. Ukraine acceded to the CoE on the 9th of November, 1995, is a participant of the Venice Commission since February 3rd, 1997, and falls under the jurisdiction of the European Court of Human Rights since September 11th, 1997. In contrast, the EU engagement in Ukraine became more or less active and deliberate only in 2004–2005, following the Eastern enlargement, the introduction of the European Neighbourhood Policy (ENP) and the so-called Orange Revolution. Until then, the EU "neither played nor endeavoured to play a role in domestic change in the Soviet successor states" (Wolczuk, 2009, p. 187). The Partnership and Cooperation Agreement (PCA) framework and technical assistance under the Technical Assistance to the Commonwealth of Independent States (TACIS) programme were basic and poorly targeted, the value dimension was underdeveloped, and the relationship with Ukraine was secondary to those with the Central and East European countries (CEEC) and Russia.[7]

Concerning the value package, the EU and the CoE pursue similar and indisputably compatible agendas, with the rule of law firmly in both. The two actors fall in line as "European organisations" that represent "European values", to the extent these can be identified. Adherence to the rule of law is a membership condition of both organisations, according to Article 49 of the consolidated Treaty on the European Union (TEU) and Article 3 of the Statute of the Council of Europe respectively. Ukraine is a CoE member state, although norm compliance did not follow norm acceptance. Similarly, Ukraine aspires to become an EU member state, although its rhetorical commitment to the values shared by EU member states is not accompanied yet by practical commitment. While the CoE already missed an opportunity to apply pre-accession conditionality, the EU still has the power to do so, as analysed in this chapter.

The concept of the rule of law is not exhaustively defined for the purposes of its promotion by either the CoE or the EU, and its exact meaning may seem fluid. Conversely, the EU, the CoE, the Venice Commission and the United Nations all advocate for the existence of a consensus on the core meaning of the rule of law and a shared pre-understanding of its essential, unquantifiable elements.[8] A coherent directing idea that law should serve its social goals by coordinating social relations, minimising arbitrariness and

---

[7] In the mid-1990s, the EU concluded ten similar partnership and cooperation agreements with all post-Soviet states minus Belarus and the Baltic states. The aims of these partnerships are to provide a general framework for political dialogue, support new democracies and develop their market economies and provide a basis for cooperation in a number of fields. TACIS was launched as early as 1991 to speed and support the domestic developments. For an overview of TACIS, see Frenz (2007).

[8] See, for instance, European Commission Communication "A new EU Framework to strengthen the rule of law" (2014; also Annex); PACE Resolution "The principle of the rule of law" (1594/2007); Venice Commission "Report on the rule of law" (2011); UNGA Resolution "On the Declaration of the High-level meeting on the rule of law at the national and international levels" (A/Res/67/1, 2012) and Joint EU pledge for a High-level meeting at the UNGA, when the said resolution was adopted. EU officials repeatedly emphasised the existence of a consensual understanding of the rule of law in interviews. The ratio of the universal and the particular in European rule of law conceptions and human rights is debated in the literature (see Leino, 2002, 2005; Leino & Petrov, 2009).

providing order in society provides the conceptual baseline on the rule of law (HIIL, 2007, p. 12; Tamanaha, 2007, p. 1). In relations with third states in the case of the EU and in relations with non-compliant states in the case of the CoE, this consensual understanding of the rule of law is common for the two organisations. In "A new EU framework to strengthen the rule of law" from March 2014, the European Commission stated explicitly that "aspects of the rule of law as a common denominator of the Union are fully reflected at the level of the Council of Europe" (Annex, p. 2). It ensures a degree of unity of their rule of law promotion efforts at a meta-level, notwithstanding differences in practical substantiation of the concept and areas of actual engagement analysed in the following section.

Being a non-specialised organisation, the EU extensively relies on the CoE concerning the rule of law standards and the assessment of a country's compliance therewith. The CoE is better placed for the task of setting the standards and evaluating the performance both politically in terms of its mandate and membership (which translate into better legitimacy) and practically in terms of its structures and expertise (which translate into monitoring tools and mechanisms). Moreover, the availability of CoE standards in a given area makes it easy for the EU to promote respective values. It is easier politically, because it relieves the EU of a need to emphasise certain issues bilaterally, which often can put the relationship under (additional) strain. It is easier technically, because the EU can build on the CoE expertise in the field and, thereby, does not need to "reinvent the wheel". A senior EU official reiterated this point as follows:

> The Council of Europe is a point of reference, absolutely. It is there, with all the standards, and those standards are included in the Copenhagen Criteria. So, perfect! And it is very convenient for us to have it as a point of reference: it allows us to put less emphasis on certain issues *ourselves*, because it is being done anyway, through a different mechanism.

In its programming documents, the EU operates widely with "European standards", directly or indirectly referring to the CoE and its elaborate networks of treaties, to which Ukraine is usually a party.[9] Similarly, in its report-

---

[9] Programming documents analysed include ENP policy papers, Country strategy papers, National indicative programmes, as well as Action Plans, Association Agendas and Annual lists of priorities.

ing documents, the EU operates widely with Parliamentary Assembly of the Council of Europe (PACE) Resolutions, Venice Commission Opinions and reports of various monitoring bodies of the CoE.[10] In fact, the dominance of the CoE and its standards in Ukraine was recognised also by non-European donors. For example, the U.S. Agency for International Development (USAID) Ukraine Rule of Law Project adopted the European model and focused its activities on rule of law components present in the Universal and European codes of standards.[11]

At the same time, the EU is enhancing its own competence. Although many questioned the appropriateness of the EU taking up a value promoting role, the EU "has assumed such a role regardless" (Greer & Williams, 2009, p. 471). On the one hand, the EU is developing its own standards and "capturing the standard-setting tasks" of the CoE in certain areas (Kolb, 2010, p. 8).[12] On the other hand the EU engages in developing new European standards under the auspices of the CoE itself, through and alongside individual EU Member States. A European Commission official emphasised that the EU is actively involved in drafting new CoE Conventions, in order to ensure that the latter contain "European standards" which are compatible with EU legislation on the subject and which the EU wants to see as such. One of the objectives behind this is precisely to make these standards binding on third state-partners of the EU that are CoE members. EU accession to the European Convention on Human Rights would increase EU leverage in the CoE forum further, making the EU a member of the Council of Europe in its own right, alongside the 28 EU Member States.[13]

The CoE is said to perceive the tendency of the EU to take up new competences and claim normative leadership as a threat, because there is "a fear

---

[10] Reporting documents analysed include Annual Country reports, as well as periodic ENP reviews and reports.
[11] Such as the Basic Principles of the Independence of Judiciary (UN GA Resolution 40/146 (1985)) and the European Charter on the Statute for Judges (1998).
[12] In particular, the new EU framework on the rule of law from March 2014 is an attempt to consolidate the EU position on the rule of law (primarily for the purposes of internal affairs, but also for the purposes of external affairs).
[13] Discussed since late 1970s, EU accession to the ECHR is a legal obligation under the Treaty of Lisbon (Article 2). For the state of affairs, see: http://hub.coe.int/what-we-do/human-rights/eu-accession-to-the-convention. Legally, EU accession to the ECHR is considered highly problematic (see Greer & Williams, 2009).

of marginalization" of the CoE and its becoming a "standard-receiver" instead of a "standard-setter" (De Schutter, 2007, p. 3). The affirmation of its standard-setting role is still an important and sensitive issue for the CoE. For example, the Summary Report on Co-operation with the European Union (Council of Europe, 2013a, p. 1) separately emphasises that "the expertise and benchmarking role of the Council of Europe in European Union policies have been confirmed and even reinforced in the context of EU Enlargement and Neighbourhood Policy", in particular in the area of rule of law promotion. In any case, regardless of how sceptical the CoE is of the EU approaching and engaging itself in the CoE core tasks, it is "unable to act independently anymore" and "has to align itself with these new EU standards" (Kolb, 2010, p. 3).

The area of engagement and operational overlap

Due to its cross-cutting nature, its "connectedness", the rule of law "constitutes a kind of structural trap that bedevils reform efforts" in any area (Tamanaha, 2011, pp. 214, 224). Just as all roads lead to Rome, progress in any area eventually hinges on the poor application of the rule of law in a country. However, speaking of the areas of actual engagement of the EU and the CoE, "rule of law promotion can only be on the agenda of these organisations if it somehow falls within the mandate or contributes to the purpose of the organisation" (HIIL, 2007, p. 28). The CoE is concerned primarily with human rights and human security. In the European Convention on Human Rights (1950) and 200 other treaties that form the body of *jus communis* and in respective CoE development efforts, the rule of law features in relation to human rights and their protection by domestic courts (Council of Europe, 2006). The major activity of the CoE Office in Ukraine is targeted at the improvement of Ukraine's domestic legislation and capacity and at the enforcement of Ukraine's international commitments with regard to the protection of human rights, and the functioning of the judiciary and law enforcement institutions (Council of Europe, 2008; Council of Europe, 2013b). In terms of the object of reform, the rule of law promotion efforts of the CoE—as an intergovernmental organisation—focus first and foremost on legislation to reform relevant institutional structures.[14] The Venice Commission is the key specialised agency and, to use the words of the former Judge at the Constitutional Court of Ukraine, "definitely enjoys the biggest influence and authority in Ukraine on constitutional issues".[15] In turn, the European Court of Human Rights embodies "the fourth degree of jurisdiction" for Ukrainians and is defined as "the most active external change agent for the past ten years (even if its judgements did not concern Ukraine)" (Petrov & Serdyuk, 2008, p. 198).[16]

As for the EU, the rule of law (or rather rule of law compliance) is relevant for virtually every EU policy area and sector of bilateral cooperation; a point stated explicitly in some EU documents and emphasised repeatedly in interviews.[17] An official at the European External Action Service commented: "Well, it is difficult to see rule of law as a 'sector', because elements of it are present in everything we do". Consequently, unlike the CoE which is a "niche player" in post-Soviet states (Merlingen & Ostrauskaite, 2004, p. 370), the EU pursues a holistic approach to rule of law promotion and refers to the rule of law for identification, authorisation, regulation and a variety of instrumental purposes.[18] In EU framework (ENP) and bilateral (Ukraine) programming documents, the rule of law appears in relation to: the democratic organisation of power and constitutional and electoral reforms; the system of justice and the functioning of judiciary and law enforcement institutions; good governance and the functioning of public administration at all levels; the relationship between society and state, and human rights protection; economic and social development; legislative adaptation of regulatory institutions, procedures and standards; and, finally, in relation to stability

---

[14] Kleinfeld (2012, Chapter 4) identifies four objects of rule of law promotion or reform: laws, institutions, power structures and social norms.
[15] Similar views were expressed by other Ukrainian experts.
[16] Ukrainians actively give recourse to the ECHR: a total of 56,427 applications have been submitted by Ukrainians as of January 1st, 2014, according to the Overview 1959-2013 ECHR (see: http://www.echr.coe.int/Documents/Overview_19592013_ENG.pdf). Out of 717 court judgements, 709 are violation judgements, as of January 1st, 2011 (see Ukraine country fact sheet, http://www.echr.coe.int/Documents/Country_Factsheets_1959_2010_ENG.pdf).
[17] For example, it is stated in the National Indicative Programme for Ukraine 2011-2013 (p. 27).
[18] Walker (2009, p. 124) identifies the above four rule of law use-values or purposes, which the rule of law can be put to serve by the EU.

and security and the management of borders and migration, fighting organised crime and corruption (Burlyuk, 2014a). Just as CoE efforts, EU rule of law promotion is targeted at transforming domestic legislative and institutional frameworks.

Being a latecomer, the EU had to carve a place amongst the activities already pursued by others. As a result, the EU cooperates with and even relies fully on other rule of law promoters as far as their understandings of the rule of law overlap and carries out its own activities as far as their understandings diverge. Constitutional reform, the reform of the system of justice, public administration and protection of human rights are traditional areas for rule of law promoters. Hence, the EU cooperates closely with the CoE, as well as with the Organization for Security and Co-operation in Europe (OSCE) and the USAID. The rule of law understood in relation to regulatory frameworks necessary for trade and investment is promoted by the EU and by the World Bank, the European Bank for Reconstruction and Development (EBRD) and others actors. At the same time, support for the adaptation of Ukrainian legislation to the EU *acquis communautaire* comes from the EU alone. Finally, the rule of law understood in relation to stability and security is promoted primarily by the EU (in cooperation with the OSCE), and no other rule of law promoter puts equal emphasis on border management, illegal migration and organised crime. Noteworthy, recent years have brought a reversal of the trend: external donors increasingly align their activities in Ukraine with the EU agenda, set out in Action Plans, Association Agendas and annual Lists of Priorities. This is because they recognise the special role of the EU due to Ukraine's European aspirations and because the EU agenda serves as a basis for Ukraine's national reform programmes, often adopted as reactions to EU-Ukraine cooperation documents (Wolczuk, 2009, p. 200). The Association Agreement between the EU and Ukraine concluded in parts in March and June 2014 makes up to 80 per cent of the EU *acquis communautaire* obligatory for Ukraine and will inflate the relevant weight of the EU and its standards, including on the rule of law.[19]

---

[19] The complete texts of the Association Agreement can be accessed at: http://eeas.europa.eu/ukraine/assoagreement/assoagreement-2013_en.htm.

Although both the CoE and the EU remain ambiguous over the precise scope of the rule of law, the core business of the CoE is clearer and narrower than that of the EU. EU rule of law promotion is broader and more all-encompassing, with less focus than that of the CoE, due to the EU's wider interests, mandates and ambitions.[20]

"Mission civilisatrice" and political overlap

In organisation theory, such substantive and operational overlap should generate competition and conflict (Grandori, 1987, p. 58; Pfeffer & Salancik, 2003, p. 2). In practice, however, there is no apparent competition among different actors, and the rule of law promotion environment in Ukraine can be characterised as "friendly". Interviews uncovered a strong and seemingly genuine ambition of all parties to avoid duplication and to ensure compatibility. In the absence of a structured government-led mechanism, semi-formal structures have been created to this end by rule of law promoters themselves. For example, the Ukraine Rule of Law Project (USAID) initiated regular monthly roundtables of all "activists" in the field of rule of law promotion; and the EU Delegation in Ukraine coordinates assistance cooperation with EU member states and other development partners. Consultation, coordination and even cooperation between various rule of law promoters in Ukraine, also non-European and non-governmental ones, can be observed. The "common product" in the form of joint publications, conferences and workshops confirms that such cooperation is not a mere imitation.[21] Nonetheless, this coordination is more about stream-lining separate efforts than about working together: ultimately, they are distinct actors with their own agendas, budgets and procedures.

The major reason for more cooperation than competition among different rule of law promoters in Ukraine in principle and the EU and the CoE in particular is the political reality and the lack of interest, motivation and capacity for reform among local partners. Notwithstanding important differences in the established objectives of the two organisations, they pursue principally

---

[20] Greer and Williams (2009, p. 480) make a similar argument concerning human rights policies of the EU and the CoE.
[21] For example, a DVD "International standards for judiciary" (2010) in Ukrainian is a joint production of three rule of law promoters: the EU, the CoE and USAID.

the same *mission civilisatrice*, or "civilising mission", in Ukraine and in the post-Soviet space overall.[22] Indeed, assessed against receiving states, the EU and the CoE have more in common than not. As discussed earlier, a shared pre-understanding of the essence of the rule of law exists in Europe. In the Report on the Rule of Law (Venice Commission, 2011, pp. 4–5), the Venice Commission explicitly stated that a consensual understanding of the essence of the rule of law is to be distinguished from a distorted, purely formalistic understanding as "rule by law", "rule by the law" or even "law by rules", found in some former socialist states.[23] In the EU context, "we can be certain of at least one thing: an oppressive legal order cannot satisfy the EU's understanding of the rule of law" (Pech, 2012, p. 27).

However, it remains a question whether the understanding of the rule of law in Ukraine and other post-Soviet states is the same, similar or at least receptive of the European one. Ukraine declared a commitment to the rule of law through its Constitution (Articles 1 and 8) and, among other things, its membership in the CoE. Yet, norm acceptance did not translate into immediate norm compliance. Moreover, little to no improvement in Ukraine's rule of law compliance in the past two decades can be reported. In the World Justice Project Rule of Law Index 2011, Ukraine received low scores for all identified rule of law factors and sub-factors, ranking last or close to last globally, regionally and by income group (Agrast, Botero, & Ponce, 2011, pp. 100, 143).[24] The systemic shortcomings are best captured by two paradoxes: the façade arrangement paradox and the Brownian motion paradox. The first means that, although spelled out thoroughly at the fundamental constitutional level, rule of law clauses fail drastically in reality. Thus, their role is reduced to a façade arrangement. The second means that, with a lot of movement overall, but no movement in a particular direction, rule of law reform processes in Ukraine resemble Brownian motion (Burlyuk, 2013, Chapter 7).

---

[22] Merlingen & Ostrauskaite (2004, p. 366) made a similar argument with respect to the OSCE and the CoE.

[23] Incidentally, the interviewed Venice Commission official revealed that this particular line was included upon the insistence of a Ukrainian delegate to the Venice Commission, with Ukraine and other post-Soviet states in mind.

[24] See also reports by KIIS (2006), Neill & Brooke (2008), Chebanenko, et al. (2011), and Allison (2012).

The reasons behind these paradoxes are deficiencies in all categories (or objects of rule of law reform)—laws, institutions, power structures and professional and popular social norms—and lie beyond the scope of this chapter. What is relevant here is the obstructive and infamous lack of political will for reform among Ukrainian elites. One of the risks of competition between the two organisations is duplication and sending mixed signals to their Ukrainian partner institutions, which are often identical for different projects. In the situation of limited interest, will and capacity for reform among local stakeholders, competition between the EU and the CoE would undermine the effects of their efforts. Forum-shopping by local stakeholders is another risk of competition in the studied context: local authorities will readily set the competing actors off against each other, exposing inconsistencies in their recommendations and expectations, interpreting these inconsistencies as signs of illegitimacy of the recommendations and expectations and so justifying the domestic status quo and their own inaction.

So, the main competition of the EU and the CoE is not with each other, but with the unwillingness of the domestic government to reform. Their common purpose, or "mission", is to promote a European understanding of the rule of law in Ukraine. Therefore, the EU and the CoE usually take similar political stances *vis-à-vis* Ukraine in cases of severe rule of law violations, as the recent cases of the Tymoshenko trials in 2010–2013 and repressions against Euromaidan protesters in 2013–2014 illustrate.

Limited resources and complementary comparative advantages

The sheer limitedness of donor resources (political, financial and human) in Ukraine further inclines the EU and the CoE to cooperate. Indeed, cooperation and complementarity with others is one of the ways for an international organisation to enhance its own effectiveness (Brummer, 2010, pp. 292–294).[25] By pooling resources, the EU and the CoE try to maximise their impact and avoid the waste of resources through "turf battle" (Kolb, 2010, p. 4). The Memorandum of Understanding (Council of Europe, 2003, p. 3) acknowledges this explicitly and states that the organisations will "take due account of the comparative advantages, the respective competences and

---

[25] Other ways, such as increasing the incentives or the scale of support, are beyond the scope of this study.

expertise" of each other. All development actors cooperate with each other to some extent. However, the relationship between the EU and the CoE is special, and even the interviewed experts spoke of them as *key* and even *natural* partners. This section revisits the particularly compatible comparative advantages that give rise to this relationship.

On the one hand, the EU-CoE cooperation is believed to enhance significantly the role of the CoE, linking it to the EU, an organisation with bigger strategic importance and larger funds (Kolb, 2010, p. 2; Merlingen & Ostrauskaite, 2004, p. 396). Compliance with the rule of law is a condition for membership in both the CoE and the EU. In the uncertain yet enthusiastic political context of the early 1990s, accession to the CoE was dominated by presumptions that "compliance could be achieved within a reasonable timeframe with the good will of governments" and that "admission would result in a continuing and indeed much stronger influence of the CoE than would be the case if the country were not a member" (Dimitrova & Pridham, 2004, p. 99; Djeric, 2000, p. 610). As a result, admission procedures were rather flexible. Ukraine and other post-Soviet states became CoE members despite their poor compliances (Jordan, 2003, pp. 667, 679). Given the wasted opportunity to apply pre-accession conditionality and its political weakness as an intergovernmental organisation, the CoE has few means to impose compliance at this point. It has the power to suspend membership of a country in violation of its principles, but is reluctant to do so. Ukraine was threatened with suspension twice, in 2000 and 2001. However, neither Ukraine, nor any other state, has been disowned yet. The Council of Europe has the monitoring tools, but rarely acts upon the monitoring results (Brummer, 2010, p. 281). Usually, the CoE does not go beyond diplomatic "naming and shaming" through Venice Commission's opinions and recommendations, PACE resolutions or CoE reports. It has vast tasks and aims, but its financial resources are "relatively modest" (Benoit-Rohmer & Klebes, 2005, p. 22). Nevertheless, it does enjoy significant socialising potential vis-à-vis Ukraine.

The EU, in turn, has the potential to induce policy change through the incentives of political and economic integration with the Union and has larger development funds to assist in policy change. Notwithstanding the fact that the mega-incentive of membership is not on the table, Ukraine's EU membership aspirations distinguish it from most other post-Soviet states and give the EU stronger political leverage in Ukraine than elsewhere in the region. Moreover, Ukraine's aspirations for EU membership give new relevance to CoE standards: they become significant not only as standards of the CoE itself, but also as pre-conditions for EU membership. Although the CoE may be displeased with such subservient political placement, its position as "an antechamber or waiting room for EU accession" in reality enhances its relevance (Joris & Vandenberghe, 2009, p. 13). Technical and financial assistance funds ten or more times the size of those of the CoE give the EU undisputed financial leadership.[26] There are examples of joint projects funded by the EU for 50, 80, 90 and 100 per cent. In 2012, EU contribution amounted to 89 per cent of the total budget of Joint Programmes. (Council of Europe, 2013)

On the other hand, having the CoE on board is advantageous for the EU. Incidentally, in interviews, the importance of the EU for the CoE was emphasised mostly by EU officials, whereas the importance of the CoE for the EU was underlined by EU *and* CoE officials, as well as independent experts. Despite its relative political and financial weakness, overlooking or reducing the role of the CoE to "a large footnote" is unjustified (MacMullen, 2004, p. 406). Most decisively, the Council of Europe possesses the necessary competence in terms of both the mandate of the organisation and the accumulated institutional memory, expertise, knowledge, know-how and experience. The wide membership (encompassing 47 states, including 28 EU Member States and all European partners of the EU apart from Belarus) gives CoE standards, activities and opinions an unparalleled degree of legitimacy. In this way, CoE standards are representative, relevant and binding at the same time, while they are also tighter and stronger than those of the United Nations as the universal organisation. By complying, member states' governments gain a sort of legitimacy themselves. Unlike the EU, whose relationship with Ukraine evolves within a highly ambiguous political paradigm, the CoE is an organisation of which Ukraine is currently a member. Ukraine has binding treaty obligations resulting from its membership in

---

[26] The total amounts of allocated development assistance can be found in EU National Indicative Programmes and Annual Action Programmes for Ukraine for respective years. Although it is difficult to isolate the amount of money directed at rule of law promotion as such, it is obvious that the amount is significantly larger than that of the CoE.

the organisation, including on the rule of law. Even though the political and legal weight of these membership commitments may be questioned, the CoE, its activities and requests enjoy a certain degree of formal authority in Ukraine. Ukraine's official rhetoric remains at all times respectful of the CoE, its recommendations, reports and statements and maintains the image of Ukraine's willingness to comply with its membership commitments (unlike Russia, for instance[27]). Furthermore, the formal relationship in place between the CoE and Ukraine allows the CoE to engage in Ukraine's domestic political processes in its own capacity, while at the same time provides a tool for domestic actors to use in domestic debates. For example, Venice Commission opinions and recommendations are an important external reference point for domestic actors.[28] A Venice Commission official revealed in interview that the Secretariat receives occasional requests from Ukrainian politicians to provide a recommendation on legislative drafts that normally would be outside of its competence, so as to obtain an authoritative opinion as a tool in domestic debates.

All this makes the CoE more than just another body for implementing EU-funded projects, which in the case of EU-CoE cooperation are framed with the Joint Programmes mechanism. The input of the CoE is significant already because it is often the one bringing the initiative and responsible for developing the content of a project and its implementation once approved.[29] Moreover, "having the Council of Europe on board opens many doors and guarantees better receptiveness on the Ukrainian side", to quote an officer from the EU Delegation to Ukraine. Precisely because Ukraine is a member of the CoE, the EU often chooses the latter as an implementer for projects dealing with the state of democracy, human rights and the rule of law in Ukraine. As an expert with 10 years of experience in monitoring develop-

---

[27] In the recent years, Russian officials stated publicly Russia's dissatisfaction with the treatment it received from the CoE and warned that Russia would revise its own attitude all the way to withdrawal.

[28] Over 70 Venice Commission Opinions on various Ukrainian laws and legislative initiatives have been issued since 1995, yet before Ukraine joined the Venice Commission in 1997. The recurring themes include constitutional reform, judicial reform, electoral legislation, legislation on prosecution, creation of a professional association of lawyers and, more recently, legislation on the right to assembly.

[29] See Joris & Vandenberghe (2009, pp. 23-24) for an overview of the operation of Joint Programmes.

ment projects in Ukraine observed, "such joint projects become a mechanism of indirect control over Ukraine's compliance with its obligations under the European Convention on Human Rights". The intergovernmental nature of the CoE allows it to carry out projects in sensitive areas that cannot be entrusted with private company-implementers. A variety of Joint CoE/EU Programmes in Ukraine deal precisely with transparency, independence and efficiency of the judicial system, ill-treatment and impunity, money laundering and terrorist financing. Projects in these areas require a high level of political and operational coordination on the part of Ukrainian partner institutions, as well as access to places of detention or disclosure of information that is otherwise not public. Therefore, Ukrainian partners are more inclined to cooperate with a project backed by the authority of the CoE rather than with a private company-implementer. In addition, the CoE is a full structure, with binding conventions and other legislation, specialised agencies and institutions, monitoring bodies and evaluative information, trained staff and experts, long-standing presence in the field and links with domestic structures and elites. It simply possesses the necessary experience and trained experts to implement the projects, which make it "better understood" among Ukrainian professionals, as experts stated in interviews. Finally, as intergovernmental organisations, the CoE and the EU have similar public statuses and decision-making procedures. This institutional compatibility, high levels of formality and rules of transparency create an atmosphere of trust between them (higher than among other rule of law promoters) and make them "fully reliable" partners, to quote an official from the European Commission's Directorate-General for Development and Cooperation. Nonetheless, the intergovernmental nature of the EU and the CoE has some negative implications at the operational level, as the actual development projects coordinated by them are extremely formal, bureaucratic and, consequently, slow.

The extensive cooperation of the EU and the CoE at the operational level mediates the perceived visibility of their involvement, visibility understood as the degree of awareness of an actor on the part of partner countries and the ease (or difficulty) with which this actor is identified among other external actors who have their own reform strategies (Bendiek, 2008, p. 4). The CoE was traditionally more familiar to domestic audiences in Ukraine and served more frequently as a point of reference and a tool of influence in domestic public debates. Although the EU lagged behind for a better part of the past two decades, the intensity and visibility of its involvement in the rule of law promotion business in Ukraine is gradually (and ever more quickly) increasing. Since 2005, the EU has intensified political dialogue and cooperation with Ukraine and enlarged the scale of technical and financial assistance provided to its rule of law reform processes. Actually, the EU is said to have finally overcome the USA as Ukraine's largest donor.[30] As a result, the EU is more frequently brought up in the domestic debate on the subject by politicians, journalists and analysts. However, in interviews, experts working in the sphere of legal reforms still named the Venice Commission and the European Court of Human Rights as external authorities in the field, not the EU. The fact that the EU is more of a financial partner than an implementing one under the Joint Programmes cooperation mechanism reduces the visibility of its rule of law promotion in Ukraine as the beneficiary country.[31]

Political and operational reality as triggers of institutional cooperation

An important observation is that the inevitability of cooperation between the EU and the CoE at the political and operational levels precedes and even triggers their cooperation at the institutional level. The two rule of law promoters work in the same field (Ukraine), deal with the same set of problems (domestic institutional context) and interact with the same counterparts (local stakeholders). Combined with the limitedness of donor resources and the lack of interest, motivation and capacity among their local partners, this reality prompts policy and institutional changes on the part of the EU and the CoE to formalise and professionalise their actual cooperation on the ground.

Indeed, looking retrospectively, the ever increasing cooperation between the two organisations has been institutionalised and formalised over the years with hesitation; a process that has been slow, based on reaction

---

[30] The above statement on the EU being the largest donor in Ukraine is based on the statements and calculations by the EU itself, for example, in Country Strategy Paper 2007-2013 (p. 9) or in the Manuscript published by the Delegation of the EC to Ukraine in 2009 (p. 1).

[31] Joris & Vandenberghe (2009, p. 24) make a general argument of a kind.

more than action, and constantly yielding to operational realities.[32] The two sets of letters that the EU and the CoE exchanged on June 16th, 1987 and November 5th, 1996 were replaced on May 23rd, 2007 by the Memorandum of Understanding between the Council of Europe and the European Union.[33] Yet, "the two organizations have not been over-zealous": the Memorandum confirmed the existing relationship rather than introduced genuine novelties (Joris & Vandenberghe, 2009, pp. 35–37). Moreover, the Memorandum was less ambitious than the one called for in the Report of Jean-Claude Juncker "Council of Europe—European Union: A sole ambition for the European continent" on April 11th, 2006.[34] Similarly, although EU/CoE Joint Programmes have been in operation since 1993, a Joint Declaration on cooperation and partnership between the Council of Europe and the European Commission was adopted only on the 3rd of April, 2001.[35] Most recently, on April 1st, 2014, ten years into the European Neighbourhood Policy, the EU and the CoE signed a "Statement of Intent" establishing a new framework for cooperation in the EU Enlargement and Neighbourhood Regions for the period 2014–2020.[36] As it is described in a press release (IP/14/356) this 5-page "administrative agreement" sets out working methods to strengthen their "strategic and programmatic", or "political and operational", cooperation in the region.[37]

The planned review of the Memorandum in 2013 celebrated "a quasi-routine of policy co-ordination on issues of common interests" that took shape and concluded that there was no need to review the Memorandum at that point (Council of Europe, 2013) Yet, many of the ideas suggested in Juncker's Report in 2006 as necessary and even urgent for efficient EU-

---

[32] See Benoit-Rohmer & Klebes (2005, pp. 127-135) and Joris & Vandenberghe (2009) for an overview of the institutionalisation of EU-CoE relations over the years.
[33] See an overview of the legal basis of EU-CoE cooperation at: http://www.coe.int/t/der/eu_EN.asp.
[34] For Juncker's final recommendations, see pp. 30-32 of the Report.
[35] The CoE/EU Joint Programmes exist since 1993 and in Ukraine since 1995, although the actual activities started in 2001. At the time of writing, there have been about 20 projects carried out in/for Ukraine, with 5 of them closely related to the rule of law. See: http://www.jp.coe.int/Default.asp.
[36] A Statement of Intent for the cooperation between the Council of Europe and the European Commission in the EU Enlargement region and the Eastern Partnership and Southern Mediterranean countries (EU Neighbourhood region), April 1st, 2014.
[37] Both phrases are used in the text of the Statement.

CoE cooperation, including EU accession to the European Convention on Human Rights, have not materialised so far. Although facilitated by the CoE Liaison Office in Brussels and recent restructuring of the CoE, their institutional cooperation remains lop-sided: the EU holds a special status in the CoE and may attend meetings of its institutions and agencies, but not the other way around (Benoit-Rohmer & Klebes, 2005, pp. 44, 131). As acknowledged in the Memorandum itself (Council of Europe, 2003, p. 5), the EU and the CoE are different organisations and retain their decision-making autonomies. However, the competition between them is concentrated largely at the institutional level, and even here it eventually gives way to cooperation under the pressure of political and operational reality, which bends the reluctant institutional structures of the two organisations.

Conclusion

This chapter analysed the relationship between the EU and the CoE as rule of law promoters in Ukraine as an instance of European value promotion in post-Soviet states. The findings reveal three important nuances (and perhaps even general tendencies) that enrich our understanding of the studied relationship, namely that cooperation prevails over competition, political and operational cooperation precedes and triggers institutional level cooperation, and the EU has recently strengthened its position vis-à-vis the CoE.

First, in this country (Ukraine) and policy area (the rule of law), cooperation between the EU and the CoE prevails over competition. Significant overlap of substantive, political and operational agendas of the two organisations in practice leads to cooperation and not competition, as theory would expect. Given the persistently low rule of law compliance levels in Ukraine and reluctance of the Ukrainian authorities to reform, the main competition of the EU and the CoE is with the country's government, not with each other. The limitedness of their political, financial and human resources further inclines the EU and the CoE to capitalise on the complementarity of their comparative advantages so as to maximise effects from their efforts. Competition is not altogether absent, but it is concentrated at (and perhaps even restricted to) the institutional level.

The second nuance is that cooperation at the political and operational levels precedes and even triggers cooperation at the institutional level. The institutions of both organisations are slow, reluctant and reactive in formalising cooperation that exists in practice. However, institutional competition also eventually gives way to cooperation. Third, the EU has strengthened its position in the last decade and claims leadership from the CoE: as a richer organisation it has taken financial leadership; as a politically stronger organisation with more incentives to offer it is fighting for political leadership; and as an organisation with a broader rule of law agenda it may eventually challenge the CoE's normative leadership. The understanding of the EU as "a payer, not a player", dominant in the 1990s and early 2000s, is losing relevance as multiple political processes continually shift the balance in favour of the EU. At the same time, the role of the CoE should not be reduced to a footnote or entirely overlooked in the analyses of value promotion in post-Soviet states, which are often limited to investigations of EU efforts. In this country (Ukraine) and policy area (the rule of law), the CoE retains special relevance, both in its own capacity and as an implementer of the (joint) projects of the EU.

The findings of this study are specific to the examined case, EU and CoE rule of law promotion in Ukraine, but can be generalised to the wider phenomenon of EU and CoE value promotion in post-Soviet states albeit with certain limitations. In the first place, it is difficult to speak of "post-Soviet states" as a group today, more than two decades after the dissolution of the Soviet Union. Even categorising them into sub-groups, such as the ENP East, South Caucasus, Central Asia and Russia, would be problematic. All states have followed individual transformation paths, and their domestic contexts and relationships with the EU and the CoE are qualitatively different. This inevitably affects the political leverage of the two organisations over domestic processes in the countries and, eventually, over each other as value promoters in each. In the second place, meaningful variation in the EU-CoE relationship across policy areas can be expected. The value agendas and mandates of the two organisations vary across policy fields, and thus the nature, degree and impact of substantive and operational overlap also differs.[38] However, one can conclude with a reasonable degree of certainty that similar *general* tendencies in the EU-CoE relationship are in

---

[38] The significance of the political context, policy area, and internal and external coordination for variation in EU external policies is analysed in Burlyuk (2014c).

place across countries and policy areas, namely: the presence of both cooperation and competition; the dominance of cooperation at substantive, political and operational levels, and the prevalence of competition at the institutional level; the determining role of the reluctance of partner states to reform and the limitedness of donor resources; and finally, the ever stronger position of the EU as compared to the CoE on all accounts—normative, political, and financial. Future research should engage in within-case and comparative studies (with comparison across countries and policy areas) in order to see the variety of formats of the EU-CoE relationship and the scope of generalisation of the findings of this study.

As for policy implications, the interconnectedness and interdependence of the EU and the CoE and their rule of law promotion efforts is apparent. It is highly unlikely that the process of assuming competences by the EU will be reversed, the overlap in mandates will be eliminated, identical membership will be achieved, one organisation will be completely replaced by the other or that the two will merge. There is no alternative but to develop better cooperation mechanisms and explore the complementarities between the two organisations further. In view of the significant and ever growing substantive, institutional and operational overlap, as well as the commonality of challenges addressed and faced, consultation between the EU and the CoE is a minimum requirement, while coordination and cooperation are desirable and appropriate ways to advance their value agendas.[39] If not automaticity, then at least effectively functioning mechanisms to realise this cooperation should be in place. Future policy should acknowledge the effective cooperation between the two actors that exists on the ground and work on institutional mechanisms to formalise, improve and facilitate this cooperation.

References

Agrast, M., Botero, J., & Ponce, A. (Eds.) (2011). *World justice project rule of law index 2011*. Washington, D.C.: The World Justice Project.

Allison, D. (2012). *The rule of law, democracy and prosperity in Ukraine: A Canadian parliamentary perspective*. Report of the Standing Committee on Foreign Affairs and International Development. Ottawa, Canada. Retrieved from http://www.parl.gc.ca/content/hoc/Committee/411/FAAE/Reports/RP5690981/faaerp04/faaerp04-e.pdf.

---

[39] Similar argument was made already in Peters (1996, p. 397).

Baracani, E. (2008). EU democratic rule of law promotion. In A. Magen & L. Morlino (Eds.), *International actors, democratization and the rule of law: Anchoring democracy?* (pp. 53–86). London/New York: Routledge.

Bartole, S. (2000). Final remarks: The role of the Venice Commission. *Review of Central and East European Law,* 26(3), 351–363.

Bendiek, A. (2008). The ENP: Visibility and perceptions in the partner countries. *SWP Working Papers,* FG2, 2008/01, 1–18.

Benoit-Rohmer, F. & Klebes, H. (2005). *Council of Europe law: Towards a pan-European legal area.* Strasbourg: Council of Europe Publishing.

Brummer, K. (2010). Enhancing intergovernmentalism: The Council of Europe and human rights. *The International Journal of Human Rights,* 14(2), 280–299.

Burlyuk, O. (2013). *European Union rule of law promotion in Ukraine: Exploring the effects of interaction between the institutional contexts.* PhD Dissertation, University of Kent, Canterbury/Brussels.

Burlyuk, O. (2014a). An ambitious failure: Conceptualising the EU approach to rule of law promotion (in Ukraine). *Hague Journal on the Rule of Law,* 6(1), 26–46.

Burlyuk, O. (2014b). A thorny path to the spotlight: The rule of law component in EU external policies and EU-Ukraine relations. *European Journal of Law Reform,* 16(1), 133–153.

Burlyuk, O. (2014c). Varition in EU external policies as a virtue: EU rule of law promotion in the neighbourhood. *Journal of Common Market Studies,* Early View (24 October 2014), 1–15.

Chebanenko, O., Golovenko, R., Kotlyar, D., & Kovryzhenko, D. (2011). *National integrity system assessment Ukraine 2011.* Kyiv: TORO Creative Union, Transparency International National Contact in Ukraine.

Council of Europe. (2003). *One Europe—a Europe of partners: Towards an associate partnership between the Council of Europe and the European Union.* Information document SG/Inf (2003)35. Memorandum by the Secretary General of the CoE, Strasbourg.

Council of Europe. (2006). *Building Europe together on the rule of law.* Leaflet on the activities of DG I – Legal Affairs, the CoE.

Council of Europe. (2008). *Action Plans for Ukraine 2008–2011 and 2011–2014.* DSP(2008)15. Directorate of Strategic Planning, Strasbourg.

Council of Europe. (2013a). *Co-operation with the European Union – Summary report.* CM Documents (2013)43. 123rd Session of the Committee of Ministers, Strasbourg.

Council of Europe. (2013b). *Action Plans for Ukraine 2011–2014.* ODGProg/INF(2013) 5 final. Revised version following the Steering Committee Meeting of 12 June 2013, Kyiv.

De Schutter, O. (2007). The division of tasks between the Council of Europe and the European Union in the promotion of Human Rights in Europe: Conflict, competition and complementarity. *Working Paper Series, REFGOV-FR-11,* 1–38.

Dimitrova, A. & Pridham, J. (2004). International actors and democracy promotion in Central and Eastern Europe: The integration model and its limits. *Democratization,* 11(5), 91–112.

Djeric, V. (2000). Admission to membership of the Council of Europe and legal significance of commitments entered into by new Member States. *Zeitschrift für Ausländisches Öffentliches Recht and Völkerrecht,* 60(3–4), 605–629.

Frenz, A. (2007). *The European Commission's Tacis Programme 1991–2006: A success story.* Retrieved from http://www.osce.org/eea/34459?download=true.

Grandori, A. (1987). *Perspectives on organization theory.* Cambridge: Ballinger.

Greer, S. & Williams, A. (2009). Human rights in the Council of Europe and the EU: Towards 'individual', 'constitutional' or 'institutional' justice? *European Law Journal,* 15(4), 462–481.

Guetzkow, J. (1998). The Council of Europe and the OSCE: How to ensure complementarity and partnership? *OSCE Yearbook 1998* (pp. 417–427). Baden-Baden: Nomos.

HIIL. (2007). *Rule of law inventory report: Academic part.* Hague: Hague Institute for the Internalisation of Law.

Jordan, P. (2003). Does membership have its privileges? Entrance into the Council of Europe and compliance with human rights norms. *Human Rights Quarterly,* 25(3), 660–688.

Joris, T. & Vandenberghe, J. (2009). The Council of Europe and the European Union: Natural partners or uneasy bedfellows? *Columbia Journal of European Law,* 15(2008–2009), 1–41.

KIIS. (2006). *Final report: Survey on corruption and service delivery in the justice system in Ukraine* (pp. 1–17). Kyiv: The Council of Europe, the European Union.

Kleinfeld, R. (2012). *Advancing the rule of law abroad: Next generation reform.* Washington, DC: Carnegie Endowment for International Peace.

Kolb, M. (2010). Friend or foe? Shedding light on the interorganizational relationship between the EU and the Council of Europe. *Paper presented at the SGIR Conference 2010.* Stockholm.

Kolb, M. (2011). *From friend to foe?* PhD Dissertation, University of Vienna. Vienna.

Kolb, M. (2013). *The European Union and the Council of Europe.* Basingstoke: Palgrave Macmillan.

Leino, P. (2002). Rights, rules and democracy in the EU enlargement proccess: Between universalism and identity. *Austrian Review of International and European Law,* 7, 53–90.

Leino, P. (2005). European universalism? The EU and human rights conditionality. *Yearbook of European Law,* 24, 329–384.

Leino, P. & Petrov, R. (2009). Between 'common values' and competing universals—the promotion of the EU's common values through the European Neighbourhood Policy. *European Law Journal,* 15(5), 654–671.

MacMullen, A. (2004). Intergovernmental functionalism? The Council of Europe in European integration. *Journal of European Integration*, 26(4), 405–429.

Merlingen, M. & Ostrauskaite, R. (2004). The international socialization of post-socialist countries: The role of the OSCE and the Council of Europe. *OSCE Yearbook 2003* (pp. 365–379). Baden-Baden: Nomos.

Neill, B. & Brooke, H. (2008). *The rule of law in Ukraine: A report produced by the Lord Slynn of Hadley European Law Foundation for the EU Ukraine Business Council* (pp. 1–43). Kyiv: The Lord Slynn of Hadley European Law Foundation.

Pech, L. (2012). Rule of law as a guiding principle of the European Union's external action. *CLEER Working Papers*, 2012/3, 1–56.

Peters, I. (1996). The relations of the OSCE to other international organizations. *OSCE Yearbook 1995–1996* (pp. 385–399). Baden-Baden: Nomos.

Petrov, R. & Serdyuk, O. (2008). Ukraine: The quest for democratization between Europe and Russia. In A. Magen & L. Morlino (Eds.), *International actors, democratization and the rule of law: Anchoring democracy?* (pp. 189–223). London/New York: Routledge.

Pfeffer, J. & Salancik, G. (2003). *The external control of organizations: A resource dependence perspective*. Stanford: Standford Business Books.

Polakiewicz, J. (2009). The European Union and the Council of Europe—competition or coherence in fundamental rights protection in Europe? In P. Canelas de Castro (Ed.), *The European Union at 50: Assessing the past, looking ahead*. Macau: University of Macau Press.

Rotfeld, A. D. (2000). For a new partnership in the new century: The relationship between the OSCE, NATO and the EU. *OSCE Yearbook 2000* (pp. 377–390). Baden-Baden: Nomos.

Sherr, J. (1998). Ukraine's new time of troubles. *IFS Info 6/1998*, 1–31.

Strohal, C. (2005). Consolidation and new challenges: The ODIHR in the OSCE's 30th anniversary year. *OSCE Yearbook 2005* (pp. 303–320). Baden-Baden: Nomos.

Tamanaha, B. (2007). A concise guide to the rule of law. *Legal Studies Research Paper Series*, No. 07-0082 (pp. 1–20). Queens, NY: St. John's University School of Law.

Tamanaha, B. (2011). The primacy of society and the failures of law and development. *Cornell International Law Journal*, 44, 209–247.

Venice Commission. (2011). *Report on the rule of law*. CDL-AD(2011) 003rev-e. 86th plenary session of the Venice Commission (Venice, 25–26 March 2011), Strasbourg.

Walker, N. (2009). The rule of law and the EU: Necessity's mixed virtue. In G. Palombella & N. Walker (Eds.), *Relocating the rule of law* (pp. 119–138). Oxford/Portland, Oregon: Hart Publishing.

Whitman, R. & Wolff, S. (Eds.) (2010). *The European Neighbourhood Policy in perspective: Context, implementation and impact*. Basingstoke: Palgrave Macmillan.

Wolczuk, K. (2004). Integration without Europeanisation: Ukraine and its policy towards the European Union. *EUI Working Papers,* RSCAS No. 2004/15 (pp. 1–25). Florence: Robert Schuman Centre for Advanced Studies, European University Institute.

Wolczuk, K. (2009). Implementation without coordination: The impact of EU conditionality on Ukraine under the European Neighbourhood Policy. *Europe-Asia Studies,* 61(2), 187–211.

List of contributors

Vera Axyonova is Postdoctoral Researcher and Lecturer at Justus Liebig University Giessen and Fulda University of Applied Sciences, Germany.

Bettina Bruns is Schumpeter Fellow at the Leibniz Institute for Regional Geography in Leipzig, Germany.

Olga Burlyuk is Assistant Professor at the Centre for EU Studies, Ghent University, Belgium.

Aron Buzogány is Researcher and Lecturer at the Free University Berlin, Germany.

Elena Kropatcheva is Researcher at the Institute for Peace Research and Security Policy, University of Hamburg, Germany.

René Lenz is Academic Coordinator of International Ph.D. Programmes at Bauhaus University Weimar, Germany.

Shushanik Minasyan is Ph.D. Candidate and Researcher at the University of Bonn, Germany.

Tsveta Petrova is Postdoctoral Fellow and Faculty MA-Student Adviser at the European Institute, Columbia University, USA.

Aijan Sharshenova is Ph.D. Researcher and Teaching Assistant at the University of Leeds, UK.

Helga Zichner is Research Assistant at the Leibniz Institute for Regional Geography in Leipzig, Germany.

AN INTERDISCIPLINARY SERIES
OF THE CENTRE FOR INTERCULTURAL AND EUROPEAN STUDIES

INTERDISZIPLINÄRE SCHRIFTENREIHE
DES CENTRUMS FÜR INTERKULTURELLE UND EUROPÄISCHE STUDIEN

CINTEUS • Fulda University of Applied Sciences • Hochschule Fulda

ISSN 1865-2255

1 *Julia Neumeyer*
   Malta and the European Union
   A small island state and its way into a powerful community
   ISBN 978-3-89821-814-6

2 *Beste İşleyen*
   The European Union in the Middle East Peace Process
   A Civilian Power?
   ISBN 978-3-89821-896-2

3 *Pia Tamke*
   Die Europäisierung des deutschen Apothekenrechts
   Europarechtliche Notwendigkeit und nationalrechtliche Vertretbarkeit einer Liberalisierung
   ISBN 978-3-89821-964-8

4 *Stamatia Devetzi und Hans-Wolfgang Platzer (Hrsg.)*
   Offene Methode der Koordinierung und Europäisches Sozialmodell
   Interdisziplinäre Perspektiven
   ISBN 978-3-89821-994-5

5 *Andrea Rudolf*
   Biokraftstoffpolitik und Ernährungssicherheit
   Die Auswirkungen der EU-Politik auf die Nahrungsmittelproduktion am Beispiel Brasilien
   ISBN 978-3-8382-0099-6

6 *Gudrun Hentges / Justyna Staszczak*
   Geduldet, nicht erwünscht
   Auswirkungen der Bleiberechtsregelung auf die Lebenssituation geduldeter Flüchtlinge in Deutschland
   ISBN 978-3-8382-0080-4

7   Barbara Lewandowska-Tomaszczyk / Hanna Pułaczewska (ed. / Hrsg.)
    Intercultural Europe
    Arenas of Difference, Communication and Mediation
    ISBN 978-3-8382-0198-6

8   Janina Henning
    In Dubio Pro Europa?
    An Analysis of the European External Action Structures
    after the Treaty of Lisbon
    ISBN 978-3-8382-0298-1

9   Claas Oehlmann
    Europa auf dem Weg zur Recycling-Gesellschaft?
    Die EU-Rohstoffinitiative im Kontext der Strategie Europa 2020
    ISBN 978-3-8382-0401-7

10 Volker Hinnenkamp / Hans-Wolfgang Platzer (ed. / Hrsg.)
    Interkulturalität und Europäische Integration
    ISBN 978-3-8382-0573-1

11 Vera Axyonova
    The European Union's Democratization Policy for Central Asia
    Failed in Success or Succeeded in Failure?
    ISBN 978-3-8382-0614-1

12 Lisa Moessing
    Lobbying Uncovered?
    Lobbying Registration in the European Union and the United States
    ISBN 978-3-8382-0616-5

13 Andreas Herberg-Rothe (ed.)
    Lessons from World War I for the Rise of Asia
    ISBN 978-3-8382-0791-9

14 Agnieszka Satola
    Migration und irreguläre Pflegearbeit in Deutschland
    Eine biographische Studie
    ISBN 978-3-8382-0692-9

15 Vera Axyonova (ed.)
    European Engagement under Review
    Exporting Values, Rules, and Practices to the Post-Soviet Space
    ISBN 978-3-8382-0860-2